Early Childhood Matters

Early Childhood Matters documents the rapid development of early years education and care from the late 1990s into the new millennium. It chronicles the unique contribution of the EPPE research to our understanding of the importance of pre-school.

The Effective Pre-school and Primary Education (EPPE) project is the largest European study of the impact of early years education and care on children's developmental outcomes. EPPE has influenced not only national policy but the everyday practices that make a difference to children's social and intellectual learning over time. Through this ground-breaking project a team of internationally-recognised experts provide insights into how home learning environments interact with pre-school and primary school experiences to shape children's progress.

The findings of this fascinating project:

- provide new evidence of the importance of early childhood experiences
- show how these experiences influence children's cognitive, social and behavioural development
- give new insights on the importance of early years education relevant to a wide audience who are interested in policy development, early years education and care, and 'effectiveness' research
- examine how the combined effects of pre-school, primary school and the family interact to shape children's educational outcomes.

This insightful book is essential reading for all those interested in innovative research methodology and policy development in early childhood education and care. It provides new evidence on good practice in early years settings and will have a wide appeal for students and those engaged in providing accredited courses of study at a range of levels in early childhood.

Kathy Sylva is Professor of Educational Psychology, University of Oxford.
Edward Melhuish is Professor of Human Development, Birkbeck College, University of London.
Pam Sammons is Professor of Education, University of Oxford.
Iram Siraj-Blatchford is Professor of Education, Institute of Education, University of London.
Brenda Taggart is Senior Research Officer, Institute of Education, University of London.

Early Childhood Matters

Evidence from the Effective Pre-school and Primary Education Project

Edited by Kathy Sylva,
Edward Melhuish,
Pam Sammons,
Iram Siraj-Blatchford
and Brenda Taggart

Routledge
Taylor & Francis Group

LONDON AND NEW YORK

First published 2010
by Routledge
2 Park Square, Milton Park, Abingdon, Oxon OX14 4RN

Simultaneously published in the USA and Canada
by Routledge
270 Madison Ave, New York, NY 10016

Reprinted 2010

Routledge is an imprint of the Taylor & Francis Group, an informa business

© 2010 Kathy Sylva, Edward Melhuish, Pam Sammons, Iram Siraj-Blatchford and Brenda Taggart

Typeset in Baskerville by
HWA Text and Data Management, London
Printed and bound in Great Britain by
CPI Antony Rowe, Chippenham, Wiltshire

British Library Cataloguing in Publication Data
A catalogue record for this book is available from the British Library

Library of Congress Cataloging-in-Publication Data
Sylva, Kathy.
   Early childhood matters : evidence from the effective
   pre-school and primary education project / Kathy Sylva...[et. al.].
      p. cm.
   Includes index.
   1. Education, Preschool – Europe – Research. 2. Education,
   Primary – Europe – Research. 3. Early childhood education –
   Europe – Research. 4. Child development – Europe – Research.
   I. Title.
   LB1140.25.E85S95 2010
   372'.94--dc22   2009026450

ISBN 10: 0-415-48242-9 (hbk)
ISBN 10: 0-415-48243-7 (pbk)
ISBN 10: 0-203-86206-6 (ebk)

ISBN 13: 978-0-415-48242-4 (hbk)
ISBN 13: 978-0-415-48243-1 (pbk)
ISBN 13: 978-0-203-86

To all the EPPE children and their families

Contents

Figures

Tables

Foreword

Gillian Pugh

Seldom, if ever, in any area of public policy, can a research project have had such a strong impact on policy and practice as the EPPE project has had on early childhood education in England. When the first government report into early years education and care – the Rumbold Report (DES, 1990) – was published twenty years ago, there was an uncoordinated patchwork of early years services across the UK, the numbers of places for young children was amongst the lowest in Europe. There were no British studies to show the effectiveness of early education, and there was no political appetite to expand services.

Within a year of coming into office in 1997 the Labour administration had sowed the seeds for the very considerable programme of expansion of early years services that continues today. Also they noted the potential importance of what was initially to be a six-year study of the effectiveness of randomly selected pre-school centres on the lives of 3,000 pre-school children. The Effective Provision of Pre-school Education (EPPE) study was subsequently extended to follow the children to the end of primary school and is now the Effective Pre-School, Primary and Secondary Education (EPPSE) project, following the children through to just beyond their GCSE year (2013).

This book focuses on the pre-school stage of children's development, though it includes one chapter on the medium term effects of pre-school at age 11. In a very welcome move, it brings together into one volume the evidence from 37 technical papers and research reports published between 1999 and 2008.

The EPPE project is the first large scale multi-level longitudinal study to show that individual pre-school centres have lasting effects on children's development and the first UK study to show that not only does pre-school education provide children with a better start to their schooling, but that these effects last and can help alleviate the effects of social disadvantage. As a research study it has brought together a rich mix of methods, both quantitative and qualitative, including rating scales, questionnaires, interviews and direct observations.

Its impact derives from a number of related issues, not the least of which is its timing. Receiving funding from a government with a strong commitment to both social justice and raising standards, and indeed to creating evidence-based policy, the EPPE findings provided the evidence that government needed to press ahead with its ambitious 10-year childcare strategy.

It is unusual for a research study to influence both policy and practice (and indeed other research studies, but that is another story), but this is what EPPE has done. The expansion of nursery places for all three and four year olds has been informed by the findings that a universal entitlement to pre-school education will benefit all children. The government's curriculum reforms and its workforce strategy have been influenced by the evidence that high quality settings, which provide an appropriate curriculum and are led by well trained staff, including a good proportion of teachers, have better and longer term effects than poor quality settings employing less well trained staff – even though the government response has been to create a new cadre of early years professionals rather than increase the number of early years teachers. The decision to create 3,000 children's centres, building on Sure Start local programmes and early excellence centres, has been supported by the findings that pre-school settings which combine care and education are the most effective and should be at the heart of service development. And the ongoing focus on narrowing the gap between children who do well and those who fall behind, and particularly the creation of a pilot scheme to provide free nursery provision for two year olds in areas of disadvantage, has been informed by EPPE's evidence that the most disadvantaged children gain the most from high quality provision, and that early intervention within the context of universal services can prevent many children requiring more costly specialist support during the primary phase.

The EPPE study has also had a notable impact in two other important areas. The very strong evidence of the impact of the 'home learning environment' on children's overall development has led to major initiatives to provide additional support to parents in their role as their children's first educator. The detailed case study evidence, showing that effective pedagogy in high quality settings is able to balance adult initiated and child led activities, that cognitive and social development are complementary and that children learn best through 'sustained shared thinking', has had a very considerable influence on the development of the first national guidelines for the foundation stage and, most recently on the Early Years Foundation Stage.

As this book shows, the impact of the research has been reinforced not just by the timing – producing findings at the time they are needed – but by the rigour of the research methodology, the reliability of the evidence and the very high commitment of the authors to providing clear summaries of their research to a wide range of audiences. Seldom can a research team have put such a high priority on providing early feedback on their findings to government policy makers, have produced so many tailored reports for the Select Committee, the Cabinet Office and the Treasury, have produced easily accessible research summaries in addition to the detailed reports, or have travelled so many miles to speak at national and international conferences.

This book is the culmination of this dissemination, bringing together as it does the main evidence from this important study. It illustrates the effectiveness of an approach which has been both bottom up and top down, placing as much importance on influencing practice in early years settings as in informing policy makers. It will be an invaluable resource to all policy makers, researchers and practitioners interested in young children and their families for many years to come.

Acknowledgements

The authors would like to thank all of the children, families, pre-school and primary school staff as well as Local Authority and Early Years Specialists who have supported the EPPE project since its inception in 1996. In addition this book would not have been possible without the help from our very large team of both field and analytical researchers and support staff who have been an essential part of the project (in particular Wesley Welcomme our Tracking Officer). We are also grateful to all our colleagues at the Department of Children, Schools and Families. Our special thanks must go to the civil servants who steered the team during the pre-school phase of the study. We are also grateful to members of the Steering Committee and our Early Years Consultative group.

The EPPE team

The EPPE longitudinal study would not have been possible without the dedication of a team of people who have worked on the project over a period of 12 years. Each has made their unique contribution and we would like to thank and acknowledge the following:

Administrative Support: Anna Keonig, Jackie Gadd, Jackie Reid, Loleta Fahad, Alison Slade and Susie Chesher

Regional Research Officers: Anne Dobson, Marje Jeavons, Isabella Hughes, Margaret Kehoe, Katie Lewis, Moria Morahan and Sharon Sadler

Senior Analysts: Dr Yvonne Anders, Dr Sofka Barreau, Karen Elliot, Dr Steve Hunt, Dr Helena Jelicic, Dr Aziza Mayo, Rebecca Smees and Wesley Welcomme

Researchers: Linda Burton, Annalise Clements, Rosemary Ellis, Elizabeth George, Anne Hall, Jill Head, Rose Jennings, Laura Manni, Helen Mirelman, Stella Muttock, John Stokes and James Walker-Hall

The EPPE research is funded by the Department for Children, Schools and Families. The views expressed in this book are those of the authors.

Chapter I

Introduction
Why EPPE?

Kathy Sylva and the EPPE Team

This introductory chapter gives the research and policy context of early childhood education in the late 1980s and early 1990s leading up to the start of EPPE.

EPPE is Europe's largest longitudinal investigation into the effects of pre-school education and care. The EPPE research examines a group of 2,800 children drawn from randomly selected pre-school settings in England toward the end of the 1990s; a group of 'home' children (who had no pre-school experience) were also recruited, bringing the sample up to 3,000. The developmental trajectories of children have been carefully investigated, with many 'enjoying, achieving and making a contribution' in the ways described so powerfully in the government's *Every Child Matters* policy (DfES, 2003). But some children have struggled in their cognitive and social/behavioural development and EPPE explores the possible reasons behind the different trajectories. It does this by collecting information not only on the children but on the educational, familial and neighbourhood contexts in which they have developed. The families and educators of the children have been interviewed for detailed information about the education and care practices that children have experienced in both home and pre-school/school contexts. At the core of EPPE are questions about how the individual characteristics of children are shaped by the environments in which they develop. The view of reciprocal influences between the child and the environment owes much to the work of Bronfenbrenner (1979) whose theory puts the child at the centre of a series of nested spheres of social and cultural influence, including home and education.

The policy context

EPPE was first conceived as a way to chart the contribution of pre-school to young children's cognitive and social development, especially to their development profiles at the start of school (at age 5) and their progress through Key Stage 1 (age 5–7). The newly elected Labour government in 1997 recognised the impact of social disadvantage on life chances and was keen to break the 'cycle of disadvantage' in which poor children received poor public services and went on to experience a range of difficulties over their life course. In 1998, the Prime Minister Tony Blair set forth the promise of his new government: 'Provision for young children's health, childcare, support – will be co-ordinated across departments so that when children start school they are ready to learn' (Blair, 1998).

Before Labour's new government, pre-school education in England, and in the UK generally, was patchy, with some services provided by the Local Authority Education or Social Services departments, some run by voluntary bodies such as the Pre-school Learning Alliance, and others provided by the private sector. The sector was poorly financed in comparison with pre-school provision in many European countries, particularly those in Scandinavia. These different forms of provision (see Chapter 2 for more details) had differing inspection arrangements and different kinds of staff, with those in the Local Education Authority appointing many trained teachers to work in nursery classes and schools while other sectors, such as playgroups, had different training and qualification structures. So, when EPPE began its research there was wide diversity of provision, only the beginning of a common curriculum (DfES Desirable Learning Outcomes, 1996), few recognised minimum 'standards', and a large un-met need for education and care for children aged 3 and 4, i.e. in the two years before entry to statutory schooling.

Since EPPE began in 1997 there has been a transformation of services for young children and families in England (Sylva and Pugh, 2005). There is currently a common entitlement curriculum for children between birth and age 5+ alongside fully specified and statutory 'standards of provision', all clearly laid out in the Early Years Foundation Stage (EYFS, DCSF, 2008). Children and families recruited into the study were experiencing pre-school during the period of change due to the government's new policy arrangements for young children and their families. Access to a free pre-school place was made available to the parents of all four year olds in 1998 and this was extended to three year olds in 2004. (It might be argued that children and families in the EPPE study were the first to benefit from the strong commitment to early childhood made by the Labour government elected in 1997.) And, although the EPPE children were the first to experience it, the policy 'offer' was constantly changing throughout the period of the EPPE research. In fact, Taggart argues in Chapter 11 that EPPE was researching the effects of early years policy at the same time as it was influencing its evolution through the opening years of the new century.

The early years of the twenty-first century saw even more initiatives for young children and families in England, particularly a major policy programme called 'Sure Start'. Announced in 1999, this ambitious programme was targeted at children and families living in the 20 per cent most disadvantaged neighbourhoods. It aimed to help 'close the gap' between the life chances of rich and poor.

Sure Start was followed by the Neighbourhood Nurseries Initiative in 2003 (Mathers and Sylva, 2007; Smith et al., 2007), nurseries catering for babies and toddlers and located in disadvantaged neighbourhoods so that their parents could move into employment. Finally, the Children's Centre programme was offered first in 2004 to families living in disadvantaged neighbourhoods and then rolled out to all communities in England (by 2010). The EPPE children attended pre-school or remained at home during a period of dramatic change.

The research context

The 'transformed' early years policy was based on sound evidence about the positive benefits of pre-school education, much of which was reviewed for government by Melhuish (2004). The most convincing studies on the effects of pre-school were experimental studies in which children were randomly assigned to an 'intervention' or to a 'control' group. Two well known examples of these carefully controlled studies were the Perry Pre-school study of the 'educational' High/Scope programme for 3 and 4 year olds (Schweinhart, Barnes and Weikhart, 1993) and the Abecedarian full-day 'care' programme for children from birth to school entry (Ramey and Ramey, 1998). Both used experimental designs in which children were randomly assigned to 'treatment' and 'non treatment' groups, and both studies reported impressive benefits of children's long term developmental outcomes from experiencing group pre-school education and care.

The most recent research in the US on the effects of child care and education on children's development was carried out by the National Institute of Child Health and Human Development (NICHD, 2002; Belsky *et al.*, 2007). This large scale but non-experimental study focused on 1,100 children, recruited at birth, and followed to age 11. Pre-school experiences before the age of 5+ were shown to have small but positive effects on children's development, although a few negative effects were seen for some children who had very early centre-based care (Belsky *et al.*, 2007).

With studies such as EPPE and the NICHD, attention has turned *away* from establishing the simple effects of early education and *towards* an understanding of the familial and educational processes that underlie change in the developmental trajectories of young children. Brooks-Gunn (2003) shows how poverty, low education and low socio-economic status work together to create a home environment of low hope, low expectations and few of the kinds of parenting interactions that stimulate young minds. It is important for current research into the effects of early education to take into account aspects of the child's home environment. Children's outcomes are the joint product of home and pre-school and any research on the effects of early education will have to take into account influences from the home. This was a major element of the EPPE research.

Until EPPE there had been little large-scale, systematic research on the effects of early childhood education in the UK. The 'Start Right' Enquiry (Ball, 1994; Sylva, 1994) reviewed the evidence of British research and concluded that small-scale studies suggested a positive impact but that large-scale research in the UK was inconclusive. The Start Right enquiry recommended more rigorous longitudinal studies with baseline measures so that the 'value added' to children's development by pre-school education could be established.

A few years after the Start Right Enquiry, Feinstein *et al.* (1998) attempted to evaluate the effects of pre-schooling on children's subsequent progress, using a birth cohort sample. The absence of data on children's attainments means that neither the British Birth Cohort Study (Butler and Golding, 1980) nor the National Child

Development Study (Davie, Butler and Goldstein, 1972) can be used to explore the effects of pre-school education on children's progress. These studies are also limited by the time lapse and many changes in the nature of pre-school provision that have occurred. Schagen (1994) attempted multilevel modelling of pre-school effects in large samples but he too did not have adequate control at entry to pre-school.

The EPPE project is thus the first large-scale British study on the effects of different kinds of pre-school provision and the impact of attendance at individual centres. In line with the recent American research, EPPE studied both the effects of pre-school experience and also the effects of family support for children's learning at home. To understand children's developmental trajectories it is necessary to take both into account.

Four questions are of particular relevance to policy:

1   What are the effects of pre-school at school entry?
2   Do early effects 'fade' over time?
3   Are the beneficial effects of early education different for children from different kinds of backgrounds?
4   Do different types of pre-school education have similar or different effects on children?

The EPPE research follows an 'educational effectiveness' design in which children's developmental progress between ages 3 and 11 is explored, through multi-level models (Goldstein, 1995) in terms of possible influences. EPPE followed the 'natural development' of a large group of children to investigate those factors that may influence children's development and identify their effects. These influences include individual child characteristics such as gender or birth weight, family influences such as parental qualifications or employment, the 'home learning' environment (HLE) created by the families to support children's learning at home, and finally the educational context of the child's pre-school or primary school. In addition to recruiting children who attended different kinds of pre-school, EPPE recruited children who had no formal, 'group care' at all (the 'home' group) and they were valuable because their development could be used for a comparison to the development of children who had attended pre-school.

The first phase of the EPPE study (between age 3–7 years) has shown the benefits to all children of attending pre-school (Sylva et al., 2004; Sammons et al., 2002; Sammons et al., 2003; Siraj-Blatchford et al., 2003). The second phase, when the children were 7 to 11 years (Sylva et al., 2008; Melhuish et al., 2008; Sammons et al., 2008a; 2008b) showed that the effects of children's pre-school experience remained until they were age 11, in both cognitive and social-behavioural outcomes.

The emerging findings of EPPE documented the gains to children's development that early childhood education could provide and influenced government policy, especially during the period 2002 onwards (Children's Plan, DCSF, 2007; Taggart et al., 2008). EPPE suggested that some early experiences were better than others both at home or in pre-school settings, providing a sound evidence base for government policy (the development of and expansion of provision). Its qualitative case studies (Siraj-Blatchford *et al.*, 2006) were influential in identifying what is meant by 'effective' early education.

EPPE has now become the Effective Pre-School, Primary and Secondary Education (EPPSE) and its children will be followed through Key Stage 3, their GCSE year and beyond to their post-16 choices (2013). This book, however, focuses on the pre-school stage of children's development, with just a glance in Chapter 7 to the medium term effects of pre-school at age 11.

In this book we seek to provide an account of the research and its main findings, we also document its impact on policy and practice over more than a decade and explore some of the implications of the research for future development of services for children and families.

References

Ball, C. (1994) *Start Right: The Importance of Early Learning*. London: Royal Society of the Arts, Manufacturing and Commerce.

Belsky, J., Vandell, D. Burchinal, M. Clarke-Stewart, K.A., McCartney, K., Owen, M. and the NICHD Early Child Care Research Network (2007) Are there long-term effects of early child care? *Child Development*, 78, 681–701.

Blair, T. (1998) *Foreword. In H.M. Treasury, Modern Public Services for Britain: Investing in Reform. Comprehensive Spending Review: New Public Spending Plans 1999–2002*. London: HM Treasury. Accessed on May 26, 2009 at: http://www.archive.official-documents.co.uk/document/cm40/4011/foreword.htm

Bronfenbrenner, U. (1979) *The Ecology of Human Development*. Cambridge, MA: Harvard University Press.

Brooks-Gunn, J., Currie, J., Emde, R.E. and Zigler, E. (2003) Do you believe in magic? What we can expect from early childhood intervention programs. *Social Policy Report*, XVII, 1, 3–15. Society for Research in Child Devlopment.

Butler, N.R. and Golding, J. (1986) *From Birth to Five: A Study of the Health and Behaviour of Britain's 5-Year-Olds*. Oxford: Pergamon Press.

Davie, R., Butler, N. R. and Goldstein, H. (1972) *From Birth to Seven*. London: Longmans.

Department for Children, Schools and Families (DCSF) (2007) *The Children's Plan: Building Brighter Futures*. Available at http://www.dcsf.gov.uk/childrensplan

Department for Children, Schools and Families (DCSF) (2008) *Early Years Foundation Stage*. Nottingham: DCSF Publications.

Department for Education and Employment (DfEE) (1996) *Nursery Education Desirable Outcomes for Children's Learning on Entering Compulsory Schooling*. London: Schools Curriculum and Assessment Authority/DfEE.

Department for Education and Skills (DfES) (2003) *Every Child Matters*. Norwich: HMSO.

Feinstein, L., Robertson, D. and Symons, J. (1998) *Pre-school Education and Attainment in the NCDS and BCSI*. London: Centre for Economic Performance.

Goldstein, H. (1995) *Multilevel Statistical Models*, 2nd edn. London: Edward Arnold.

Mathers, S. and Sylva, K. (2007) *National Evaluation of the Neighbourhood Nurseries Initiative: The Relationship between Quality and Children's Behavioural Development*. London: DCSF. Accessed at http://www.dcsf.gov.uk/research/data/uploadfiles/SSU2007FR024.pdf on 26 May 2009.

Melhuish, E. (2004) *A Literature Review of the Impact of Early Years Provision upon Young Children, with Emphasis Given to Children from Disadvantaged Backgrounds.* Report to the Comptroller and Auditor General. London: National Audit Office.

Melhuish, E., Sylva, K., Sammons, P., Siraj-Blatchford, I., Taggart, B., Phan, M. and Malin, A. (2008) Pre-school influences on mathematics achievement. *Science*, 321, 1161–1162.

National Institute of Child Health and Development (NICHD) (2002) Early child care and children's development prior to school entry: results from the NICHD Study of Early Child Care. *American Educational Research Journal*, 39(1), 133–64.

Ramey, C.T. and Ramey, S.L. (1998) Early intervention and early experience. *American Psychologist*, 53, 109–120.

Sammons, P., Sylva, K., Melhuish, E.C., Siraj-Blatchford, I., Taggart, B. and Elliot, K. (2002) *The Effective Provision of Pre-School Education (EPPE) Project: Technical Paper 8a – Measuring the Impact of Pre-School on Children's Cognitive Progress over the Pre-School Period.* London: DfES/Institute of Education, University of London.

Sammons, P., Sylva, K., Melhuish, E.C., Siraj-Blatchford, I., Taggart, B. and Elliot, K. (2003) *The Effective Provision of Pre-School Education (EPPE) Project: Technical Paper 8b – Measuring the Impact of Pre-School on Children's Social/Behavioural Development over the Pre-School Period.* London: DfES/Institute of Education, University of London.

Sammons, P., Sylva, K., Melhuish, E., Siraj-Blatchford, I., Taggart, B. and Hunt, S. (2008a) *The Effective Pre-School and Primary Education 3–11 (EPPE 3–11) Project: Influences on Children's Attainment and Progress in Key Stage 2: Cognitive Outcomes in Year 6.* London: DCSF/Institute of Education, University of London.

Sammons, P., Sylva, K., Melhuish, E., Siraj-Blatchford, I., Taggart, B. and Jelicic, H. (2008b) *The Effective Pre-School and Primary Education 3–11 (EPPE 3–11) Project: Influences on Children's Development and Progress in Key Stage 2: Social/Behavioural Outcomes in Year 6.* London: DCSF/Institute of Education, University of London.

Schagen, I. (1994) Multilevel analysis of the Key Stage 1 National Curriculum assessment data in 1991 and 1992. *Oxford Review of Education*, 20, 163–71.

Schweinhart, L.J., Barnes, H. and Weikhart, D. (1993) *Significant Benefits: The High/Scope Perry Pre-School Study through Age 27.* Ypsilanti, MI: High/Scope Press.

Siraj-Blatchford, I., Sylva, K., Taggart, B., Sammons, P., Melhuish, E. C. and Elliot, K. (2003) *The Effective Provision of Pre-School Education (EPPE) Project: Technical Paper 10 – Intensive Case Studies of Practice across the Foundation Stage.* Nottingham: DfES Publications.

Siraj-Blatchford, I., Sammons, P., Sylva, K., Melhuish, E., and Taggart, B. (2006) Educational research and evidence-based policy: the mixed method approach of the EPPE project. *Evaluation and Research in Education*, 19, 2, 63–82.

Smith, T., Smith, G., Coxon, K., Sigala, M., Sylva, K., Mathers, S.L, LaValle, I., Smith, R., Purdon, S., Dearden, L., Shaw, J. and Sibieta, L. (2007) *National Evaluation of the Neighbourhood Nurseries Initiative.* London: DCSF. Accessed at http://www.surestart.gov.uk/_doc/P0002386.pdf on 26 May 2009.

Sylva, K. (1994) School influences on children's development. *Journal of Child Psychology and Psychiatry*, 35, 135–70.

Sylva, K. and Pugh, G. (2005) Transforming the early years in England. *Oxford Review of Education*, 31, 1, 11–27.

Sylva, K., Melhuish, E., Sammons, P., Siraj-Blatchford, I. and Taggart, B. (2004) *The Effective Provision of Pre-School Education (EPPE) Project: Final Report.* London: DfES/Institute of Education, University of London.

Sylva, K., Melhuish, E., Sammons, P., Siraj-Blatchford, I. and Taggart, B. (2008) *The Effective Pre-School and Primary Education 3–11 (EPPE 3–11) Project: Final Report from the Primary Phase: Pre-school, School and Family Influences on Children's Development during Key Stage 2 (Age 7–11)* London: DCSF/Institute of Education, University of London.

Taggart, B., Siraj-Blatchford, I., Sylva, K., Melhuish, E. and Sammons, P. (2008) Influencing policy and practice through research on early childhood education. *International Journal of Early Childhood Education*, 14, 2.

Chapter 2

The EPPE settings in the context of English pre-schools

Iram Siraj-Blatchford

This chapter describes the context in which pre-schools exist in England. It describes the settings in which the children in the EPPE sample started their pre-school experience. It covers what these early experiences look like day-to-day and how this relates to the Early Years Foundation Stage curriculum framework (DCSF, 2008). The term pre-school is employed here as a generic term for *all* types of providers.

The United Kingdom consists of four nations: England, Wales, Scotland and Northern Ireland with a population of over 60 million people. There are growing differences in curriculum and in statutory provision across the country. For example, while compulsory schooling begins at the age of 4 in Northern Ireland, elsewhere it begins at the age of 5. In England the early years curriculum is reflected in the Early Years Foundation Stage (EYFS) framework for birth to 5 year olds whereas in Wales it is called the Foundation Phase and covers curriculum for children 3–7 years of age. At the outset it is therefore important to note that the following account of provision is therefore focused on England, where EPPE drew the sample of pre-schools from and where an estimated 83 per cent of the total UK population currently resides. The chapter focuses further on the provisions made for 3–5 year olds in the EPPE study. Chapter 10 looks at a sister study in Northern Ireland which has very similar findings.

In order to understand the different approaches taken by different settings within the pre-school sector, a short description of the 'big-picture' of pre-school education and care in England is necessary. As the EPPE study embarked on its investigation. The Audit Commission (1996) stressed the diversity prevalent in pre-school provision that included:

- local authority (LA) maintained (state funded) nursery education (within the school system such as nursery schools and nursery classes attached to primary school);
- reception classes in maintained primary schools;
- local authority day nurseries;
- private settings such as private day nurseries;
- playgroups (often part of the voluntary sector);
- combined care and education family centres and
- childminders.

In 2007, 112,600 providers of childcare and early years education offered 2,494,000 childcare and early years places (registered with The Office for Standards in Education, the English inspection and regulatory body (Ofsted)). Most types of childcare and education providers have increased in number since the EPPE project started. The following brief description of the types of settings provides some additional details:

Local authority (LA) nursery schools

According to Mooney *et al.* (2006), in 2004 there were 470 maintained nursery schools with an average of 83 children per school. These are 'traditional' nursery schools under the local education authority (and fully funded by the state) with adult:child ratios of 1:13. The head teacher would typically be a four-year graduate qualified teacher with an early years background. They would include a high proportion of qualified teachers, typically with one in every two adults being a four-year graduate qualified teacher and the other adult having 2 years' childcare training. This type of provision would usually offer half-day sessions (with some children going full time before they enter primary school) throughout the week for children 3–5 years of age. Many nursery schools have now become Children's Centres offering many more extended services, see below. Nursery schools were included in the EPPE sample.

Local authority (LA) nursery classes

These are normally separate units, part of primary schools and they accept children from age 3, having an adult:child ratio of 1:13 (one in every two adults is normally a 4 year graduate qualified teacher and the other adult has had two years childcare training) and usually offer only half-day sessions in term time, five days per week. Nursery classes currently cater for the needs of 131,200 four year olds and 119,200 three year olds (Hughes, 2009). This type of provision was included in the EPPE sample.

Reception classes in primary schools

While parents are not obliged to send their child to school until the term after their fifth birthday, in 2009, 83,800 4 year olds were reported to be attending reception classes (Hughes, 2009). The admission policies can vary between local authorities with children entering reception classes at different time points throughout the year. A common pattern used to be for an intake of children in September and another in January. Almost all reception classes would be led by a qualified graduate teacher who may or may not have a specialised early years background. Reception teachers have the same pay and conditions of service as their primary school teacher colleagues. Reception class teachers are usually assisted by trained (early years specialised) or untrained support staff.

Voluntary playgroups

Mooney *et al.* (2006) reported that in 2005 there were 9,900 playgroups in England providing a total of 241,100 places. These have an adult:child ratio of 1:8 and typically accept children from age 2+ (training of adults is variable from none to graduate level). The most common type of training is based on short Pre-school Learning Alliance (their national organisation) courses. All offer sessional provision in term time. Many children attend fewer than 5 days/week. Playgroups usually have fewer resources (facilities, materials and sole use of space) than other types of centres. They often share the use of community accommodation, e.g. church halls or community centres. Playgroups were included in the EPPE sample.

Day care centres and private nurseries

The Office for Standards in Education (Ofsted) reported that in 2005 there were 12,900 day nurseries in 2005 offering 553,100 places (Ofsted 2006). These have an adult:child ratio of 1:8 (normally the adults have a two year childcare training, but some have less training). All offer full day care for children age 0–5 on a fee paying basis. However, many children attend part-time and most private nurseries are run as for-profit businesses, although some are co-operatives. In 1999 there were 400 local authority (day care) centres that were originally developed by the social service sector, although in recent years most have come under the authority of the new local authority Children's Trusts. Some in this group combined care and education with one or more teachers per centre or a peripatetic teacher shared with other centres. These types of settings were included in the EPPE sample.

Integrated or combined centres

In 2009 there are 3,000 centres combining education, health and care and are now called *Sure Start Children's Centres*. When EPPE started there were only 70 such centres. There has been considerable government investment in expanding this type of provision and the current national policy is to increase the number of these types of setting to 3,500 by the year 2010. These were similar to nursery schools (see above) but had developed their provision of extended care to include full day care and parent involvement. They would usually have adult:child ratios of 1:9 for 3–4 year olds (staffing used to be the same as nursery schools for the over 3s but in the new Sure Start Children's Centres there is only entitlement to one teacher for the entire centre) and they accept children 0–5. The newer Children's Centres are much more integrated to deliver services for parents and families, especially to support parenting and employment skills. These settings were included in the EPPE research where they were often referred to as 'integrated' or 'combined' settings.

Childminders or family daycare

Childminders currently provide for 33,500 3 year olds and 24,000 4 year olds in England (Hughes, 2009). They undergo strict registration with the local authority and are inspected by both the LA and Ofsted. Childminders provide education and care for children under the age of five (or over) in their own homes for short or extended hours per day, for which parents pay a fee. Recommended ratios are 1:3 for children under five. Childminders may also be looking after their own children at the same time as receiving payments for looking after other children, and their own children have been included in the 1:3 ratio. Because of the small numbers of children being looked after by individual childminders they could not be included in the EPPE sample. Only larger group settings could be included to provide for a statistical centre effect. However, more details on childminding is included in Researching Effective Pedagogy in Early Years study (REPEY, Siraj-Blatchford *et al.*, 2002).

Characteristics of the centres in the EPPE study

The EPPE sample was originally recruited in 1997 and structured to ensure sufficient of each form of provider to allow for the identification of the effectiveness of centre 'types' (see Chapter 3 for details of the research design). Initially we learnt most about our centres through research officers' visits and interviews with the centre managers. In total, 140 centre managers in five regions (six local authorities) in England were interviewed (Taggart *et al.*, 2000). The numbers of managers interviewed in each pre-school type were as follows: 24 in nursery classes, 20 in nursery schools, 24 in local authority day care centres, 34 in playgroups, 31 in private day nurseries and 7 in local authority combined centres.

This interview was designed to provide information likely to help differentiate effectiveness in pre-school settings by contextualising information from observational profiles (Sylva *et al.*, 1999; Siraj-Blatchford *et al.*, 1999) and help in the development of case studies (Siraj-Blatchford *et al.*, 2003).

The interview schedule explored the following areas: *general information*, i.e. age of centre, opening times, major objectives, etc.; *centres and parents*, i.e. opportunities for parent/staff contact, written materials provided to parents, parent education, etc.; *the staff*, i.e. conditions and benefits, qualifications, turnover, etc.; *the children*, i.e. numbers, provision for special educational needs, etc.; *perceptions of quality in child care and education*, and *organisational practices*, i.e. planning and record-keeping, etc. (for full details of the interviews see Taggart *et al.*, 2000).

The interviews revealed the wide differences in provision across the sectors. In general the LA state-maintained provision (nursery classes, nursery schools and combined centres) had superior resources, training, professional facilities and support, plus better staff pay and conditions and lower rates of staff turnover compared to the private and voluntary sector. The emergence of integrated/combined centres means that younger children were cared for in settings where the standards of working conditions are higher for staff on a year round, full time basis whereas the playgroups and private day nurseries lagged behind in terms of resources, etc., as illustrated below.

Staffing

The private day nurseries had the youngest staff profiles of all, while the oldest staff were found in nursery classes. The most ethnically diverse staff were employed by local authority day care and combined centres both of which were normally found in inner-city areas.

The longest hours worked by centre managers was reported in the combined centres (now Children's Centres) which would reflect the longer hours of opening associated with extended services. However the longest hours worked by staff were reported in private day nurseries.

Recruitment of regular staff posed few problems across the providers; however, there were difficulties across the sector as a whole for the recruitment of suitable 'substitute/supply' cover. Overall, full-time staff had access to better staff development opportunities than part-time staff. This has implications for types of pre-schools employing more part-time than full-time staff such as the playgroups and private day nurseries.

Providers could meet (or better) the statutory requirements for adult/child ratios without the help of unpaid workers, except for some playgroups where unpaid workers were essential to maintaining statutory ratios. All providers had some unpaid workers in regular contact with children. Both nursery classes and nursery schools appeared to offer ratios that were notably lower than the statutory requirements for their sector.

Qualifications and staff development

The most highly qualified staff (for childcare and early education qualifications) were in the LA maintained (state) settings, where the highest salaries were also to be found. The centre managers with the highest childcare qualifications, e.g. degrees (Bachelor of Education) or post graduate qualifications (Post Graduate Certification in Education) were predominately in the 'education' rather than 'care' sectors. Combined centres also had high levels of staff with higher childcare and education qualifications. Playgroups had the least qualified centre managers with over 50 per cent with vocational rather than academic qualifications (National Vocational Qualifications at Level 2 or below). The most commonly held childcare qualification amongst pre-school staff was the two year further education training validated by the Nursery Nursing Education Board award (NNEB –which now equates to a Diploma in childcare and education) with the second most common category being 'no qualifications'.

Training opportunities for staff working in playgroups were poorer than for staff working in any other types of pre-school provision. Playgroup staff had fewer opportunities to be appraised, fewer secure training resources, less access to training materials and fewer opportunities to have their training paid for by their centres.

What do managers value in their staff?

When considering issues of 'quality' in care and education, managers at interview reported that they sought staff that had relevant experience and training, with personal attributes appropriate to working with young children. They wanted staff who could meet the individual needs of children, helping them to develop social skills, self-confidence and independence, in a happy environment. They also thought it important to nurture environments that encouraged parental involvement and were 'child friendly'. Managers of pre-schools, in addition to providing care, rated the development in children of language and reasoning, friendship and sharing and encouraging positive self-concepts as the most important objectives of their centres.

Planning and monitoring children's development

Staff working in the maintained rather than the voluntary sector were more likely to have been trained to assess and monitor children's development. They conducted assessments more regularly and used a wider repertoire of assessment strategies.

The interviews and visits to settings revealed that there was widespread use of daily timetables and collegiate planning but the maintained sector was more likely to refer to aspects of the curriculum when planning activities. There was good use made of a range of curriculum documents (at the time the most used was the Desirable Learning Outcomes [DLO]), but playgroups made less use of curriculum documents when planning activities than other forms of provision. This may be because some playgroups had very few four year olds at whom the DLOs were targeted during the late 1990s.

Centre managers in the maintained sector reported higher numbers of children with special needs and were unanimous in having systems for early identification. The use of the Code of Practice for Special Educational Needs (which is a framework for supporting children with additional needs – see Chapter 9) was much more common in the maintained sector, as was the practice of having a named person responsible for children with special needs.

Parental involvement

While the majority of pre-school centres reported providing opportunities for regular contact with parents, the reality of 'take up' fell short of the rhetoric. The greatest differences were seen in private day nurseries. The voluntary sector reported fewer incidents of scheduled formal meetings with parents but may have relied on more informal contacts. When reporting parental contact the issue of working parents must be borne in mind and the availability of some form of accommodation (parents' room) to encourage this to happen. The maintained sector was also found to provide more information to parents than the voluntary sector. Combined centres, nursery schools and nursery classes reported a greater emphasis on giving parents information on 'education' issues, whilst playgroups were more likely to provide parents with leaflets on a broad range of topics.

The descriptions of the EPPE settings above provide only a 'snap-shot' of what our settings were like in the late twentieth century. However these need to be considered in the light of the dominant legislation and political climate at the time. The rest of this chapter will consider the historical context in which these settings were placed and outline some key developments in early years education and care which will update policy and practices into the twenty-first century during the 'life' of the EPPE study.

Developments to regularise 'uneven' provision

Prior to the Labour government of 1997, services had been characterised by unevenness in access, effectiveness, quality and costs (The Audit Commission, 1996, p.30, see Chapter 1). For instance, the voluntary sector had half-day parent-run, parent-financed playgroups which catered for the largest number of children under age 4, whilst the state sector education nurseries provide free, half-day provision. At the same time social services continued to contribute to full-time care programmes in daycare centres and combined nurseries.

The majority of social services (local authority daycare) settings in the initial EPPE sample became administered by education departments at both the local and national level. However the deep historical 'split' between 'care' and 'education', evident in the unevenness and diversity of pre-school types, created divisions and these will continue for some time despite national initiatives to set-up Early Years Childcare and Development Partnerships and now Children's Trusts under Children's Services in each local authority to deliver a coordinated and more integrated service. One move in the direction of 'coherence' across pre-school types has been for LAs to provide joint training programmes to which all members of early years services are encouraged to attend.

In terms of pedagogy there has been the same unevenness, with the 'patchwork' of diverse forms of provision matched by an equally diverse workforce (Sylva et al., 1992; Taggart et al., 2000). Traditionally, the initial training of those who work in the education and care sectors has differed. Teachers along with nursery nurses can be found mainly in the maintained ('education') nursery sector, normally attached to primary schools. These teachers have had three or four years of higher education. Those trained for the 'care' sector have normally had two years of mainly childcare and development training in further education. In addition the voluntary sector and childminders receive training locally based on programmes devised by their national organisations. Different early childhood 'educators' therefore hold differing perceptions of the nature of early childhood, educational assessment, play and how all of these elements are integrated in early childhood curriculum and pedagogy (Siraj-Blatchford *et al.*, 1999).

Since 2000 there has been a concerted effort on the part of government to bring in similar standards of provision across the range of providers to ensure that children have more equal access and entitlement to quality provision whilst maintaining parental choice. This has been in part a response to the growing critique of the pre-2000 position, and an effort to 'standardise' the education and care that young children receive. Most notable was the introduction of a common set of early learning goals for all children. The government introduced the Curriculum Guidance for the Foundation Stage (QCA, 2000) which all providers have been required to work towards if they educate 3–5 year olds. In 2008 the early learning goals were adapted and integrated with the Birth to Three Framework to produce the Early Years Foundation Stage (EYFS – DCSF, 2008) Framework for all children from birth to age 5 to promote positive outcomes in six areas of learning. These curriculum arrangements are dealt with later in this chapter.

Childcare and education for the twenty-first century

Over the last ten years there has been considerable policy development in early years education and care in England. From a system which was largely uncoordinated and uneven we now have tighter regulations with all provision for 0–5 year olds inspected by Ofsted, and the inspection reports outline how far settings cater for and enable children to achieve the identified early learning goals and how they meet the statutory care standards. In addition we have free pre-school education (currently 12 hours per week but to increase to 15 hours by 2010 and then 20 hours) available for all 3–4 year olds whose parents choose to take up the offer. This is coordinated by the 150 local authorities and financed by central government.

But perhaps the most radical development during this period has been government funding to develop Sure Start Children's Centres. These began between 1999 and 2002 when twenty-nine Early Excellence Centres (EECs) were identified. These settings, many of which were ex-nursery schools and combined centres were supported by the (then) Department for Education and Employment (DfEE) in developing a more 'integrated' or 'combined' service which supported parents and offered 'outreach' programmes, including health and employment information to families. The piloting of these settings was followed by a government commitment to expand this provision to a further hundred such centres by 2004. This initiative was then subsumed in the 'Sure Start' community programme, a major community based service targeted at improving a range of outcomes for families and children living in disadvantaged areas. A major element of this ambitious programme (which covered health and associated outcomes) was the development of Sure Start Local Programmes into Sure Start Children's Centres (SSCC). The EECs were developed to build on the strengths of the 70 early established (1970s–1990s) combined centres to provide 'joined up thinking' and 'one-stop-shops' for families and children through integrated care and education services delivered through inter-agency partnership. In one of three annual evaluations, Bertram *et al.* (2002) identified four defining features of the integrated services being developed through that initiative at the time:

1 shared philosophy, vision and agreed principles of working with children and families;
2 perception by EEC users of cohesive and comprehensive services;
3 perception by EEC staff teams of a shared identity, purpose and common working practices;
4 commitment by partner providers of EEC services to fund and facilitate integrated services.

(Bertram *et al.*, 2002)

A major piece of legislation, the Green Paper *Every Child Matters* (HM Treasury 2003), suggested that Extended Schools (for school age children) and Children's Centres (birth–5 year olds) would be the most appropriate means of enabling inter-agency teams to work with children, families, schools and communities. As stated earlier, 3,500 Children's Centres should be developed by 2010 to provide integrated services to pre-school children and their families. This is to coincide with the development of extended schools for older children, and some Children's Centres are being developed on the same sites as primary/secondary schools to provide continuity of provision for children as they grow up (Siraj-Blatchford and Siraj-Blatchford, 2009).

The development of early years practice

The early 1990s saw a focus on standards in primary education particularly with the publication of international league tables (see Chapter 11). The 1997 Labour government saw the need to improve standards across the board, particularly in primary schools and introduced explicit targets for schools to achieve. One of the most significant of these targets was to improve achievement in Mathematics and English in primary schools by the year 2002. In the efforts to achieve these targets, support was provided through reducing class sizes for 5, 6 and 7 year olds and through the development of 'Educational Action Zones' that were set up in areas of educational under-performance. At the point at which the EPPE data were collected, the government was also in the process of setting up early excellence centres, literacy summer schools, out-of-school-hours learning activities, and family literacy schemes to improve outcomes, particularly for children living in disadvantaged areas. In addition, high profile literacy and numeracy strategies were introduced in 1998 and 1999 later evolving into the National Primary Strategy.

Having concentrated for some time on the years of compulsory schooling, the government in 1996 turned to provision for children who are under five. Research evidence from the United States, like the High/Scope Perry Pre-school programme and research in other countries (see Chapter 1) had convinced government that high quality pre-school provision can benefit children for the rest of their lives, particularly children from low socio-economic classes. We now know that good pre-school education encourages learning dispositions which favour life-long learning and the development of social and behavioural competencies (Sylva et al., 2008) that are of particular benefit in our increasingly complex and interdependent communities. Good pre-school provision has been shown to reduce future dependency on educational remediation. The evidence also suggests that it can also reduce crime and future social and welfare expenditure (Schweinhart et al., 1993). However this research was largely conducted in the US and amongst more disadvantaged groups, therefore the extent of benefits for children in the UK was less evident at the time EPPE was conceived. Increased pre-school provision also addressed in part the government's agenda to get more women out to work (see Chapter 11).

Given this evidence it wasn't at all surprising that the government embarked upon a programme of educational reform that included the development of pre-school provision in England. The government's declared intention has been to raise the educational achievement of the majority of children. One of the key questions to be answered was therefore whether this would result in breaking the cycle of underachievement related to social class or whether it would merely re-establish the class divisions at another level. In fact interest in the development of early childhood education as a social leveller has a very long history in the UK. When Robert Owen opened the very first infant school early in the nineteenth century it was because he believed that there were no justifiable reasons why the educational performance of any one social group should be superior to that of any other. He also believed that schools could be influential in supporting poor and working class families in breaking the cycle of underachievement (Siraj-Blatchford, 1997).

In 1996 the Audit Commission was asked to investigate and report on provision for under fives in England and Wales. The results of this extensive investigation were published in the document *Counting to Five: Education of Children Under Five*. This document reported some of the research into the value of early years education and concluded that 'Children's early educational experience is crucial for developing the socialisation and learning skills that they will need throughout their lives' (The Audit Commission, 1996, p.4).

The first major landmark in developing equal access for all young children to quality experiences was published in The Curriculum Guidance for the Foundation Stage (CGFS, QCA, 2000), now the Early Years Foundation Stage (DCSF, 2008) which describes six broad areas of learning, that would enable children to move seamlessly into the English National Curriculum (introduced in the 1980s and statutory for all pupils in state education). Adults working with children between the ages of birth to 5 need to ensure they monitor children's development in the following areas:

- Personal, Social and Emotional Development
- Communication, Language and Literacy
- Problem Solving, Reasoning and Numeracy
- Knowledge and Understanding of the World
- Physical Development
- Creative Development.

These areas of learning were also identified as far back as the Rumbold Report (DfES 1990) as appropriate for young children, although some aspects identified in the Rumbold Report were left out of the *CGFS* (QCA, 2000, see also Siraj-Blatchford, 1998). The document *Nursery Education: The Next Steps* (DfEE, 1996) had clearly demonstrated the relationship between the earlier *Desirable Outcomes* and the National Curriculum via a set of tables which show how the areas of learning link to Key Stage One (ages 5–7 in primary education) of the primary school National Curriculum. The reforms continue. The Rose Review of Primary Education during 2009 is concerned with how the EYFS can lead seamlessly into a revised primary curriculum.

Developing a skilled workforce

One of the key findings of the EPPE research has been the relationship between the qualifications of staff and the quality of the settings (see Chapter 5). EPPE has also reported on the relationship between quality and child outcomes (see Chapters 6 and 7). The evidence above illustrates the inequality that exists with regard to the qualifications across early years as a whole. Given the importance of the workforce it is worth exploring further what kind of early years workforce England had and how the government has intervened through a range of initiatives to try and increase the skills and qualifications for those who want to work with very young children.

The Department for Education and Skills developed a Children's Workforce Strategy, published in April 2005. It set out the key areas of reform for the early years workforce and the Children's Workforce Strategy update, published in March 2007 gave an update on some of the progress made. The previous Children's Workforce Strategy set challenges which included: the ten year childcare strategy which set out a vision for the sector of a strengthened role for early yearsprofessionals, more people trained to professional levels, and more graduate-led settings.

Table 2.1 shows the scale of the task in achieving widespread graduate leadership across early years services in the private and voluntary (PVI) sector, where the overall graduate level is under 5 per cent. This contrasts with the position in schools where there is a requirement that early years provision is led by a school teacher, who will in most cases be a graduate.

Table 2.1 Graduate leadership of childcare provision – 2005[1] (from DCSF Early Years Workforce Reform Discussion Paper, 2007)

Type of provider	Number of providers	Senior managers with qualifications at level 6 and above	
	n	n	%
Full day care	11,811	1,450	13
Sessional	9,966	750	8
Out-of-school	8,609	1,050	13
Childminders (working)	57,650	1,200	2

Note:
1 See DCSF (2006).

The Children's Workforce Strategy (DfES, 2006) set out the government's aim for all full daycare settings to employ a graduate Early Years Professional (EYP) by 2015, and since early 2006 the Children's Workforce Development Council (CWDC) has worked with its partners to develop the Early Years Professional Status (EYPS).

In Children's Centres, it is a requirement of their designation that they must employ a minimum 0.5 of a qualified teacher who assigns at least half their time to the development of young children. The government also intends for all Children's Centres to employ someone with EYPS by 2010. It is probable that many EYPs working in Children's Centres will be qualified teachers who have undertaken one of the training pathways to achieve EYPS. However, EYPS is not a requirement for the maintained sector where there are teachers with Qualified Teacher Status (QTS).

The strategy set out its vision and commitment to have a better qualified workforce and a higher proportion of the workforce qualified to at least Level 3 by 2008. The *National Standards for Under 8s Day Care and Childminding* (DfES, 2003) states that all supervisors of full daycare provision should hold at least a Level 3 qualification appropriate for the care and education of children. At least half of all the other childcare staff should hold a Level 2 qualification appropriate for the care or education of children.

We know from the 2005 Childcare and Early Years Providers Survey that the number and proportion of those with Level 3 qualifications continues to increase.

The government also launched the Transformation Fund to provide funding for increased training. This has now become the Graduate Leader Fund which includes investment both in the supply of early years professionals through the CWDC, and support to incentivise their employment. The Children's Plan increased the amount available to a total of £305 million between 2008 and 2011. This fund is made up of £232m for settings via LAs and £73m for CWDC to deliver early years professionals with Early Years Professional Status. However, none of this addresses the need for more teachers in the early years. The EPPE

Table 2.2 Proportion of all paid staff with at least a Level 3 qualification

Types of providers	2003	2005
	%	%
Full day care providers	57	63
Sessional providers	44	55
After school providers[1]	37	52
Childminders	16	43[2]

Notes:
1. Different methods of sample selection were used for the 2003 and 2005 surveys for this group of providers; the percentages are not directly comparable and should be treated as indicative of the trend.
2. This increase should be treated with caution as there is some evidence that it could be due to some childminders counting one unit towards the Level 3 qualification as a 'full' Level 3 qualification when answering this question (from DCSF Early Years Workforce Reform Discussion Paper, 2007).

project has shown that higher qualified staff are better for children's development, however the highest association was with qualified teachers. It is true that EYPS did not exist during our study of preschools, and a study comparing EYPS with QTS is desirable. It seems that the legacy of a muddle in provision is now being followed by a muddle in training, with an even more diverse workforce; different qualifications being more prolific in different types of provision, namely lower paid EYPS staff in largely the private and voluntary sector and QTS in the maintained (state) sector. The need for improved training of teachers to deliver the full EYFS also remains unresolved.

The challenges for early years

One of the main issues for local authorities is how to coordinate the diverse and many initiatives coming from government departments. Nevertheless, the drive to raise standards in pre-school education, to expand childcare, coordinate training and policy has to be welcome after years of un-coordinated and under-financed services. The vision for comprehensive and coordinated service will take time to develop. An extended programme of training in collaboration with institutes of higher education is needed to ensure that staff working with young children understand and implement effective teaching and learning practices leading to dispositions for lifelong learning (Siraj-Blatchford, 1999). The bringing together of education and the social services departments along with other relevant partners from all strands of early years and childcare provides an opportunity to address these important and complex issues. As recognised by the government there is a need to rationalise the existing systems of inspection, and a new early years branch of Ofsted, the inspection body, is some way to developing this. Local authorities and early childhood organisations will need to maintain pressure for a consistent approach and high quality inspections across all sectors providing education and childcare in the early years. In terms of training, the inequity in qualifications and conditions of service and remuneration need to be addressed.

The EYFS and the associated assessment profile provides an opportunity to get in place common curriculum and assessment practices and for staff development towards a consistent approach across all early years settings. However, the fact that early years provision is now firmly rooted in the welfare state, under the Child Care Act 2006 (sections 39–48 introduce the Early Years Foundation Stage which will build on and bring together the existing Birth to Three Matters, Foundation Stage and national standards for day care and childminding; this new framework aims to support providers in delivering quality integrated early education and care for children from birth to age 5) and although the training focus has shifted from graduates with an education specialism (teachers) to a broader qualification (EYPS) often without financial remuneration, the aims of EYFS will be difficult to achieve quickly.

During the EPPE study, and arguably even today, there is no level playing field across the range of early childhood provision in England. There is, and remains diversity in staff qualifications; their conditions of service, salaries, age profile and other fundamental experiences. In the chapters that follow, EPPE will explore whether these variations and pre-school factors make a difference to children's development and their day to day learning experiences.

For those interested in more detail on training, inspection and curriculum in England, further information can be obtained from the following websites:

- England's inspection body for all sectors of early education and care – www. ofsted.gov.uk
- The main government department for education and now responsible for the early years – www.dcsf.gsi.gov.uk
- The main body with information on early years curricula and assessment – www.qca.org.uk

Does such diversity in provision matter? In the next chapter we move on to describe the EPPE research design and the way we studied the effects of different types of pre-school provision and the effects of individual pre-school settings on children. In later chapters we also examine the important topic of quality of provision (Chapter 5) and provide detailed case studies of more effective centres that explore what constitutes good practice and pedagogy in early years (Chapter 8).

References

The Audit Commission (1996) *Counting to Five: Education of Children Under Five*, London: HMSO.

Bertram, T., Pascal, C., Bokhari, S., Gasper, M. and Holtermann, S. (2002) *Early Excellence Centre Pilot Programme: Second Evaluation Report 2000–2001* (DfES research report 361), London: DfES (available at http://publications.dcsf.gov.uk/eOrderingDownload/RR361.doc, accessed 9 January 2009).

Department for Children, Schools and Families (2006) *Childcare and Early Years Providers Survey 2006 – Technical Appendix*, DCSF-RW017, London: DCSF.

Department for Children, Schools and Families (2007) *Early Years Workforce Strategy Action Plan: Discussion Paper*, Early Years Workforce Development Team, 19 July 2007, London: DCSF.

Department for Children, Schools and Families (2008) *Early Years Foundation Stage Framework*, London: DCSF.

Department for Education and Employment (1996) *Nursery Education Desirable Outcomes for Children's Learning on Entering Compulsory Schooling*. London: Schools Curriculum and Assessment Authority/DfEE .

Department for Education and Science (1990) *Starting with Quality*, London: HMSO.

Department for Education and Science (DfES) (2003) *National Standards for Under 8s Day Care and Childminding: Childminding*, London: DfES.

Department for Education and Science (DfES) (2006) *Children's Workforce Strategy: Building an Integrated Qualifications Framework*, London: DFES.

HM Treasury (2003) *Every Child Matters* (Cm 5860), London: The Stationery Office (available at http://publications.everychildmatters.gov.uk/eOrderingDownload/CM5860.pdf, accessed 18 March 2009).

Hughes, B. (2009) Written Answers: Pre-School Education, London, Commons Hansard, 3 March 2009 Col 1561W.

Mooney, A., Boddy, J., Statham, J. and Warwick, I. (2006) *Diversity in Early Years Provision, Healthy Early Years Study*, London: Thomas Coram Research Unit.

Office for Standards in Education (Ofsted) (2006) *Quarterly Childcare Statistics as at: 31 December 2005*, London, Ofsted.

Qualifications and Curriculum Authority (2000) *The Foundation Guidance*, London: DfEE and QCA.

Schweinhart, L.J., Barnes, H.V., and Weikart, D.P. (1993) *Significant Benefits: The High Scope Perry Pre-school Study through Age 27*. Monograph of the High/Scope Educational Research Foundation, No 19, Ypsilanti, MI: High Scope Press.

Siraj-Blatchford, I. (ed.) (1998) *A Curriculum Development Handbook for Early Childhood Educators*, Stoke-on-Trent: Trentham Books.

Siraj-Blatchford, I. (1999) Early childhood pedagogy, practice, principles and research, in P. Mortimore (ed.) *Understanding Pedagogy and its Impact on Learning*, London: Paul Chapman.

Siraj-Blatchford, I. and Siraj-Blatchford, J. (2009) *Improving Development Outcomes for Children through Effective Practice in Integrating Early Years Services*, London: Centre for Excellence and Outcomes (C4EO).

Siraj-Blatchford, I., Sylva, K., Melhuish, E., Sammons, P. and Taggart, B. (1999) *The Effective Provision for Pre-School Education Project, Technical Paper 3. Contextualising the EPPE Project: Interviews with Managers and LEA Cco-ordinators*, London: DfEE and University of London, Institute of Education.

Siraj-Blatchford, I., Sylva, K., Muttock, S., Gilden, R. and Bell. D. (2002) *Researching Effective Pedagogy in the Early Years*, Research Report 356 Nottingham: Department for Education and Skills.

Siraj-Blatchford, I., Sylva, K., Taggart, B., Sammons, P., Melhuish, E.C. and Elliot, K. (2003) *The Effective Provision of Pre-School Education (EPPE) Project: Technical Paper 10 – Intensive Case Studies of Practice across the Foundation Stage*, DfES Research Brief No. RBX 16–03 October 2003. Nottingham: DfES Publications.

Siraj-Blatchford, J. (1997) *Robert Owen: Schooling the Innocents*. Nottingham: Educational Heretics Press.

Sylva, K., Siraj-Blatchford, I. and Johnson, S. (1992) *The Impact of the UK National Curriculum on Pre-school Practice, International Journal of Early Childhood*, 24, 41–51.

Sylva, K., Melhuish, E., Sammons, P., Siraj-Blatchford, I. and Taggart, B., (2008) *Effective Pre-School and Primary Education (EPPE 3–11) Project: Final Report from the Primary Phase: Pre-school, School and Family Influences on Children's Development during Key Stage 2 (age 7–11)* DCSF Research Report RR061, Nottingham; DCSF.

Sylva, K., Siraj-Blatchford, I., Melhuish, E.C., Sammons, P., Taggart, B., Evans, E., Dobson, A., Jeavons, M., Lewis, K., Morahan, M. and Sadler, S. (1999) *The Effective Provision of Pre-School Education (EPPE) Project: Technical Paper 6 – Characteristics of the Centres in the EPPE Sample: Observation Profiles*. London: DfEE/Institute of Education, University of London.

Taggart, B., Sylva, K., Siraj-Blatchford, I., Melhuish, E.C., Sammons, P. and Walker-Hall, J. (2000) *The Effective Provision of Pre-School Education (EPPE) Project: Technical Paper 5 – Characteristics of the Centres in the EPPE Sample: Interviews*. London: DfEE / Institute of Education, University of London.

Chapter 3

The EPPE research design

An educational effectiveness focus

Pam Sammons

This chapter describes the main aims of the EPPE research and the way we identified our pre-schools and child sample. It also outlines the data collection procedures, including how children were assessed at different time points throughout the study. It discusses the rationale for our choice of research design and why we chose to focus on exploring 'educational effectiveness' in the pre-school, and describes the methodology and analysis strategies.

The EPPE project is the first longitudinal research to apply an *educational effectiveness* design to the study of children's development and the effects of early years education and care. We chose this design to investigate the impact of pre-school on children's developmental outcomes (both cognitive and social behavioural) over time, from pre-school through to the end of primary school. Although EPPE's research methods draw upon several well known traditions of investigation, the questions it seeks to answer about 'effective' ways to educate and care for young children, are both contemporary and practical. The research team brought together researchers and approaches used in different and previously separate research traditions to provide a rigorous analysis that could be presented with quantitative breadth and sufficient qualitative depth to achieve impact upon policy and practice and contribute to the further understanding of the influence of pre-school on young children.

This chapter provides an account of the background to the research design, why mixed methods were chosen as the most appropriate design to answer the kind of research questions the team set out to explore and outlines the kinds of data and other evidence we collected. Further details of the instruments and measures used are given in Appendix 1. The research was originally designed to examine pre-school influences on young children's development in the early years following children up to age 7 years (the end of Key Stage 1 in primary school in England) but was later extended to investigate whether pre-school effects still continue to influence children's development in the longer term up to the end of primary school (Key Stage 2, age 11 years). The two phases of the research (pre-school and primary) are therefore described separately.

This chapter describes the research design and what it intended to accomplish. However, it is worth noting what EPPE was not constructed to do. Our study did not attempt to study specific pre-school interventions and their impact, for which an experimental design would be needed (for example see Ramey and Ramey, 1998 for a discussion of the impact of early intervention). Instead we sought to study naturally occurring variation in children's pre-school experiences in England and follow up a sample of children who had attended different types of pre-school into primary education to investigate longer term outcomes.

We chose a large scale design involving large numbers of children and centres, because we wanted to study variation in outcomes, and identify statistical patterns and effects. We therefore do not provide the thick description that qualitative case studies of individual children and families can offer (although in subsequent research we have followed up individual children and families to explore their experiences and perspectives, see Siraj-Blatchford, 2006). We have, however, included detailed case studies of more effective centres and these provide rich insights into practice and pedagogy that increase our understanding of effectiveness. Nor have we been able to give an account of individual's unique perspectives and voices as has been done in other largely qualitative and small scale studies.

Background

In the US, McCartney and Jordan (1990) suggested that the study of child care effects and of school effects should be more closely aligned. They argued that these two fields had developed separately through attempts to address three broadly parallel phases of research questions:

- Early Phase – does educational environment matter?
- Second Phase – what matters?
- Third Phase – what matters for which types of children?

The EPPE study, planned in 1996, explicitly sought to draw together these two separate fields of research to investigate the impact of pre-school education and care on young children. A mixed method design was judged most appropriate to facilitate such integration and to provide the rich mix of evidence needed to answer the research aims which were to inform both policy makers and practitioners.

Quantitative analysis was first applied to try to isolate the child, family, home learning and pre-school factors of most statistical significance in explaining variations in the progress and social behavioural development of young children during their time in pre-school, and to investigate the influence of attending pre-school. Multilevel statistical models were used to explore variations in the effectiveness of pre-school institutions in terms of different child outcomes and to identify 'outlier' pre-school centres for further study.[1] This approach was supported by a series of qualitative enquiries that both extended and triangulated the quantitative analysis and simultaneously provided the illustrational and

---

1   Multilevel models are a form of hierarchical regression analysis (Goldstein, 1995) that are particularly well suited to the study of institutional influences.

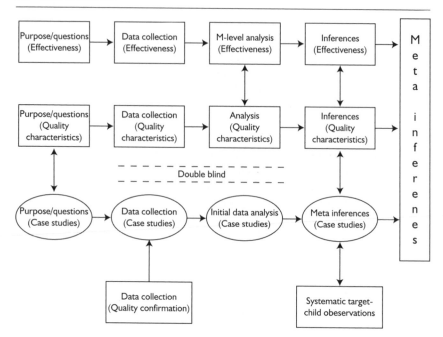

Figure 3.1 The mixed methods research design

practical exemplar resources that were needed in the development of early years educational practice.

While the *School Effectiveness* research field has developed quite separately from that of *School Improvement* in the UK until fairly recently, the EPPE study sought to address both of these concerns simultaneously through its innovative design. Figure 3.1 provides a simplified overview of the mixed method approach that was adopted. The multilevel modelling and data collection processes are described in detail in various technical papers (Sammons *et al.*, 2002, 2003; Siraj-Blatchford *et al.*, 2003). This chapter therefore outlines the relationships between the quantitative (effectiveness and quality characteristics) and the qualitative (case study) components of the project. The diagram illustrates the analytical process that allowed us to combine these two methodological components. Following the convention adopted by Tashakkori and Teddlie (2003), the rectangular blocks show the quantitative and the ovals show the qualitative stages in the research process. The diagram highlights three parallel aspects of analysis: the effectiveness study, the identification of quality characteristics and the case studies (Siraj-Blatchford *et al.*, 2006).

Research on the effects of early education

In the UK there is a long tradition of variation in pre-school provision between types of provider (voluntary, private and maintained) and in different parts of the country reflecting particular local authority (LA) emphases and funding and geographical conditions (e.g. urban or rural) during the mid-1990s. A series of reports questioned whether Britain's pre-school education was as effective as it might be and called for both better co-ordination of services along with research into the impact of different forms of provision (Siraj-Blatchford, 1995).

However, there has been little systematic longitudinal research on the effects of pre-school in the UK. One exception was the Child Health Education Study which indicated that children with some form of pre-school education had better outcomes at school (Osborn and Milbank, 1987). Other evidence had been provided concerning the influence of different pre-school environments on children's development (Melhuish, 1993; Sylva and Wiltshire, 1993). Some researchers adopted cross-sectional designs to explore the impact of different types of pre-school provision (Davies and Brember, 1997). The absence of data about children's attainments at entry to pre-school meant that neither the Birth Cohort Study (1970) nor the National Child Development Study (1958) could explore children's developmental progress over the pre-school period. Moreover, there have been significant changes and expansion in pre-school provision and use, as well as changes in the school system during the last 30 years, and thus the 1970 Cohort cannot provide evidence relevant to recent practice. A major enquiry into early years education and care, The 'Start Right' Enquiry (Ball, 1994) recommended the use of longitudinal studies with baseline measures so that the 'value added' to different child outcomes by pre-school education could be investigated and the results used to inform policy makers.

The most detailed and widely known studies of early education have been carried out in the USA. Slavin *et al.* (1994) used 'best evidence synthesis' to identify successful programmes for disadvantaged children. They concluded the more successful interventions combined several 'strands', involved intensive participation by children and families and lasted for a substantial number of years. The Perry Pre-school Project, later called High/Scope intervention, showed striking long term social and economic benefits for very disadvantaged children (Schweinhart *et al.*, 1993). The study adopted an experimental randomised control trial (RCT) design. There are however limitations (practical and ethical) on the use of randomised experimental designs in studies of pre-school influences. It is argued that the random allocation of young children to alternative pre-school 'treatments' would be unacceptable to most parents in England where policies emphasising parental 'choice' have been encouraged, particularly given the non-statutory nature of pre-school provision. Also RCT approaches, while appropriate to test the impact of specific interventions, can be difficult to generalise to other populations and contexts and cannot indicate which features of an intervention are most important.

Research into the effects of pre-school education requires longitudinal designs which separate pre-school influences from those related to the individual child's personal and family characteristics. It also needs to study a wide variety of children including a range of groups (disadvantaged children and others). Such research should also seek to identify and illuminate the educational processes, including pedagogy, associated with positive effects on children (Sylva, 1994), and so needs to sample from a wide range of different types of pre-school providers and settings. When EPPE was designed no research had sought to investigate the impact of both types of provision and to identify individual pre-school centre effects using appropriate longitudinal data sets and methodologies. The EPPE research aims included:

- comparing and contrasting the developmental progress of 3,000+ children from a wide range of social and cultural background who had differing pre-school experiences;
- separating out the effects of pre-school experience from the effects of the home and that of primary school education in the period between Reception and Year 2 (5–7 years);
- establishing whether some pre-school centres were more effective than others in promoting children's cognitive and/or their social/emotional development during the pre-school years (ages 3–5);
- discovering the individual characteristics (structural and process) of pre-school education in more effective centres.

In addition, when the research was extended to follow up the children in the sample to the end of primary schooling (age 11 years) the research aims were expanded to establish:

- whether pre-school influences continue to influence children's development in the mid- to longer term (after six years in primary school);
- how pre-school influences interact with those of the primary school in shaping children's developmental outcomes.

The effectiveness component to the design

Educational effectiveness designs explicitly seek to explore and model the impact of educational institutions by working with the natural clustered samples that are found in everyday settings such as pre-schools or schools (e.g. taking into account the fact that children or young people are grouped into schools or other institutions such as pre-school centres). The growing field of school effectiveness research has developed an appropriate methodology for the separation of intake and school influences on children's progress using so-called 'value added' multilevel models (Goldstein, 1995). But at the time the EPPE study was designed, such techniques had not been applied to the pre-school sector.

School effectiveness studies can be summarised as addressing the question 'Does the particular school attended by a child make a difference?' (Mortimore *et al.*, 1988). More recently the issues of internal variations in effectiveness, teacher/class level variations and stability in effects of particular schools over time have assumed importance. EPPE represents the first large scale longitudinal attempt to examine the impact of individual pre-school centres in promoting different kinds of child outcomes (cognitive and social/behavioural). The inclusion of a 'home' sample of children recruited at primary school entry is another important feature of the overall research design. It enables further comparison of the impact of experiencing different types of pre-school, different durations of time or quality of provision in a pre-school centre with a reference group (the home children) who had no experience of such group care. The analyses involving the home group, however, do not explore progress or social behavioural gains made over the pre-school period using value added approaches to identify individual centre effects. Such longitudinal analyses are conducted only on the main pre-school sample, for whom baseline data were collected at entry to a target pre-school when they were aged 3 years plus.

The child sample

Using a birth cohort sample would have been inappropriate for the EPPE research aims because insufficient numbers of children attending any one pre-school centre would be recruited and, because a cohort sample is intended to approximate a random selection, too few children would be included from certain types of provision. In order to maximise the likelihood of identifying both centre and type of provision effects, the sample was stratified by type of pre-school centre (e.g. nursery class, playgroup, etc.) and from a number of regions across the country (see Figure 3.2):

- six English Local Authorities (LAs) in five regions were chosen to cover provision in urban, suburban and rural areas and a range of ethnic diversity and social disadvantage;
- six types of group provision were included: playgroups, local authority day nurseries, private day nurseries and nursery schools and classes, and integrated/combined centres (which combined care and education see Chapter 2 for more details).

The project sought to recruit 500 children, 20 in each of 20–25 centres, from each of the six types of provision to ensure a clustered sample. However, in some LAs certain forms of provision were less common. Due to the small size of some centres (e.g. rural playgroups), more of this type were recruited than originally proposed, bringing the total to 141 centres and over 3,000 children in the study.

An additional sample of 300+ 'home' children who had no group pre-school experience was recruited from the reception classes to which children from the

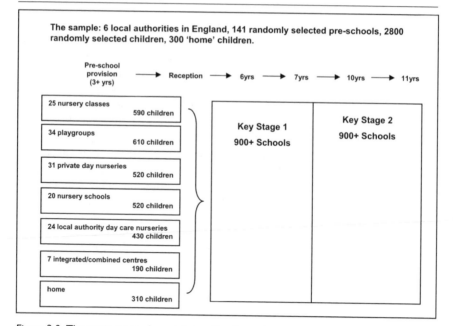

Figure 3.2 The project sample and data collection points

pre-school sample transferred. The numbers of children varied in the five regions, reflecting differences in provision and access to centres, and home children were found to be geographically clustered in some areas and over-represented amongst certain ethnic and social groups. Because of this an important part of our design was to ensure that detailed child, family and home environment background data were collected about each child in the sample when they were recruited. This is necessary to facilitate statistical control for potentially confounding influences related to a child's background, when we make any comparisons of the effects of pre-school type duration or quality.

It was not possible to recruit children at a 'common age' because in reality children can enter pre-school at different ages depending on the availability of places and parents' requirements. Children were recruited to the EPPE sample and baseline assessed within ten weeks of entry to the target centre from the ages of 3 years to 4 years 3 months. Children who had been at a centre before their third birthday were assessed as close to their third birth date as possible. Because children could enter at different ages it was important to take account of age as well as other background factors in our analyses and also to take account of how long children were in pre-school (in months) before they moved on to primary school.

Details about the number of sessions for which a child was registered and attendance were collected to enable the amount and duration of pre-school centre experience to be quantified. Significant variation in children's age at starting date at the 141 target centres was found, and the length (in months) of pre-school experience prior to baseline assessment at the start of the EPPE research was investigated. On average children attended one of our pre-school centres for around 18 months part time before starting primary school.

We followed the progress and development of EPPE children over four years until the children were 7 years old. Child mobility is a complicating factor because children can move from one form of pre-school provision to another. Mobile children were followed up so that separate analyses of this group could be conducted. A measure of change of centre was included in the statistical models to control for this mobility (in calculating pre-school centre effects reported in Chapter 6).

Child assessments

Common points of assessment were used, tracking children from age 3 years plus to end of Key Stage 1, so that the longer term influence of pre-school could be followed up to age 7 years. Children were later followed up in Years 5 and 6 in Key Stage 2. Appendix 1 lists all the assessments used. In this chapter we focus on those used to identify pre-school effects where we studied children's developmental progress from age 3 years plus to school entry.

Entry to pre-school (age 3.0 to 4 years 3 months)

Assessments provided a baseline against which later progress and development could be measured for the pre-school sample. The British Ability Scales II (BAS, Elliot et al., 1996) are designed for use with this age range and provided a measure of General Cognitive Ability (GCA) including both verbal and non-verbal sub-scales.[2] Centre staff familiar with the child completed an Adaptive Social Behaviour Inventory (ASBI, Hogan et al., 1992) to provide measures of children's social/behavioural development.

Entry to reception class (age rising 5 years)

Children were assessed at entry to primary school. The assessments were chosen to be compatible with the Desirable Learning Outcomes for Pre-School Education (DfEE, 1996): BAS II sub-scales were administered by researchers providing verbal and non-verbal measures, including Early Number Concepts. Pre-reading skills were measured by Letter recognition (Marie Clay) as well as Rhyme and Alliteration (Bryant and Bradley, 1985)[3]. The ASBI was adapted and extended to cover a greater range of behaviours and renamed the Child Social Behavioural

---

2   Children not fluent in English: assessed only on Block Building and Picture Similarity and social and emotional behaviour.

3   Children not fluent in English: assessed on Picture Similarity, Pattern Construction and social behaviour. In addition BAS II Copying, a measure of spatial ability.

Questionnaire with four sub scales: Self-regulation, Hyperactivity, Anti-social behaviour and Peer sociability.

End of Key Stage 1 (Year 2 age 7 years) and end of Key Stage 2 (age 11 years)

Children's national assessment results in English and Mathematics were collected and in addition, class teachers completed the Child Social Behavioural Questionnaire for each child in our sample.

Child and family background characteristics

Parent interviews at recruitment provided rich information about parent education, occupation and employment history, and family structure and a very high (97 per cent) response rate was achieved. Details about the child's day care history and health problems, and parental involvement in educational activities/play (e.g. reading to child, teaching nursery rhymes, etc.) were also collected and an index of the Home Learning Environment (HLE) was created (Melhuish et. al., 2008 and Chapter 4). Later on in primary school a parental questionnaire was used to provide some additional background data on family income, employment details, follow up changes in children's family circumstances and home learning. Here the response rate was approximately 80 per cent.

Identifying pre-school centre effects

The first phase of the study explored the impact of child, family and home environment characteristics on young children's attainment and their social behaviour measured at the start of the study age 3 years plus. The second phase focused on measuring their progress and development over the pre-school period, controlling for children's baseline scores and background influences (Sammons et al., 2002, 2003a; Sammons et al., 2004). *Contextual* models explored the influence of background factors on attainment or social behaviour at a given time point, while our *value added* models control for baseline scores plus background factors to explore progress or change in children's developmental outcomes over time.

The value added models show how much of the variation in child outcomes can be attributed to differences between individual children and that which lies between pre-school centres. The influences of age at assessment, amount and duration of pre-school experience and attendance record were investigated. Age at assessment is particularly important and the baseline BAS measures at entry to target pre-school (taken on average at 39 months) were internally standardised by the NFER for the EPPE study. Age at subsequent assessment was also modelled (the mean age at which children entered primary school was 4 years 9 months).

Predictor variables tested in the value added models included prior attainment (BAS total verbal and non-verbal scores) when we studied later cognitive or academic outcomes or prior social behaviour (ASBI factor scores on different dimensions of social behaviour) when we studied later social behavioural outcomes. In addition we included various background characteristics (personal, social and family, including early years HLE) in the models because much research has shown that such factors influence children's outcomes. In this way we could also take account of intake differences between pre-schools.

We examined differences in the attainments and social behaviour of different groups of children at entry to pre-school and again at entry to reception classes. Identifying the extent and strength of such differences is relevant to the discussion of equity issues and to current policy interest in the potential role of pre-school education as a means to promote inclusion.

Our models allowed us to create indicators of *relative effectiveness* for each of the 141 centres in our study for each of our different child outcome measures. Table 3.1 illustrates how individual centre residuals were classified into five centre effectiveness categories, ranging from significant positive outlier (95 per cent confidence limits lie above the expected value of zero) through to significant negative outlier (95 per cent confidence limits lie below zero) and gives the number of centres in each group for the five cognitive outcomes analysed.[4]

Most pre-school centres had relatively small numbers of children in the EPPE sample, thus the number of centres identified as outliers is likely to be a fairly conservative estimate of the extent of 'real' differences in relative effectiveness.

Table 3.2 illustrates two contrasting centre (fictitious) profiles for cognitive outcomes, one classified as broadly more effective in terms of positive outcomes (Park Lane nursery) and one broadly less effective (Elm Road nursery), based on the classification of pre-school centre residuals into five categories as described above. None of the EPPE centres were found to be highly effective in *every* area. However profiles tended to be generally either more positive or generally less positive; few centres had very mixed profiles. Similar profiles were constructed for each of the four social behavioural outcomes we measured and these profiles were also examined to select case studies.

Results from the analysis of the effectiveness profiles of the 141 centres were used to identify those that were effective and highly effective. This information was used to select case study centres for further in-depth investigation in the qualitative component of the research, described in a later section of this chapter (see also Chapter 8).

Effect sizes (ES) can provide measures of the relative importance of different predictors in educational research. ES are based on the difference in means between two groups divided by an estimate of the standard deviation. Usually used in reporting the results of intervention studies (particularly RCTs) they can be adapted for multilevel analyses (Tymms et al., 1997). EPPE used ES calculations

---

4   Residual estimates and their associated confidence limits were used to provide estimates of individual centre effects. The number of children within centres affects the identification of statistically significant outliers. Where the number of children is small, the confidence limits associated with the residual estimates are wider.

Table 3.1 Classification of pre-school centres for cognitive outcomes by effectiveness category*

Centre effectiveness category	Pre-reading		Early number concepts		Language		Non-verbal reasoning		Spatial awareness/ reasoning[1]	
	n	%	n	%	n	%	n	%	n	%
Significantly above expected (95% CI)**	10	7.1	7	5.0	1	0.7	1	0.7	3	2.1
Above expected (68% CI)	18	12.8	20	14.2	16	11.3	13	9.2	8	5.7
As expected	83	58.9	95	67.4	108	76.6	113	80.1	118	84.3
Below expected (68% CI)	24	17.0	14	10.0	14	9.9	12	8.5	9	6.4
Significantly below expected (95% CI)	6	4.3	5	3.5	2	1.4	2	1.4	2	1.4

Notes:
* n of centres in each category
**CI = confidence interval
1 For spatial awareness/reasoning, 140 centres were included in the analysis due to missing data

Table 3.2 Examples of two contrasting value added centre profiles (fictitious) for cognitive outcomes

Centre effectiveness category	Pre-reading	Early number concepts	Language	Non-verbal reasoning	Spatial awareness/ reasoning
'Excellent' – significantly above expected (95% CI*)	Park Lane				
'Good' – above expected (68% CI)			Park Lane	Park Lane	
Typical – as expected	Elm Road	Park Lane			Park Lane and Elm Road
'Below average' – below expected (68% CI)		Elm Road		Elm Road	
'Poor' – significantly below expected (95% CI)			Elm Road		

Notes:
Park Lane has a broadly positive (more effective) centre profile
Elm Road has a broadly negative (less effective) centre profile
* CI = Confidence interval

to illustrate the relative impact of different child, family and home environment factors and also for other measures such as duration, quality and type of pre-school (Elliot and Sammons, 2004). Table 3.3 illustrates selected results of the net impact of different child characteristics based on estimates from the value added models, compared with the impact of the quality and duration of pre-school on child progress in two important areas: Pre-reading and Early number concepts.

Comparisons with children who did not go to pre-school: results for the 'home' group

When comparisons of outcomes were made with the home group compared with children who did attend a pre-school, it was not possible to use value added models that control for prior attainment as this was not available for the home group. Contextualised multilevel models including significant child, family, home environment measures and duration of pre-school in months (versus none for the home group) as predictors of attainment at entry to primary school were therefore employed. Both the presence and absence of pre-school centre experience and also its duration could thus be tested. Such models enable direct comparison of the net impact of specific background characteristics on attainment (e.g. a child's gender, etc.) with those of different durations of pre-school.

Table 3.3 Illustrative examples of effect sizes for selected background factors – for progress in pre-reading and early number concepts over the pre-school period*

	Pre-reading ES	Early number concepts ES
FSM	0.12	ns
Gender	0.21	0.09
Low birth weight	0.19	ns
Very low birth weight	0.23	0.47
Mother academic 18yrs+	0.21	0.23
Quality of pre-school	0.18	0.16
Duration of pre-school	0.38	0.28

Note:
* ES calculated from value added multilevel models controlling for prior attainment and child, family and home environment influences, pre-school sample only.

Quality characteristics

Field Officers made regular visits to centres, maintained notes, observed staff and children and interviewed centre directors. They collected information on: group size, child–staff ratio, staff training, aims, policies, curriculum, and parental involvement. Process quality characteristics studied included child-staff interaction, child–child interaction, and structuring of children's activities. Information was also obtained from the Early Childhood Environment Rating Scale Revised (ECERS-R) (Harms *et al.*, 1998). The ECERS-R includes the following sub-scales:

- Space and furnishings
- Personal care routines
- Language and reasoning
- Activities
- Interaction
- Programme structure
- Parents and staffing.

Further measures of quality were collected using the Caregiver Interaction Scale (CIS, Arnett 1989), covering 'Positive relationships', 'Punitiveness', 'Permissiveness and 'Detachment'.

Sylva *et al.* (2003) developed the Early Childhood Environment Rating Scale-Extension, an instrument which included four sub-scales covering educational quality in terms of: Language, Mathematics, Science and Environment, and Diversity. The ECERS-R and E and CIS ratings were compared and showed general agreement in identifying higher quality centres. Statistically significant differences in quality measures at the centre level within and between types of provider were revealed (Sylva *et al.*, 1999, 2006). We discuss the way we measured quality in more detail in Chapter 5. Overall, integrated centres and nursery schools had higher quality ratings, whereas playgroups and private day nurseries had significantly lower average scores. Private day nurseries showed greater variation in quality evidenced by a larger standard deviation for each scale.

Our multilevel analyses tested our various measures of children's pre-school experience (attendance or not, duration of attendance in months, the various measures of quality) to see whether they indicated that they were significantly related to children's outcomes and developmental progress. In other words, after we take account of children's background factors, does pre-school make a difference – predict better outcomes when children start primary school? In Chapters 6 and 7 we show the size and statistical significance of pre-school effects. In addition to examining whether pre-school gave children a better start to primary school (in terms of improved cognitive and social behavioural outcomes at reception entry) we also followed the sample up at ages 7 and 11 years. This was done to see whether pre-school effects continue to influence children's development in the mid- to longer term after three to six years in primary school or whether they are only evident in the short term and tend to 'wash out'. This is a very important matter given the resources devoted to pre-school, in terms of providing a lasting benefit. Of particular interest also is whether pre-school benefits all children and to what extent it can help disadvantaged children in particular.

The diagram below illustrates our quantitative analysis strategy for studying the influence of different factors (related to the five main groups of interest to our research) on child outcomes at different time points. In order to explore continuing pre-school influences up to the end of Key Stage 1 and then later to the end of Key Stage 2 we had to include details about the primary school attended in the models because we knew from past research on school effectiveness that the

Different influences on child outcomes

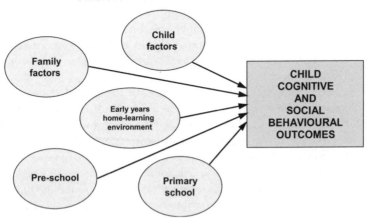

Figure 3.3 The modelling strategy for the quantitative multilevel analyses of children's attainment and social-behavioural outcomes

primary school would also be likely to have an important impact on children's attainment, progress and social behavioural development.

The qualitative methodological component

A systematic (although non-linear) process that we describe as 'iterative triangulation' characterised much of the general approach in applying the mixed methodology design for EPPE. Apart from exploiting the usual benefits of triangulation in achieving greater internal validity, we were concerned to work 'back and forth between inductive and deductive models of thinking' (Creswell, 1994, p.178). The regular, weekly meetings of the central team and their varied research backgrounds greatly facilitated this dialogue. Despite this commitment to collaborative practice it was decided that the initial analysis of the twelve case study pre-school centres should be conducted 'blind' to avoid any possibility of (subconscious) analytic bias. Neither the principal qualitative investigator nor any other researcher engaged in the initial qualitative data collection and analysis therefore knew the specific outcomes achieved by each of the selected case study centres. The initial analysis was also conducted without reference to the analyses of correlations between the various outcomes and pre-school quality characteristics.

Case studies

The effectiveness study had shown that none of the 141 individual centres performed statistically significantly either above or below expectations across all of the child outcomes studied. But some centres were found to have particular strengths, and others areas of apparent weakness. A purposive sample of twelve centres was selected to include those classified as having 'good' (68 per cent confidence level), to 'excellent' (95 per cent confidence level) developmental progress in one or more of the cognitive, or social/behavioural outcomes. The case study sample thus provided a number of contrasting centre profiles for in-depth comparison. An important feature of the research process was that the field workers did not know which were the 'good' and which the 'excellent' centres in terms of child outcomes.

Since the EPPE children had left the centres by the time of the case studies, it was necessary to ensure the centres selected had not changed greatly. The ECERS-E was therefore re-administered and the centres were only included if they achieved a similar or better ECERS-E score than previously recorded. It was also important that centres had experienced no major management changes (keeping the same manager/deputy and senior management team), and that there were no difficult circumstances associated with the centre around the time of the field work that might affect staff behaviour or aspects of the provision observed (e.g. pending/recent inspection by Ofsted).

The overall aim of the case studies was to explore what helped to make some centres more successful at achieving better child outcomes in particular domains.

The aim was to tease out specific pedagogical and other practices associated with achieving 'excellent' outcomes as compared to 'good' outcomes. The decision not to compare 'excellent' with 'poor' performance was made for ethical reasons and also to maximise the potential impact of the data for use in dissemination and engagement with practitioners. The comparison of excellent with poor practice was deemed to be less fruitful and illuminating than the contrast of good and excellent. The case studies applied a variety of methods of data gathering, including documentary analysis, interviews and observation. The researchers were trained to:

- conduct more naturalistic observations, followed by discussion with staff;
- engage in semi-structured interviewing of staff and parents;
- collect and analyse documents such as policies, plans and information booklets.

Each researcher had made up to 40 previous visits to their case study centres for child assessments and ECERS ratings, and spent two weeks in each of their centres collecting qualitative data. This was supplemented by a further week of fieldwork to carry out structured child observations using a systematic 'target child observations' procedure (Sylva, 1997). The analytic codes that were initially derived through a process of grounded induction from the observation and interview data, were continually reworked and adapted through the subsequent analyses of data and in consideration of the findings of other studies identified in the literature review of early years pedagogy (Strauss and Corbin, 1990). As soon as the first phase of this process was complete, and all of the qualitative data had been initially coded, and 'thick descriptions' produced for the individual case study accounts (Siraj-Blatchford et al., 2003), the 'reduced data' were interrogated further seeking pedagogic process explanations for the cognitive and social outcomes provided by the effectiveness study. Where the pedagogic findings appeared to provide explanatory support for any particular EPPE outcome, theoretical sampling (of the full data set) was employed to investigate more closely the centres achieving the best results in those terms. In order to illustrate the analytical processes involved in identifying 'effective pedagogies' we provide the example of 'sustained share thinking'. While our observations showed it was less commonly employed by practitioners, sustained shared thinking came to be identified as a particularly effective pedagogy and is described in Chapter 8.

The case study analysis was further supported by data from the systematic target child observations (Sylva, 1997). A total of 254 target child observations were carried out in each of the case study centres, involving 10 boys and 10 girls, identified by practitioners to show a range of ability and age. These systematic observations allowed us to focus on individual children within a centre and record their social participation, their activity, curriculum experience and interactions with adults. These events were sampled every 30 seconds, for a total of 20 minutes on each occasion. The training and piloting of the Target Child Observation system took place in a range of centres unrelated to the case studies. Inter-rater reliability was calculated using Kappa, and the results for all codes ranged between 0.57 and 0.84.

Of the 254 target child observations, 141 were randomly selected for more fine-grained qualitative analysis. The 20-minute target child observation was divided into various learning episodes. The learning episodes recorded in this detailed way were continuous, coherent activities which were initiated either by children or adults, and lasted for at least one minute. The episodes were examined to provide an analysis that included who initiated and chose each activity (staff member or child), and the cognitive challenge involved (see Sylva et al., 1980).

All pedagogical interactions made by adults to the target child during the systematic timed observations were recorded and assigned to different categories, e.g. 'adult models'. These smaller categories were then grouped together into higher order categories based on the qualitative findings. For example, 'modelling' and 'questions' were grouped together to form part of the higher order category 'sustained shared thinking' (Siraj-Blatchford, 2009).

Overview

In this chapter we have provided a rationale for our choice of a mixed methods research design to study pre-school influences and described the quantitative and qualitative components and how the two sources of evidence were analysed and interrelated. Our longitudinal 'educational effectiveness' design enabled statistical modelling of the effects of different features of pre-school experiences (amount, type, quality, duration of attendance at pre-school) on children's attainment and social behaviour at different time points, and on children's developmental progress over the pre-school period and in primary school across different Key Stages. The inclusion of a 'home group' enabled further important comparisons about the impact of pre-school to be made. An important feature of our design was modelling the influences of child, family and home learning environment characteristics on the various child outcomes we studied and exploring how these change as children move through school. Our design has advantages in studying naturally occurring variation in children's pre-school experiences and their impacts at different ages; in particular it allows us to establish whether such effects continue to influence children's development in primary school in the mid- to long term. For further in-depth discussion of our mixed methods rationale see Sammons et al. (2005) and Siraj-Blatchford et al. (2006), two articles that focus particularly on this feature of the EPPE research design.

The EPPE research design was influenced by both pragmatic and philosophical arguments that suggest mixed methods can offer complementary strengths and minimise the weaknesses associated with reliance on only one paradigm (for further discussion see Johnson and Onwuegbuzie, 2004). The longitudinal mixed methods design brought together a large-scale quantitative survey approach that involved the assessment of children and both structured and non-structured observation of practitioners and children in the in-depth case studies that illuminate and enhance understanding of what constitutes good and excellent practice. While our diagram (Figure 3.1) suggests a fairly linear sequence of quantitative-qualitative-quantitative analysis, the reality involved a more complex iterative approach. The use of mixed methods has, we believe, enabled a study of pre-school influence that is more meaningful, and provides a wider evidence base for both policy makers and practitioners than reliance on only one form of data gathering and approach to analysis. We argue that complex and pluralistic social contexts demand analysis that is informed by multiple and diverse perspectives. Our conclusions, and our inferences, are therefore stronger for having applied a mixed method approach.

EPPE findings are generally in line with those of the National Institute of Child Health and Development study in the US (NICHD, 2002). However, the NICHD study did not employ an educational effectiveness design and so could not investigate the impact of *individual* pre-school centres. EPPE sought to include children from the full range of provision, plus an additional group of home children in the design. This improved the ability to detect pre-school effects. The large EPPE data set has enabled additional research on children with special educational needs, developing understanding of those children most 'at risk' in the pre-school period and the impact of multiple disadvantage (Sammons *et al.*, 2003b; Taggart *et al.*, 2006).

The correspondence in findings on the importance of early child care between EPPE and the NICHD suggests the conclusions concerning the impact of pre-school experience in terms of both quality and quantity (duration) are robust. EPPE goes further, however, by examining variation in the effectiveness of *individual* pre-school centres as well as exploring the impact of pre-school type in England. Case studies are an important feature with the qualitative and quantitative strands creating an ongoing research dialogue and illuminating the study of processes. They have proved particularly valuable in the development of explanations and models of effective pedagogical practices, while the quantitative results on pre-school effects have informed the development of pre-school policy in England as we describe later in Chapter 11.

First however we need to examine the characteristics of the EPPE child sample and investigate the importance of child family and home learning environment influences on young children's social behavioural and cognitive development. These features are of considerable interest in their own right but it is also important to examine such influences before we seek to investigate the contribution of pre-schools. They help us to set pre-schools in the context of the communities and families they serve and show why intake matters in any study of pre-schools.

References

Arnett, J. (1989) Caregivers in day-care centres: does training matter? *Journal of Applied Developmental Psychology*, 10, 541–552.

Ball, C. (1994) *Start Right: The Importance of Early Learning*, London: RSA.

Bryant, P. and Bradley, L. (1985) *Children's Reading Problems*, Oxford: Blackwell.

Creswell, J. W. (1994) *Research Design: Qualitative and Quantitative Approaches*, Thousand Oaks, CA: Sage.

Davies, J. and Brember, I. (1997) The effects of pre-school experience on reading attainment: a four year cross-sectional study, *Educational Psychology*, 178 (3), 255–266.

Department for Education and Employment (1996) *Desirable Outcomes for Children's Learning*, London: DfEE.

Elliot, C.D., with Smith, P. and McCulloch, K. (1996) *British Ability Scales Second Edition BAS II)*, Windsor: NFER-Nelson.

Elliot, K. and Sammons, P. (2004) Exploring the use of effect sizes to evaluate the impact of different influences on child outcomes, in K. Elliot and I. Schagen (eds) *What Does it Mean? The Use of Effect Sizes in Educational Research*, Slough: NFER.

Goldstein, H. (1995) *Multilevel Statistical Models*, 2nd edn, London: Edward Arnold.

Harms, T., Clifford, R. and Cryer, D. (1998) *Early Childhood Environment Rating Scale Revised*, New York and London: Teachers' College Press.

Hogan, A.E., Scott, K.G. and Bauer, C.R. (1992) The adaptive social behaviour inventory (ASBI): a new assessment of social competence in high-risk three year olds, *Journal of Psycho Educational Assessments*, 10(3), 230–239.

Johnson, R. and Onwuegbuzie. A. (2004) Mixed methods research: a research paradigm whose time has come, *Educational Researcher*, 33, 7, 14–26.

McCartney, K. and Jordan, E. (1990) Parallels between research on child care and research on school effects, *Educational Researcher*, 19 (1): 24–27.

Melhuish, E.C. (1993) Pre-school care and education: lessons from the 20th and the 21st century, *International Journal of Early Years Education*, 1, 19–32.

Melhuish, E., Sylva, K., Sammons, P., Siraj-Blatchford, I., Taggart, B. and Phan, M. (2008) Effects of the home learning environment and preschool center experience upon literacy and numeracy development in early primary school, *Journal of Social Issues*, 64(1), 95–114.

Mortimore, P., Sammons, P., Stoll, L., Lewis, D. and Ecob, R. (1988) *School Matters: The Junior Years*, Wells: Open Books.

National Institute of Child Health and Development NICHD (2002) Early child care and children's development prior to school entry: results from the NICHD Study of Early Child Care, *American Educational Research Journal*, 39, (1): 133–164.

Osborn, A.F. and Milbank, J.E. (1987) *The Effects of Early Education: A Report From the Child Health and Education Study*, Oxford: Clarendon Press.

Ramey, C.T. and Ramey, S.L. (1998) Early intervention and early experience, *American Psychologist*, 53, 109–126.

Sammons, P., Sylva, K., Melhuish, E., Siraj-Blatchford, I., Taggart, B. and Elliot, K. (2002) *Measuring the Impact of Pre-school on Children's Cognitive Progress over the Pre-School Period*, EPPE Technical Paper 8a, London: DfES/Institute of Education.

Sammons, P., Sylva., K., Melhuish, E., Siraj-Blatchford, I., Taggart, B. and Elliot, K. (2003a) *Measuring the Impact of Pre-school on Children's Social Behavioural Progress over the Pre-School period*, EPPE Technical Paper 8b, London: DfES/Institute of Education.

Sammons, P., Siraj-Blatchford, I., Sylva, K., Melhuish, E., Taggart, B. and Elliot, K. (2005) Investigating the effects of pre-school provision: using mixed methods in the EPPE research, *International Journal of Social Research Methodology, Theory and Practice*, special issue on mixed methods, *Educational Research*, 8(3), 207–224.

Sammons, P., Smees, R., Taggart, B., Sylva., K., Melhuish, E., Siraj-Blatchford, I. and Elliot, K. (2003b) *The Early Years Transition and Special Educational Needs (EYTSEN) Project*, Technical Paper 1, London: DfES/Institute of Education.

Sammons, P., Elliot, K., Sylva, K., Melhuish, E., Siraj-Blatchford, I., Taggart, B., and Smees, R., (2004) The impact of pre-school on young children's cognitive attainments at entry to reception, *British Educational Research Journal*, 30 (5), 691–712.

Siraj-Blatchford, I. (1995) Expanding combined nursery provision: bridging the gap between care and education, in P. Gammage and J. Meighan *The Early Years: The Way Forward*, Nottingham: Education New Books.

Siraj-Blatchford, I. (2009) Conceptualising progression in the pedagogy of *Play and Sustained Shared Thinking* in early childhood education: A Vygotskian perspective, *Educational & Child Psychology*, 26(2), 77–89.

Siraj-Blatchford, I., Sylva, K., Taggart, B., Sammons, P. and Melhuish, E. (2003) *The EPPE Case Studies*, Technical Paper 10, London: Institute of Education/DfEE.

Siraj-Blatchford, I., Sammons, P., Sylva, K., Melhuish, E. and Taggart, B. (2006) Educational research and evidence based policy: the mixed method approach of the EPPE Project, *Evaluation and Research in Education*, special issue – 'Combining Numbers with Narratives', guest edited by S. Gorard and E. Smith, 19(2), 63–82.

Slavin, R.E., Karweit, N.L. and Wasik, B.A. (1994) *Preventing Early School Failure*, Needham Heights, MA: Allyn and Bacon.

Strauss, A. and Corbin, J. (1990) *Basics of Qualitative Research*, Newbury Park, CA: Sage.

Sylva, K. (1994) School influences on children's development, *Journal of Child Psychology and Psychiatry*, 35(1), 135–170.

Sylva, K. (1997) The target child observation, in K. Sylva and J. Stevenson *Assessing Children's Social Competence*, Slough: NFER Nelson.

Sylva, K. and Wiltshire, J. (1993) The impact of early learning on children's later development: a review prepared for the RSA Enquiry 'Start Right', *European Early Childhood Education Research Journal*, 1(1),17–40.

Sylva, K., Roy, C. and Painter, M. (1980) *Childwatching at Playgroup and Nursery School*, London: Grant McIntyre.

Sylva, K., Sammons, P., Melhuish, E., Siraj-Blatchford, I. and Taggart, B. (1999) *The Effective Provision of Pre-school Education (EPPE) Project. Technical Paper 1 – An Introduction to the EPPE Project*, London: DfES/Institute of Education, University of London.

Sylva, K., Siraj-Blatchford, I. and Taggart, B. (2003) *The Early Childhood Environment Rating Scales: 4 Curricular Subscales*, Stoke on Trent: Trentham Books.

Sylva, K., Siraj-Blatchford, I., Taggart, B., Sammons, P., Melhuish, E., Elliot, K. and Totsika, V. (2006) Capturing quality in early childhood through environmental rating scales, *Early Childhood Research Quarterly*, 21, 76–92.

Taggart, B., Sammons, P., Smees, R., Sylva, K., Melhuish, E., Siraj-Blatchford, I., Elliot, K. and Lunt, I. (2006) Early identification of special needs and the definition of 'at risk': the Early Years Transition and Special Education Needs (EYTSEN) Project, *British Journal of Special Education*, 33 (1), 40–45.

Tashakkori, A. and Teddlie, C. (2003) (eds) *Handbook of Mixed Methods in Social and Behavioural Research*, Thousand Oaks, CA: Sage.

Tymms, P., Merrell, C. and Henderson, B. (1997) The first year at school: A quantitative investigation of the attainment and progress of pupils, *Educational Research and Evaluation*, 3(2), 101–118.

Chapter 4

Why children, parents and home learning are important

Edward Melhuish

This chapter describes the characteristics of the EPPE children and their families including a range of background characteristics and social demographics. It investigates the relationships between such child, family and home factors and various measures of young children's social behavioural and cognitive development at different ages. It also includes a discussion of the importance of the early years home learning environment (HLE) experiences and illustrates the way social disadvantage affects children's development and increases the risk of poor outcomes.

The families in the EPPE study

Parental characteristics in terms of levels of employment, marital status, age and educational qualifications all show associations with the socio-economic status or level of disadvantage of the family, and they differ for the groups in the study. We can illustrate these differences with regard to mothers' qualifications as shown in Tables 4.1 and 4.2.

The EPPE sample is over-represented (as compared with a national sample) at the bottom end of the socio-economic spectrum with some over-representation at the top end of the spectrum. This is illustrated with mothers'educational qualifications in Table 4.1, and other measures linked to socio-economic status

Table 4.1 Educational qualifications of mother: EPPE versus national sample.

Qualification	EPPE sample %	National sample %
Degree or higher	16.9	12.9
HND, 18+ vocational	13.4	12.1
A level	8.4	12.7
GCSE level	37.0	44.1
Less than GCSE level	23.4	16.2
Other miscellaneous	0.9	1.9

Table 4.2 Educational qualifications of mother by pre-school type (% within each pre-school type).

Education-al qualifica-tions	Pre-school groups						
	Nursery class	Play-group	Private day nursery	LA day nursery	Nursery school	Integrated centre	'Home' group
Degree or higher	12.9	10.9	36.9	18.3	14.6	16.5	3.9
HND, 18+ Vocational	11.8	14.1	9.9	16.6	16.8	18.2	6.6
A level	6.4	8.2	13.8	6.8	8.9	11.4	3.5
GCSE	43.5	46.3	31.2	27.6	40.1	27.8	27.1
Less than GCSE	23.6	19.7	6.5	29.8	19.4	26.1	58.1

reveal a similar pattern. This was done for two reasons: (a) to provide sufficiently large numbers of disadvantaged/ethnic minority children for robust findings related to them, and (b) to lead to a representative sample at age 7 after (anticipated) selective attrition in more disadvantaged groups.

The groups in the EPPE study differ significantly in terms of mothers' qualifications. The mothers in the private day nursery group show a distinctly higher level of educational qualifications than the rest of the sample. The LA centre group has the next highest percentage of mothers with a degree or better qualifications but this group also has the second highest percentage of mothers with no qualifications. This reflects the admissions policies of several local authorities to their pre-school centres, where they maintain a quota of fee-paying places, usually used by parents with higher socio-economic status and educational qualifications but with many places kept for families of low socio-economic status who are non fee-paying. The combined centres group has a similarly diverse make-up in terms of mothers' qualifications. The playgroup, nursery class, and nursery school groups are in the middle of the range. The home group mothers have by far the highest proportion with no qualifications. Similar differences exist across other parental characteristics reflecting differences in terms of socio-economic status or disadvantage.

As other measures of disadvantage vary in a similar way to mothers' education (as shown by Melhuish *et al.*, 1999, Melhuish *et al.*, 2001), we can say in summary that the home group has by far the highest proportion of disadvantaged families, LA centres and combined centres are next most disadvantaged and similar to each other. The playgroup, nursery class and nursery school families are towards the middle of the range of disadvantage seen in the EPPE sample. The families using private day nurseries are by far the most advantaged in the sample.

The EPPE project considered how a wide range of factors influence children's development. For example, when looking at attainment in English, we consider how child, family, neighbourhood, pre-school and school influenced a child's English attainment. When progress is considered, the child's prior attainment is added into the statistical model (for details of the methodology and analytical strategy see Chapter 3 and for details of pre-school effects see Chapter 6). The large sample size and the statistical methods allow the separate influence of each of these background characteristics (predictors) to be estimated, so that when an effect for pre-school is shown (see Chapter 6) it is after allowing for all the relevant background factors. Although much of the emphasis in this study is the short, medium and long term impact of pre-school, it would be nonsensical to study this without first examining the children and families who use these settings. So, before looking at the impact of pre-school it is important to consider the individual attributes that children themselves and their families bring to the study. In this chapter we refer to the strength of influences upon children's development in terms of effect size (ES)[1] for easy comparison.

The importance of child characteristics

Sylva *et al.* (2004) summarised how EPPE children's own individual characteristics (gender, birth weights, etc.) exerted an influence on their cognitive and social/behavioural outcomes up to the age of 7 and drew attention to the importance of these background variables. This chapter refers to some of those associations but adds to the findings of the first phase of the study, by reporting on the enduring influences and how some of these change as children get older (to age 11 at the end of primary school).

It is important to recognise that we refer here to patterns of statistical association and prediction. When we report on gender effects we refer to differences between girls and boys as groups, although we may find that, as a whole, girls show better language development than boys at age 3 or 5 years, this does not of course mean that all girls have better language than all boys. There is a great deal of individual variation within as well as between groups. It is important to be aware of such patterns and to control for such differences in investigating pre-school effects, but the individual teacher or early years staff member should not let such information colour their judgements and expectations of individual children. A child's disadvantaged background should not lead to lower expectations, rather teachers

---

1 The effect size is a statistical measure (in standard deviation units) of how much the outcome measure (e.g. maths attainment) is related to the predictor measure (e.g. age, mothers' education) having allowed for other factors that also influence the outcome. Effect sizes of less than 0.1 are very small and relatively unimportant, an effect size of 0.2 would be small but potentially important, effect size of 0.5 would be medium and very important and 0.8 would be large and extremely important (Howell, 1989). Note that all effects sizes quoted are after allowing for all other influences and hence are conservative estimates.

and staff need to assess children carefully so that they can identify strengths and support children appropriately. The evidence on the impact of background is best used to help target resources and monitor equity gaps, with early intervention strategies to support vulnerable groups and those children showing developmental delay compared with other children of their age group.

Gender differences

Sammons *et al.* (2008a, 2008b) reported on how, as a group, young girls out-performed boys on most outcomes up to age 11. At age 11, girls are still doing better than boys in English (ES=0.29) but boys now have slightly better attainment in Mathematics (ES=–0.19). This is in contrast to earlier ages where girls showed higher attainment than boys in both subjects. Also there are marked gender differences in social/behavioural development. Boys were rated by teachers as displaying more Hyperactive and 'Anti-social' behaviour than girls, whereas girls were rated more highly on Self-regulation and 'Pro-social' behaviour than boys at age 11. Differences between the genders are especially large for 'Pro-social' behaviour and 'Hyperactivity' (where the effect size is 0.71 for both measures).

Birth weight and early developmental problems

Throughout the study low birth weight (LBW) has been adversely related to children's development. At age 11 children with very LBW still showed significantly lower attainment in English (ES=–0.47) and Mathematics (ES=–0.48) than children with normal birth weight.[2]

Independent of the birth weight effects, child developmental problems reported by parents before age 3 frequently were related to later development. Children whose parents reported early developmental problems showed lower attainment in English and Mathematics at age 11 than children for whom no early developmental problems were reported (ES=–0.24 English, –0.15 Mathematics). Children who had one early behavioural problem, reported by parents, also had lower Self-regulation (ES=–0.25) and 'Pro-social' behaviour (ES=–0.24) and significantly higher 'Hyperactivity' (ES=0.31) and 'Anti-social' behaviour (ES=0.24) at age 11. In contrast, having early developmental problems was found to be a significant predictor only for later Self-regulation (ES=–0.47) at age 11.

Children with English as an additional language (EAL)

Most children with EAL had similar scores to their peers. However, children who still needed support for English as an additional language (EAL) at age 11 showed

---

2   We used three classifications for birth weight: above 2,500 gms is regarded as normal birth weight, between 1,501 and 2,500 gms is regarded as low birth weight and below 1,500 gms is regarded as very low birth weight.

lower attainment in English (ES=–0.59) and Mathematics (ES=–0.64) than others. Possibly the effect of EAL support is slightly stronger for Mathematics than English because EAL support is often targeted at reading rather than mathematics in primary schools. Also the need for EAL support was associated with lower Self-regulation (ES=–0.65) and greater 'Hyperactivity' (ES=0.46).

Season of birth

A child's age within a year group was also found to be a significant influence on their development. Specifically, the younger the pupil (in their academic year) the poorer their performance tends to be, compared with older pupils (Crawford *et al.*, 2007). In our study we have used age standardised tests when measuring cognitive attainment, as the exact age of a pupil can exercise an influence on their cognitive performance.

To illustrate this effect of age within year we compared children born in different school terms. The Autumn-born (September to December) were older than the Spring-born (January to April) and the youngest are the Summer-born (May to August). When comparing children's attainment in their Key Stage 2 (age 11) assessments the Autumn-born more often achieved highest level attainment (Level 5) than the Spring-born who had greater attainment than the Summer-born. Table 4.3 shows the differences between these three groups in terms of the percentage reaching each level of attainment in English. Similar patterns are evident for Mathematics attainment at this age.

One possible consequence of such differences by age in year is a greater likelihood of younger children being identified, possibly erroneously, as having special educational needs (SEN). Table 4.4 indicates that there is such a difference, with a greater proportion of younger pupils being identified as having an SEN in KS2 compared to older pupils.

These findings are similar to other studies (see Crawford *et al.*, 2007) which have identified the 'age' effect. Traditionally, entry to school in England is during the

Table 4.3 English attainment level at KS2 and season of birth (*n*=2810)

| Key Stage 2 academic level | Season/term child born | | | | | |
| | Autumn | | Spring | | Summer | |
	n	%	n	%	n	%
No level awarded	39	4.2	57	5.5	60	7.0
Level 2	8	0.9	9	0.9	12	1.4
Level 3	116	12.6	166	16.1	148	17.2
Level 4	448	48.5	511	49.7	438	51.0
Level 5	313	33.9	285	27.7	200	23.3
Total	924	100	1028	100	858	100

Table 4.4 Special educational needs (SEN) identified up to the end of KS2 by season of birth (n=2718)

| | Season/term child born | | | | | |
| | Autumn | | Spring | | Summer | |
SEN status	n	%	n	%	n	%
SEN identified	318	35.8	402	40.4	375	45.0
Not SEN identified	571	64.2	593	59.6	459	55.0
Total	889	10.00	995	100.0	834	100.0

year of a child's fifth birthday. Children entering in the Autumn term (September to December) experience longer in a 'reception' (or first class) than their summer born peers. Recently attention has been drawn to this inequity (see Crawford *et al.*, 2007) and many local authorities are experimenting with different patterns of intake and practices (one intake per year, modified curriculum, etc.) to help ameliorate this disadvantage.

The importance of parent characteristics

Having established the child characteristics which independently influence a child's overall development, the study then looked at the children's families.

Melhuish *et al.* (2001) and Sylva *et al.* (2004) described how the social class characteristics of parents such as levels of education, occupational status and family income were all associated with a wide array of cognitive, and socio-emotional outcomes for children during their early years. It is often proposed that where parents are advantaged in these characteristics they afford their children an array of services, goods, parental actions, and social connections that greatly benefit their children and there is a concern that children of many lower status parents lack access to such resources and experiences, which puts the children at risk of developmental problems (Duncan and Brooks-Gunn, 1997). We report here on the enduring influences of parents and how some of these change as children get older (to age 10 and 11, upper end of primary school).

It is important to look at the net effect of different factors because the results indicate that parents' education is a much stronger predictor of outcomes than either family income or SES. This needs to be remembered because if only SES or income are studied, different conclusions might be reached about the impact of social disadvantage. In policy terms, improving the educational level of the next generation of parents is likely to show greater long term benefits than addressing only income differences.

Parental education

Parents' education, as measured by highest level of qualification, has shown a consistent pattern of strong and positive effects throughout the study and these effects have become stronger as children get older.

Figures 4.1 and 4.2 show details on effect sizes for various levels of parent's qualifications compared to no qualification upon children's English and Mathematics performance at age 11 having allowed for all other background, pre-school and primary school factors. While both mothers' and fathers' education are important, the effects are particularly pronounced for mothers' education. We have compared groups where the parent has various levels of qualifications with a group where the parent has no qualifications. The greatest effects of mothers' education for both English and Mathematics (ES=0.76, and 0.71) are clearly stronger than for fathers' education (ES=0.39, and 0.34).

With regard to social/behavioural outcomes at age 11, parents' education is again an important influence (for details of the pre-school and early primary school period see Sylva *et al.*, 2004). For mothers' education there was a moderately strong relationship with all four social/behavioural outcomes measured at age 11. Higher mothers' qualification levels are associated with increased Self-regulation (ES=0.55) and 'Pro-social' behaviour (ES=0.36) as well as lower levels of 'Hyperactivity' (ES=−0.45) and 'Anti-social' behaviour (ES=−0.27). These findings are in line with the results of analyses for previous years, but slightly stronger. Fathers' education was not such a strong predictor of social/behavioural development at age 11, but there was a relationship for Self-regulation and 'Hyperactivity'. Children whose fathers had a degree have higher levels of Self-regulation (ES=0.29) and lower levels of 'Hyperactivity' (ES=−0.30) than children

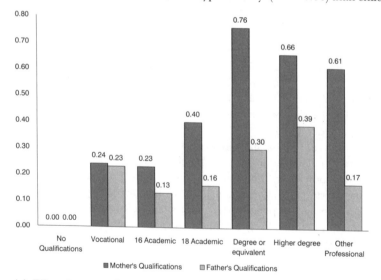

Figure 4.1 Effect sizes upon English at age 11 for various levels of parents' education

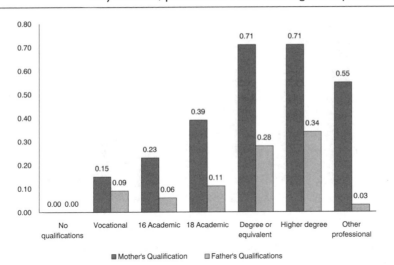

Figure 4.2 Effect sizes upon Mathematics at age 11 for various levels of parents' education

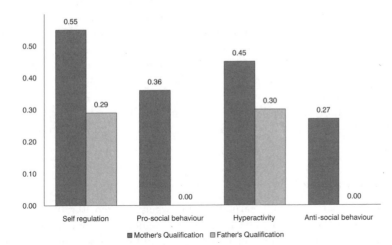

Figure 4.3 Social development at age 11 and parents' education

whose father had no qualifications. The effects for parents' education upon social behavioural outcomes is illustrated in Figure 4.3.

Parental socio-economic status (SES)

Parents occupational or socio-economic status (SES) measured by parents' highest social class of occupation was also independently linked to children's development. Where a parent had a 'professional non-manual' occupation children consistently showed higher attainment in English and Mathematics at age 11. The effects of

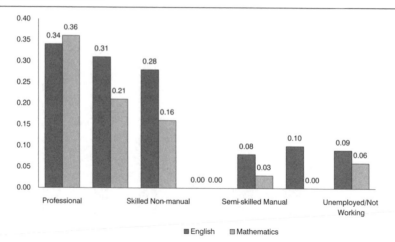

Figure 4.4 Net effects of SES upon English and Mathematics attainment at age 11

parental SES having allowed for all other variables are illustrated for children's attainment in Key Stage 2 (KS2, age 11) assessments in Figure 4.4.

For social/behavioural outcomes at age 11, parents' occupational status related only to 'Anti-social' behaviour. Where a parent was of professional occupational status (e.g. lawyer, doctor) children were rated by teachers as showing less 'Anti-social' behaviour than children from families in the skilled non-manual (e.g. bank clerk) (ES=0.23), unskilled manual (e.g. labourer) (ES=0.28) and unemployed (ES=0.20) groups. Overall the differences for parental SES are relatively modest but most evident for those children with a parent in a non-manual occupation compared to those children with parents in manual occupations or unemployed.

Parental income

We collected data on family earned income when children were 6–7 years of age. Controlling for all other effects there were significant but modest net effects associated with family earned income. Children in families with higher income (£37,500–£67,499 per annum – using 2002 base data) have better scores in English at age 11 than children whose parents have no earned income (ES=0.23). For Mathematics, effect sizes in the range of 0.15 to 0.25 are found for different income groups between £17,500 per annum and more than £67,000 per annum. Family earned income was also associated with social/behavioural development. Children from families with medium and high earned income have higher levels of Self-regulation (ES=0.33 to 0.38) and 'Pro-social' behaviour (ES=0.22 to 0.23) at age 11 than children from families with low income or no earned income. In addition, children from families with a low–medium income level have lower levels of 'Hyperactivity' (ES=0.24) at age 11 than children from families with low income or no earned income.

In line with these effects of parental income, similar effects occur when children from poor and not poor families are compared. Where a child is deemed to be eligible for free school meals (FSM), this is often taken as a proxy measure of family poverty. This FSM measure has been consistently associated with poorer child development. At age 11 the differences were moderate to weak for academic outcomes (ES=-0.23 for English, ES=-0.15 for Mathematics), and for social/behavioural outcomes (ES=-0.23 for Self-regulation, ES=0.21 for 'Hyperactivity', and ES=0.27 for 'Anti-social' behaviour).

Taken together the results show that children of higher social status parents do better academically and in terms of social development other things being equal. However, of the variables linked to social status, parental education is relatively more important than either parental occupational status or income in affecting children's developmental outcomes.

The importance of family characteristics

As well as focusing on the child and their parents, the EPPE study also looked at the other characteristics which make up 'families'. The important attributes which exert an independent influence on children are described below. Again, findings from the early years are seen in the context of children's later development.

Family size

Children from larger families (three or more siblings) showed, on average, lower attainment in reading at age 10 (ES=0.21) but not in Mathematics. This may reflect reduced opportunities for parental time with a child in larger families during the early years (see below for discussion of the early years home learning environment). However, the effects of family size in the early years were no longer statistically significant in predicting children's outcomes at age 11.

Marital status

Mother's marital status (measured at age 6–7) was a significant predictor of 'Pro-social' behaviour at age 11. The findings suggest that children of separated or divorced mothers have lower levels of teacher rated 'Pro-social' behaviour (ES=-0.18) than children of married mothers, while there is no significant difference for children's 'Pro-social' behaviour where mothers are single and never married compared to where mothers were married. In addition, we looked at the predictive influence of change in marital status (i.e. change in marital status from when children were in the pre-school period to when children were in KS1) with children's social/behavioural outcomes at age 11.

Changes in marital status were coded into four categories: (1) couple at both times, (2) single at both times, (3) change from couple to single and (4) change from single to couple. Interestingly, after controlling for other background characteristics there were significant differences in 'Hyperactivity' and 'Anti-social' behaviour among children coming from different marital status change groups. The findings suggest that children whose mothers made a change from being single to either getting married or living with a partner tend to have higher levels of 'Hyperactivity' (ES=0.24) and 'Anti-social' behaviour (ES=0.25) than children of stable couples. These findings are in line with other research on families where it was found that a parent's transition into a new marriage is linked with children's increased negative behaviour (Dunn et al., 1998; Dunn, 2002).

What kinds of families attend different types of pre-schools?

Pre-schools, for a variety of reasons (geography, opening hours, etc.) often attracted families from different socio-economic groups or levels of disadvantage. Melhuish et al. (1999) described these patterns in detail but the following is of importance in this chapter as it demonstrates variations across families which had to be taken into account by EPPE's analytical strategy.

Types of pre-school in the EPPE sample differed significantly in terms of the qualifications of the children's mothers. The mothers in the private day nursery group show a higher level of educational qualifications than those in other types of centres. The local authority (LA) day nurseries have the next highest percentage of mothers with a degree or better qualifications but this group also has the second highest percentage of mothers with no qualifications. This reflects the admissions policies of several LAs to their pre-school centres, where they maintain a quota of fee-paying places, usually used by parents with higher socio-economic status and educational qualifications but with many places kept for families of low socio-economic status who are non fee-paying. The combined centres had a similarly diverse make-up in terms of mothers' qualifications. The playgroup, nursery class, and nursery school are in the middle of the range. The home group mothers (those with no pre-school experience) have by far the highest proportion with no qualifications. Similar differences exist across other parental characteristics reflecting differences in terms of socio-economic status or disadvantage.

In summary the home group has by far the highest proportion of disadvantaged families. LA centres and combined centres are next most disadvantaged and similar to each other. The playgroup, nursery class and nursery school families are towards the middle of the range of disadvantage seen in the EPPE sample. The families using private day nurseries are by far the most advantaged in the sample.

Non-parental child care before 3 years and its effects upon children

Our parental interviews discussed child care 'history' before their child entered the study. This revealed that non-parental child care before three years of age had several effects.

High levels of 'group care' before the age of three (and particularly before the age of two) were associated with slightly higher levels of anti-social behaviour for a small group of children when assessed at age 3 (Melhuish *et al.*, 2001). This effect was largely restricted to children attending LA day nurseries and private day nurseries where substantial numbers of children attended from infancy onwards. If children with higher anti-social behaviour attended a high-quality setting between 3 and 5 years, then their anti-social behaviour decreased.

Although moderate levels of childminder care were not associated with increased anti-social behaviour, the levels were extremely high (45+ hours/week). Where there was substantial care from a relative (usually grandmothers) there was less anti-social behaviour and more co-operative behaviour in children (Melhuish *et al.*, 2001) as reported by pre-school workers.

The possible association between early day care and anti-social behaviour has attracted a lot of attention, largely because this relationship has been reported in a well-known American study (NICHD ECCRN, 1998) at 2 years and at 4.5 years of age (NICHD ECCRN, 2004). However by 8 years of age the relationship between the amount of day care to anti-social behaviour had disappeared but a relationship with more conflicted relationships with teachers and mothers emerged (NICHD ECCRN, 2005). Subsequent analyses by Van IJzendoorn *et al.* (2004) found that the effects of day care on anti-social behaviour were specifically related to group day care rather than any other type of care. In a follow-up at 11–12 years of age of the children in the NICHD study a relationship between higher levels of early group care and problem behaviours was again found (Belsky *et al.*, 2007).

We have examined this possible link between early group care and anti-social behaviour in more detail in the much larger EPPE sample in England. We used longitudinal multilevel models to simultaneously investigate the variables affecting anti-social behaviour at 3, 5, 6, 7 and 10 years of age. This statistical strategy is preferable to considering each age alone as it takes account of the correlation between behaviour at each age and gives greater power and discrimination in the analysis. We found that the earlier finding of a relationship between amount of group care in the first three years and later anti-social behaviour was confirmed at 3, 5 and 6 years, and to a reduced extent at 7 years of age, but by 10 years of age the effect had disappeared. We further explored this relationship by looking at age of starting group care. We found that only where group care had started under the age of 2 years was the relationship between high levels of group care and anti-social behaviour maintained. In particular the relationship between early group care and anti-social behaviour was strongest where the group care had started in the first year of life. Where group care had started in the second year there was still a relationship but it was considerably weaker.

In summary, high levels of group care in the first two years are related to higher levels of anti-social behaviour, but this effect disappears by 10 years of age. The effect is linked to high levels of group care starting in the first year of life particularly, with a reduced effect where group care starts in the second year of life and no effect with any later start.

Does where parents live (the neighbourhood) affect educational achievement and social development?

Some existing evidence indicates some small effects for young children's development associated with the neighbourhood. In the USA, Chase-Lansdale *et al.* (1997) found around two per cent of the variation in behaviour problems and academic achievement for 5 and 6 year olds was linked to neighbourhood effects (deprivation and ethnic diversity). Similarly in the UK McCulloch and Joshi (2001) found 4–5 year olds achieved lower cognitive scores if they came from poorer rather than more affluent neighbourhoods independently of other socio-economic measures. Also in the analysis of data for over 500,000 children per year for three successive years (2002–2004) in all state primary schools in England, Melhuish *et al.* (2006a, 2006b) found that children's progress from Key Stage 1 (age 7) to Key Stage 2 (age 11) was also influenced to a small extent by the level of deprivation of their neighbourhood. However, it is possible that such 'neighbourhood' effects may reflect unmeasured differences in families resulting from the non-random distribution of families across neighbourhoods.

All research discussed so far deals with the issue of neighbourhood effects by seeing whether there is a separate influence associated with neighbourhood deprivation after standard child and family demographic factors, such as child gender, ethnicity and age, and parental socio-economic status (SES) and education, have been taken into account. Such research does not include data on families as rich as that in the EPPE research. Thus it is possible to investigate neighbourhood influences including more control of child and family factors than has previously been achieved. In particular the EPPE research has developed a measure of the learning opportunities provided within the home – the early years home learning environment (HLE) index – and this measure has proved to be a powerful predictor of educational achievement (e.g. Melhuish *et al.*, 2008a and b) and social/behavioural development (e.g. Sammons *et al.*, 2008b). The last part of this chapter explains in full the HLE and how it impacts on children's outcomes.

We used three measures when considering the influence of neighbourhood. Two measures reflected the parents' perceptions of their neighbourhood in terms of social cohesion and safety (collected through questionnaires when the children were 7 years old), and the third was the Index of Multiple Deprivation (IMD, ODPM 2004).

First, we considered children's outcomes at age 6 and 11 years. These outcomes were analysed firstly in terms of the standard child and family demographic characteristics, then the neighbourhood measures were added to the analysis to see if they showed an additional effect, and finally the early years HLE measure was added to see if neighbourhood effects were altered when the early years HLE was included.

There were no significant effects associated with any of the neighbourhood measures for reading and the social/behavioural outcomes once the HLE was added to the analysis. For Mathematics, the IMD score had a small but significant additional effect (ES=0.13) on Mathematics at 6 years of age, whereby children in areas of higher deprivation scored lower even after taking account of all child, family, and HLE effects. At age 11 years all effects of neighbourhood disappeared once the HLE was added to the analysis.

This pattern of results whereby initial neighbourhood effects disappear once the HLE is added suggests that inter-family differences may mediate neighbourhood effects for young children. Family characteristics and neighbourhood characteristics can co-vary, and when examined together family characteristics tend to overpower neighbourhood effects so that we find little evidence of independent neighbourhood effects up to age 11. It may be that neighbourhood influences become more evident when children are older (e.g. teenage years) when peer group effects may be expected.

Does changing pre-school/school impact on a child's development?

Having looked at a range of family background characteristics, e.g. marital status, etc. and whether or not being in a particular neighbourhood impacts on children, the EPPE team also considered another characteristic associated with families: the extent to which parents move children from one institution to another. There are a number of reasons why parents interrupt their children's' education. They may:

1 relocate in which case a move is inevitable;
2 be unhappy with their child's progress and feel they would do better in a different environment;
3 make a strategic move to secure a place at a more desirable school.

An extremely important aspect of any longitudinal study is knowing where children are, particularly in the run up to an 'assessment point'. EPPE has been fortunate in having a dedicated Tracking Officer (Wesley Welcomme) who has liaised with schools and families to ensure that the whereabouts of the sample was known at all times. This has contributed to the low attrition and high response rates associated with the success of the study. Because of these carefully kept records, the EPPE team have been able to look at 'mobility' of the sample at different time points.

We use the term mobility to refer to a change of pre-school or primary school that does not result from school closure, amalgamation, or transfer across phases of schooling. Prior research has only dealt with mobility during school age, and has indicated that mobility, specifically moving school, is associated with lower levels of academic attainment. Machin *et al.* (2006) found that children aged 5 to 16 who change schools are more likely to have a low previous academic attainment record than children who do not change. However, Machin *et al.* (2006) also found that 'pupils who move school and home simultaneously are typically more socially disadvantaged than otherwise'. Furthermore, Strand and Demie (2006) have found that although 7 to 11 year old pupil mobility is associated with poorer attainment, when other background factors (e.g. disadvantage) are taken into account this association is reduced, and it completely disappears when looking at progress, i.e. controlling for prior attainment. These findings suggest that it is social disadvantage rather than mobility that accounts for the lower academic attainment that has been associated with mobility as it co-varies with disadvantage rather than exerting an independent influence on academic attainment. However with secondary school pupils, this perspective should be qualified by the findings of Strand and Demie (2007) who found that mobility did have a significant negative association with academic performance by age 16 (GCSEs and other measures).

In the EPPE study we have shown a clear difference in level of social advantage, between families whose children moved between pre-school centres and those who moved in primary school, i.e. pre-school mobility and primary school mobility. More advantaged families, defined in terms of mothers' highest qualification, were more likely to move during pre-school; and those eligible for free school meals (FSM) less likely to move during pre-school. In terms of pre-school centres the majority (81 per cent) of the children who moved pre-schools attended playgroups, private day nurseries and local authority day nurseries initially. Additionally, children who attended pre-school for a longer length of time (two years or more) were more likely to move pre-schools. Most mobile children (60 per cent+) moved to nursery classes either for their first (or second) change of pre-school. It is likely that parents chose to move from fee paying to free provision at age 3 plus.

Mobility during Key Stage 1 (KS1, 5–7 years old) of primary school had the reverse characteristic: those more socially disadvantaged, in terms of FSM and those with absent fathers, were more likely to move during KS1. Mobility during Key Stage 2 (KS2, 8–11 years old) was also typified by social disadvantage but not to the same degree as during KS1.

Children who were mobile during pre-school were more likely to come from socially advantaged families and to attend a more academically effective primary school. By contrast, children who were mobile in KS1 were more likely to come from socially disadvantaged families and have been attending a primary school with a significantly lower academic effectiveness before moving school.

The pattern evident in Figure 4.5 shows the more advantaged children, who had the lower scores on the Multiple Disadvantage Index (see Chapter 6 for details on multiple disadvantage), had higher rates of pre-school mobility and lower rates in KS1. There was little discernable difference by advantage in terms of KS2 mobility, except in the cases of those with the highest levels of disadvantage, who also had the highest rates of mobility.

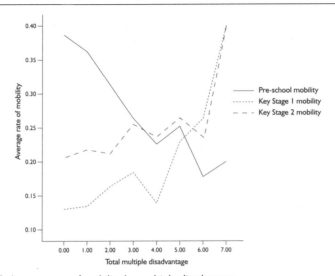

Figure 4.5 Average rate of mobility by multiple disadvantage

Does mobility affect academic achievement?

The EPPE results, controlling for background characteristics and prior attainment, indicate that mobility itself – moving pre-school centre – is not a significant predictor of poorer academic progress. That is mobility does not empirically produce diminished or increased academic progress during the pre-school years. The results were similar considering mobility in KS1. However, by the end of KS2 there was evidence of an association between lower levels of progress in Mathematics in KS2 and mobility in the KS2 period. Mathematics may cause special difficulties for children as they struggle with an unfamiliar curriculum or pedagogy (Mantizicopoulos and Knutson, 2000), which would point to the need for greater flexibility and personalisation on the part of teachers in this subject. These findings are broadly consistent with previous research (Strand and Demie, 2006). Mobility, that is at least one change of setting either during pre-school or KS1, has little independent impact on cognitive outcomes when background and prior attainment are taken into account and when the estimate is made against a simple non-mobility group for the same period.

Does mobility affect social/behavioural development?

However, later mobility is associated with diminished social/behavioural outcomes, specifically Self-regulation and 'Pro-social' behaviour at KS1 (age 7 years), and all social/behavioural outcomes (Self-regulation, 'Pro-social' behaviour, 'Hyperactivity' and 'Anti-social' behaviour') at KS2 (11 years). While these diminished outcomes are associated with primary school mobility, it is not clear whether this is a causal relationship or whether mobility reflects unmeasured family characteristics leading to the association between mobility and social/behavioural outcomes. Possible unmeasured family characteristics that might be influential include parental personality such as being go-getting or achievement oriented or sub-cultural factors related to child achievement. Also movement might be job related, or due to family breakdown, or increase in family size. However, it is also possible that poor social/behavioural development might dispose parents to move their child to another school.

The importance of the early years (pre-school period) home learning environment (HLE)

Having considered earlier in this chapter child, parental and family characteristics, we now turn in the final part to what parents do with their children in the home, which EPPE will demonstrate is as important as many of these background characteristics.

Whilst the main focus of EPPE was on pre-school provision it would have been naive to imagine that young children arrive at pre-school as 'empty vessels'. Many studies have indicated the importance of parenting generally (e.g. Melhuish et al., 2008a; Sylva et al., 2008) in the early years and more specifically parental practices which engage children in 'learning'. Parenting practices such as reading to children, using complex language, responsiveness, and warmth in interactions have been shown to be associated with better developmental outcomes (Bradley, 2002). Hess et al. (1982) investigated the links between SES and developmental outcomes and found that higher SES parents use more developmentally enhancing activities.

Stimulating activities may help children with specific skills-enhancing development (e.g. linking letters to sounds), but also, and perhaps most importantly, by developing the child's ability and motivation concerned with learning generally. Additionally, it is possible that a feedback loop is operating whereby parents are influenced by the child's level of attainment, which would lead to children with higher ability possibly receiving more parental stimulation. Thus there may be context in which there is a 'reciprocal' relationship with parental interactions and the learning environment, see Bronfenbrenner (1979) whose theory puts the child at the centre of a series of nested spheres of social and cultural influence, including education.

Given the importance of learning in the home, EPPE needed to take this into account when looking at children nested in families. We wanted to know what aspects of the home environment produce effects upon children's competencies. We needed to have some indication of which children were coming from more or less stimulating early HLE.

To address this question, parents were asked at interview (Melhuish et al., 2001) about the kinds of activities they engaged in at home with their children, which had the potential to provide learning experiences and/or contributed to their social skills. The HLE includes such activities as reading to children, singing songs and nursery rhymes, playing with friends, etc.

Each of the 14 home activity items that were in the parental interview was individually tested (in regression analysis) to see if it predicted over- or under-achievement.[3] The seven social/routine activities (play with friends at home, and elsewhere, visiting relatives/friends, shopping, TV, eating meals with family, regular bedtime) were not significantly related to under- or over-achievement in literacy and numeracy at age 5. Conversely, the seven activities providing clear learning opportunities (frequency of being read to, going to the library, playing with numbers, painting and drawing, being taught letters, being taught numbers, songs/poems/rhymes) each had significant positive effects on boosting cognitive and over achievements beyond that expected. Since the items are conceptually and statistically linked, this supports the creation of a combined measure, the early years Home Learning Environment (HLE). The frequency of each of the seven activities was coded on a 0–7 scale (0=not occurring, 7= very frequent), and the seven scores were added to produce an index with a possible range of 0–49, which was normally distributed with a mean of 23.42 (SD = 7.71).

To support the conclusions that the HLE added to the prediction of achievement over that provided by family and background characteristics for children, new multilevel models for literacy and numeracy were created including the HLE index in addition to the significant family and child background factors. By adding the HLE to the demographic model, the explained variance at the child level showed a 21 per cent increase for age 5 literacy and an 18 per cent increase for age 5 numeracy, thus supporting the conclusion that the HLE is an important independent predictor of development.

The results clearly support the importance of the HLE, and the influence of the HLE was over and above that of standard parenting proxy measures of parental education and occupational status. The results also demonstrate that this interview method is useful for identifying variability in parenting. While other family factors such as parents' education, SES and income are also important, the HLE exerts a greater and independent influence on educational attainment. The comparison of over, average, and under-achieving groups indicates that at age 5 the HLE is effective in differentiating both over and under-achieving groups from children achieving as expected, i.e. across the ability range.

---

3   Children's characteristics and family background were included in a multilevel model to predict children's age-adjusted achievement at age 5 using child, family, and pre-school characteristics as predictors. Three categories of performance (unexpected over-achievers, expected, and unexpected under-achievers) for literacy and numeracy were constructed based on children's adjusted scores deviating by at least ±1 standard deviation from that expected from background characteristics. Sixteen per cent of children were achieving higher than predicted from their background in both literacy and numeracy, and similar proportions (16 per cent literacy, 15 per cent numeracy) were achieving less well than would be predicted.

The HLE is important for school readiness yet it is only moderately associated with parents' SES and education (correlations = 0.28–0.33) indicating that low status homes sometimes score highly and, conversely, high status homes at times score poorly on the HLE measure.

The effects of the HLE and parenting upon children's development may partly be due to the teaching and learning of specific skills, e.g. letter-sound relationships and improved language and vocabulary. However, the multiplicity of learning opportunities included in the HLE suggests that the effects may also be related to more generalised and motivational aspects of child development, e.g. learning to learn. Also children may internalise aspects of parental values and expectations (implicit in the activities of the HLE) as they form a self-concept of themselves as a learner. Such a perspective is congruent with Vygotsky's theory (1978) that children learn higher psychological processes through their social environment and specifically with adult guidance operating within a child's 'zone of proximal development' (stimulation within the child's comprehension) and reinforces the idea that children acquire cognitive skills such as literacy through interaction with others who aid and encourage skill development.

Also it is possible that the strong relationship between the HLE and cognitive scores is mediated by some intervening unmeasured factor. Those parents who answer the questions in a way leading to a high score may have other characteristics that lead their children to have higher cognitive scores. However, even if this were so, the HLE would still be an efficient proxy measure of such unmeasured factors. Moreover, the fact that some activities such as teaching songs and nursery rhymes in pre-school related most strongly to language development, while teaching letters and numbers and reading to the child was a better predictor of pre-reading skills at age 5, suggests that these specific activities do have a measurable impact on learning.

Whatever the mechanisms, the influences of parenting upon child development are pervasive. Similar results are reported by Bradley et al. (2001) using another strategy to measure parenting activities. Also, research involving 0–3 year olds from the evaluation of the Early Head Start (EHS) programme, which provided combinations of home-visits and centre childcare intervention for disadvantaged families, found that the intervention increased both the quantity and quality of parents' interaction with children, as well as children's social and cognitive development (Love et al., 2005).

Support for these views also comes from other studies of interventions. A review of early interventions concluded that, to gain the most impact, interventions should include both parent and child together with a focus on enhancing interactions (Barnes and Freude-Lagevardi, 2003). Such work indicates that parenting behaviours are learnable, and changes in parenting are associated with improved child development (e.g. Sylva et al., 2008). Similar conclusions derive from a study (Hannon et al., 2005) where children showed better literacy progress when parents received a programme on ways to improve child literacy during the pre-school period.

EPPE also measured the home learning environment at age 7 and age 11. However it was only the HLE measured in the pre-school period (early years HLE) that predicted substantial variance in developmental outcomes at all ages up to 11 years, and therefore the results reported here use the early years HLE as the unit of analyses. There are two possible reasons for this: first, early learning at home is more powerful, or second, the interview conducted when the child was 3–4 years old yields more accurate data than the postal questionnaires used later in the study.

What predicts the level of the pre-school home learning environment (HLE)?

We have shown above that the HLE is strongly associated with better cognitive and social development, including Self-regulation. The effects associated with the HLE upon children's development are stronger than for other traditional measures of disadvantage such as parental SES, education or income up to age 7 years.

Gender and parental education

The HLE varies between boys and girls similarly across all ethnic and social class groups, with girls' homes having higher overall HLE scores than boys' homes. Parents' education has similar effects upon HLE scores for all ethnic groups, with higher parents' education (particularly mothers') being associated with higher HLE scores (correlation 0.3).

Ethnic group

The HLE shows similar predictive relationships with both cognitive and social/behavioural outcomes in all minority ethnic groups. This indicates that the HLE measure is useful for understanding factors affecting children's development across all the minority ethnic groups studied. We also find that for all ethnic groups the HLE is associated with differences in child and family characteristics. Also when examining the impact of the HLE upon children's under- or over-achievement in literacy and numeracy (relative to expectations) the effects of the HLE are strong across most ethnic groups with some minority ethnic groups showing HLE effects stronger than the White UK group. This clearly indicates that the HLE is important for these ethnic groups in determining how children reach different levels of attainment.

Family size, developmental problems and gender

Where a child has more than three siblings (defined as large family size) this depressed the HLE score, as does the presence of early developmental problems for the child, and these influences upon the HLE are stronger for boys than for girls.

Mothers' qualifications and the compositional effect in pre-schools

Where children attended a pre-school, the composition of the pre-school was associated with differences in the HLE for all groups. Where more of the other mothers using the pre-school had a degree then the HLE was higher. This suggests that opportunities for mixing with other parents who are better educated may have some benefits for parenting, i.e. the possibility of a peer-group learning effect amongst mothers or parents. This pre-school influence appears somewhat stronger for girls than boys.

Neighbourhood effect

Similarly suggestive of peer-group effects amongst parents is the finding that if children lived in more deprived areas their HLE was depressed, and this effect was stronger for boys than girls.

The variation in the HLE for different groups

The above analyses led the EPPE team to further examine whether the HLE varies between different groups in the population, e.g. by SES or ethnic group. The factors that influence the HLE can be examined through statistical analysis (in this case multilevel models) and those showing significant effects upon the HLE together with effect sizes are shown in Table 4.5. The effect sizes are shown separately for analyses with the total sample, low SES only, White UK low SES, boys and girls.

The HLE tends to vary by socio-economic status (SES) and by ethnic group as can be seen from raw average scores shown in Table 4.6.

Within ethnic groups there is usually a pattern of the professional groups having higher HLE scores than the middle SES groups who are higher than the low SES group. The ethnic groups vary with the White UK group showing the highest overall HLE scores and the Pakistani group the lowest.

The HLE and educational achievement at the end of primary school

The HLE remained a powerful predictor of better cognitive attainment at age 11 even after 6 years in primary school. We compared the effects of various levels of HLE with the lowest level (0–13). The effect size (ES) for Mathematics between the highest and the lowest scoring groups on the HLE index was ES=0.42 'net' of other child and family factors, while for English the ES=0.69 (see Figures 4.6 and 4.7). At earlier time points the impact of learning experiences at home on attainment in Mathematics were found to be slightly stronger, and still the results illustrate the continued importance of these experiences. A high HLE rather than a low one

Table 4.5 Effect sizes for influences upon the HLE for different groups

	Total sample	Low SES	White UK Low SES	Boys	Girls
Gender	+0.38***	+0.35***	+0.38***	–	–
Home language not English (i.e. EAL)	–0.60***	–0.61***	–	–0.53***	–0.76***
3+ siblings	–0.30***	–0.34***	–0.46*	–0.41***	–0.18
Developmental problems	–0.23**	–0.34***	–0.42*	–0.31***	–0.10
Mother's education	+0.46***	+0.45***	+0.40*	+0.49***	+0.58***
Father's education	+0.23***	–	–	+0.30***	+0.20
Pre-school composition – % mother's degree	+0.25**	+0.20*	+0.25	+0.18	+0.38***
Area deprivation	–0.25***	–0.30**	–0.13	–0.34**	–0.20*

* $p < 0.05$, ** $p < 0.01$, *** $p < 0.001$

Table 4.6 Average HLE by SES and ethnic groups (heritage)

Ethnic heritage	Prof SES	Mid SES	Low SES	Total (rank)	n
White UK	26.8	23.3	20.3	24.1 (1)	2205
White European	27.0	20.5	15.1	22.7 (3)	116
Black Caribbean	25.1	21.0	19.3	21.4 (4)	105
Black African	18.0	21.5	19.3	20.4 (5)	63
Indian	23.7	18.5	17.1	20.1 (6)	61
Pakistani	19.1	14.8	14.2	15.2 (9)	146
Bangladeshi	23.8	15.5	19.6	17.5 (8)	33
Other ethnic minority	22.1	19.5	17.2	19.7 (7)	180
Mixed	26.8	21.2	21.2	23.4 (2)	83

has a similar positive effect on later outcomes at Year 6 to having a mother with a degree versus one with no qualifications. It should be noted that there are only modest correlations (0.28 to 0.33) between the HLE and parents' qualification level. In analyses the HLE and parents' qualification level are two independent predictors. It was found that some parents provide a high scoring HLE irrespective of their own qualification level and support the development of their children in this way.

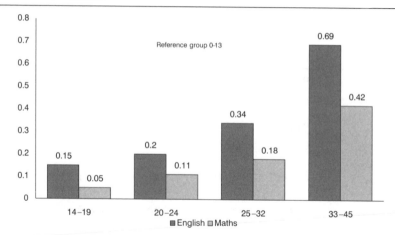

Figure 4.6 Net effects of HLE upon English and Mathematics attainment at age 11

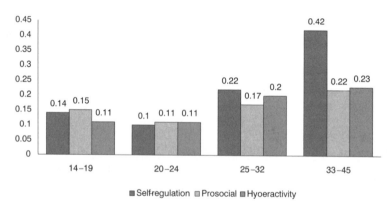

Figure 4.7 Net effects of HLE upon Social/behavioural development at age 11

Effects of early years HLE on social/behavioural outcomes at the end of primary school

In addition to the strong effects upon cognitive outcomes associated with the HLE, there were consistent effects for social/behavioural outcomes. These can be illustrated by considering social/behavioural outcomes at age 11 as shown in Figure 4.7.

After controlling for child and family characteristics, the pre-school HLE had a significant effect on children's Self-regulation, 'Pro-social' behaviour and 'Hyperactivity' at age 11. For these three outcomes, children with a score of 25+ on the HLE had significantly more positive ratings of their behaviour than children with a low score (0–13). The findings suggest that children with a higher early HLE have higher levels of Self-regulation (ES=0.42) and 'Pro-social' behaviour (ES=0.22) and lower levels of 'Hyperactivity' (ES=–0.23). Thus a child's HLE in the early years has a continuing effect on their later social/behavioural development and this is moderately strong for Self-regulation.

Summary

This chapter clearly demonstrates the importance of the child's background in influencing cognitive and social development, and their effects are roughly twice as important as any effects of pre-school or primary school (see Chapters 6 and 7). There is a wide range of child and family factors that exert long-term influences upon children's development. In particular the effect of mothers' education is strong throughout the study but with some variation at different time points compared to other factors. The Home Learning Environment (HLE) in the pre-school period has association with all aspects of children's cognitive and social development and for much of a child's life is one of the most powerful influences upon development.

While certain background factors such as parents' educational level and the early years HLE have a stronger influence than pre-school on its own (as we discuss in Chapters 6 and 7), educational influences such as pre-school and primary school have a similar size impact to factors such as family income and SES. This has important implications for policy makers who are concerned to promote equity and combat disadvantage.

It is also of interest that the HLE is clearly important for all ethnic groups and it is the most powerful influence upon self-regulation, the aspect of children's social development that most influences academic achievement. In contrast neighbourhood effects are small and disappear once the HLE is taken into account, and while mobility varies with social class it does not appear to be significantly related to children's development.

Child, family and earlier HLE characteristics are important predictors of children's cognitive and social/behavioural development at age 11, although the combined strength of this influence is slightly weaker than when children were age 7. This change probably reflects the growing importance of primary school and peer influence.

With the major effects that background influences exert, it has been critical to the EPPE research that these influences have been fully taken into account in establishing the pre-school and school effects upon children's development that are discussed in subsequent chapters.

References

Barnes, J. and Freude-Lagevardi, A. (2003) *From Pregnancy to Early Childhood: Early Interventions to Enhance the Mental Health of Children and Families*, London: Mental Health Foundation.

Belsky, J., Vandell, D., Burchinal, M., Clarke-Stewart, K.A., McCartney, K., Owen, M. and The NICHD Early Child Care Research Network *(2007)* Are there long-term effects of early child care? Child Development, 78, 681–701.

Bradley, R. (2002) Environment and parenting, in M. Bornstein (ed.) *Handbook of Parenting*, 2nd ed, Hillsdale, N.J: Lawrence Erlbaum Associates.

Bradley, R.H., Corwyn, R.F., Burchinal, M., McAdoo, H.P. and Coll, C.G. (2001) The home environments of children in the United States Part II: relations with behavioral development through age thirteen, *Child Development*, 72, 1868–1886.

Bronfenbrenner, U. (1979) *The Ecology of Human Development: Experiments by Nature and Design*, Cambridge, MA: Harvard University Press.

Chase-Lansdale, L., Gordon, R., Brooks-Gunn, J. and Klebanov, P. (1997) Neighborhood and family influences on the intellectual and behavioral competence of preschool and early school-age children. In J. Brooks-Gunn, G. Duncan and L. Aber (eds.) *Neighborhood Poverty: Context and Consequences for Children*. 119–145. New York: Russell Sage Foundation.

Crawford, C., Dearden L. and Meghir, C. (2007) *When You are Born Matters: The Impact of Date of Birth on Child Cognitive Outcomes in England*, London: Institute for Fiscal Studies.

Duncan, G.J. and Brooks-Gunn, J. (1997) *Consequences of Growing Up Poor*, New York: Russell Sage Foundation.

Dunn, J. (2002) The adjustment of children in stepfamilies: lessons from community studies, *Child and Adolescent Mental Health*, 7, 154–161.

Dunn, J., Deater-Deckard, K., Pickering, K., O'Connor, T.G. and Golding, J. (1998) Children's adjustment and pro-social behaviour in step-, single and non-step family settings: findings from a community study, *Journal of Child Psychology and Psychiatry*, 39, 1083–1095.

Hannon, P., Nutbrown, C., and Morgan, A. (2005) *Early Literacy Work with Families*, London: Sage.

Hess, R.D., Holloway, S., Price, G. and Dickson, W.P. (1982) Family environments and the acquisition of reading skills, in L.M. Laosa and I.E. Sigel (eds) *Families as Learning Environments of Children*, New York: Plenum, pp. 87–113.

Howell, D.C. (1989) *Fundamental Statistics for the Behavioral Sciences*, Boston, MA: PWS-Kent.

Love, J.M., Kisker, E.E., Ross, C., Constantine, J., Boller, K., Chazan-Cohen, R. *et al.* (2005) The effectiveness of Early Head Start for 3-year-old children and their parents: lessons for policy and program, *Developmental Psychology*, 41, 885–901.

Machin, S., Telhaj, S. and Wilson, J. (2006) *The Mobility of English School Children*, London: Centre for the Economics of Education, London School of Economics.

Mantzicopoulos, P. and Knutson, D. J. (2000) Head Start children: school mobility and achievement in the early grades, *The Journal of Educational Research*, 93(5), 305–311.

McCulloch, A. and Joshi, H. (2001) Neighbourhood and family influences on the cognitive ability of children in the British National Child Development Study, *Social Science and Medicine*, 53, 579–591.

Melhuish, E.C., Sylva, K., Sammons, P., Siraj-Blatchford, I. and Taggart, B. (1999) *The Effective Provision of Pre-school Education Project, Technical Paper 4: Parent, family and Child Characteristics in Relation to Type of Pre-school and Socio-economic Differences*, London: Institute of Education/DfEE.

Melhuish, E.C., Sylva, K., Sammons, P., Siraj-Blatchford, I. and Taggart, B. (2001) *The Effective Provision of Pre-school Education Project, Technical Paper 7: Social/behavioural and Cognitive Development at 3–4 Years in Relation to Family Background*, London: Institute of Education/DfES.

Melhuish, E., Romaniuk, H., Sammons, P., Sylva, K., Siraj-Blatchford, I. and Taggart B. (2006a) *Effective Pre-school and Primary Education 3–11 (EPPE 3–11) Project. The Effectiveness of Primary Schools in England in Key Stage 2 for 2002, 2003 and 2004.* DfES Research Brief X06-06, Nottingham: DfES.

Melhuish, E., Romaniuk, H., Sammons, P., Sylva, K., Siraj-Blatchford, I. and Taggart, B. (2006b) *Effective Pre-school and Primary Education 3–11 Project (EPPE 3–11): The Effectiveness of Primary Schools in England in Key Stage 2 for 2002, 2003 and 2004. Full Report.* London: Institute of Education, University of London. http://eppe.ioe.ac.uk/

Melhuish, E., Sylva, K., Sammons, P., Siraj-Blatchford, I., Taggart, B. and Phan, M. (2008a), Effects of the home learning environment and pre-schools centre experience upon literacy and numeracy development in early primary school, *Journal of Social Issues,* 64, 157–188.

Melhuish, E.C., Sylva, K., Sammons, P., Siraj-Blatchford, I., Taggart, B., Phan, M. and Malin, A. (2008b) Pre-school influences on mathematics achievement, *Science,* 321, 1161–1162.

NICHD Early Child Care Research Network (1998) Early child care and self-control, compliance, and problem behavior at twenty-four and thirty-six months, *Child Development,* 69, 1145–1170.

NICHD Early Child Care Research Network. (2004) Type of child care and children's development at 54 months. *Early Childhood Research Quarterly,* 19(2), 203–30

NICHD Early Child Care Research Network (2005) Early child care and children's development in the primary grades: results from the NICHD study of early child care and youth development, *American Education Research Journal,* 43, 537–570.

Office of the Deputy Prime Minister (2004) *The English Indices of Deprivation 2004 (revised),* London: ODPM.

Sammons, P., Sylva, K., Melhuish, E., Siraj-Blatchford, I., Taggart, B. and Hunt, S. (2008a) *The Effective Pre-School and Primary Education 3-11 (EPPE 3–11) Project: Influences on Children's Attainment and Progress in Key Stage 2: Cognitive Outcomes in Year 6,* London: DCSF.

Sammons, P., Sylva, K., Melhuish, E., Siraj-Blatchford, I., Taggart, B. and Jelicic, H. (2008b) *The Effective Pre-School and Primary Education 3–11 (EPPE 3–11) Project: Influences on Children's Development and Progress in Key Stage 2: Social/Behavioural Outcomes in Year 6,* London: DCSF.

Strand, S. and Demie, F. (2006) Pupil mobility, attainment and progress in primary school, *British Educational Research Journal,* 32, 551–568.

Strand, S. and Demie, F. (2007) Pupil mobility, attainment and progress at secondary school, *Educational Studies,* 33, 313–331.

Sylva, K., Melhuish, E., Sammons, P., Siraj-Blatchford, I. and Taggart B. (2004) *The Effective Provision of Pr-School Education (EPPE) Project: Final Report,* Report No. SSU/FR/2004/01, Nottingham: Department for Education and Skills.

Sylva, K., Scott, S., Totsika, V., Ereky-Stevens, K. and Crook, C. (2008) Training parents to help their children read: a randomized control trial, *British Journal of Educational Psychology,* 78, 435-455.

Van IJzendoorn, M.H., Tavecchio, L.W.C., Riksen-Walraven, J.M.A., Schipper, J.C., de Gevers Deynoot-Schaub, M. and Schaub, M. (11 July 2004) Center day care in the Netherlands. What do we know about its quality and effects? Paper presented at the biennial meeting of the International Society for the Study of Behavioural Development, Ghent, Belgium.

Vygotsky, L.S. (1978) *Mind in Society,* Cambridge, MA: Harvard University Press.

Chapter 5

Quality in early childhood settings

Kathy Sylva

Introduction

The EPPE research design allowed us to create thousands of individual developmental trajectories, one for each child in the study. To understand the impact of pre-school on the development of any one child, it was necessary to investigate the duration of attendance (in months) and how old the child was at the start of pre-school experience. But this is only part of the story: two children might begin pre-school at age 3 but one attends a nursery class in a local primary school for part of the day and the other attends a private day nursery for up to nine hours each day. The quality of their experiences may vary. Many studies on the effects of pre-school education focus exclusively on *attendance* at some form of nursery school, childcare centre or playgroup (Osborn and Millbank, 1987; Berrueta-Clement *et al.*, 1984, Schweinhart and Weikart, 1997) along with hours' or months' experience. But EPPE wished to go much deeper than the type of provision and the hours of attendance; it sought to 'open the nursery's door and look inside the room'. It did this in several ways, but one of the most important ways was using direct observation to assess the quality of interactions, pedagogy, resources and relationships.

Concepts of quality

Researchers have been debating for years about the concept of 'quality' in early childhood education and care. Judgement of quality involves values, and what is a 'high quality' centre to one parent may be quite low in the eyes of a local authority officer or indeed another parent. Katz (1993) has written perceptively about the different perspectives of quality, one from 'insiders' such as staff and children; and the other from 'outsiders' such as inspectors or researchers. Katz warns that these different perspectives may lead to different definitions of quality; children may think a centre is high in quality if they have fun all day long, where inspectors might want them to be 'learning' and 'gaining social skills' as well.

Munton *et al.* (1995) have focused on different quality indicators, rather than the perspective of the individual making the judgement. Munton *et al.* have suggested that there are three basic dimensions of quality: these are the *structure* which includes both facilities and human resources; the educational and care *processes* which children experience every day such as their conversations with staff; and the *outcomes* or the longer term consequences to individual children of the education and care the child receives. This last is complex because it is not easily observable and requires longitudinal research showing the developmental progress made by children attending different kinds of centre. The quality measures described in this chapter focus on observed educational and care processes but also includes some structural dimensions such as staff qualifications or turnover.

In this more objective view of quality (see Soucacou and Sylva, in press), quality in Early Years environments can best be understood as a set of measurable characteristics. Specifically, quality is conceived as an objective reality consisting of agreed criteria measured in standardised ways that allow generalisability across contexts (Siraj-Blatchford and Wong, 1999). In the research literature, objective definitions of quality are often based on the most common aspects that have been shown to predict children's learning, including such things as the physical environment, tangible resources, curriculum/learning experiences for children, teaching strategies, staffing, planning, assessment and record keeping, relationships and interactions, parental and community partnership and management. Using objective, measurable definitions of quality has produced a wealth of research showing a clear relationship between the quality of early childhood provision and children's developmental outcomes (Burchinal *et al.*, 2000; Gallagher and Lambert, 2006; Peisner-Feinberg and Burchinal, 1999; Sylva *et al.*, 2004; Sammons *et al.*, 2008a, 2008b.)

Quality measures can include: *structural elements*, including adult–child ratio, or teacher education and training; and *process elements*, including the nature of adult–child interactions, or the nature of activities and learning opportunities available to the children (Phillipsen *et al.*, 1997). A main research issue facing investigations into process quality is the question of measurement. Some process quality measures focus strongly on specific aspects of the adult–child interaction (e.g. Caregiver Interaction Scale, CIS; Arnett, 1989); other more global process quality measures focus on multiple processes (e.g. Early Childhood Environment Ratings Scale, ECERS-R; Harms *et al.*, 1998). Both these instruments have been widely used in research assessing childcare quality (Burchinal *et al.*, 2002; De Kruif *et al.*, 2000; Gilliam, 2000; Jaeger and Funk, 2001; Phillipsen *et al.*, 1997; Sheridan *et al.*, 2009, Whitebook *et al.*, 1989).

In order to assess pre-school quality, the EPPE project focused particularly on process elements. The main process measurements employed were the observational rating scales ECERS-R (Harms, Clifford, and Cryer, 1998) and a newly developed extension supplementing the ECERS-R, called the ECERS-E (Sylva, Siraj-Blatchford and Taggart, 2003).

EPPE also used the Caregiver Interaction Scale (CIS; Arnett, 1989). The administration of the rating scales was carried out on the same day by one trained researcher who had familiarised herself with the centre and knew the staff and children well enough that all felt comfortable with the 'visitor'. In addition to a whole day of observation, certain items on the ECERS-R and ECERS-E were completed by interview with staff and by consulting centre records or displays.

The word 'environment' in the rating scale is taken in its broadest sense to include social interactions, pedagogical strategies and relationships between children as well as adults and children. Matters of pedagogy are very much to the fore in ECERS-R. For example the sub-scale Organisation and Routine has an item 'Schedule' which gives high ratings to a balance between adult-initiated and child-initiated activities. In order to score a 5, i.e. a rating of 'good', the centre must have 'a balance between structure and flexibility' but a 7, an 'excellent' rating, requires 'variations to be made in the schedule to meet individual needs, for example a child working intensively on a project should be allowed to continue past the scheduled time'. Further attention to pedagogy can be found in the item 'Free Play', where to earn a score of 5, centres must have 'free play occurring for a substantial portion of the day/session both indoors and outdoors. These few examples should make clear that this observational instrument is entitled '*Environmental* Rating Scale' and that it actually describes processes of the educational and care environment much more than the physical space and materials on offer.

As the ECERS-R was developed in the United States and intended for use in both care and educational settings, the EPPE team thought it desirable to devise a complementary early childhood environment rating scale which was focused on provision in England as well as good practice in catering for diversity (Siraj-Blatchford and Wong, 1999; Sylva *et al.*, 2003). They decided to measure the quality of the learning environment when the children were in pre-school in order to study its effects when children were older. The EPPE researchers needed a measurement instrument that was robust and relevant to English curriculum policy and practice. The development of the ECERS-E is described in Soucacou and Sylva (in press 2008). The new scale was devised after wide consultation with experts and practitioners and was piloted extensively. It was based on part of the English national curriculum for early childhood called 'Desirable Learning Outcomes' (Department for Education and Employment, 1996).

The English curriculum was revised and expanded in 2000 and 2008. It now includes six areas of development, three of which are included in the ECERS-E: Communication, Language and Literacy; Problem Solving, Reasoning and Numeracy; and Understanding the World. However, the remaining three (Creative Development; Physical Development; and Personal, Social and Emotional Development) were already covered adequately by the ECERS-R and so the team decided to focus on the cognitive domains of development and rely on the ECERS-R to assess quality related to other aspects of development.

Both the ECERS-R and ECERS-E are based on a conceptual framework which takes account of pedagogical processes and curriculum. They are described in more detail below, along with the Caregiver Interaction Scale, which was used in EPPE to measure the quality of interactions between caregivers and the children in their care.

The Early Childhood Environment Rating Scale – Revised (ECERS-R; Harms et *al.*, 1998)

This observational scale consists of 43 items across seven sub-scales (see Introduction) and has been shown to possess good psychometric properties and good predictive validity in significantly relating to children's developmental outcomes (De Kruif *et al.*, 2000; Gilliam, 2000; Jaeger and Funk, 2001; Peisner-Feinberg and Burchinal, 1997; Phillips, McCartney and Scarr, 1987). Its sub-scales are:

Items 1–8	Space and furnishings
Items 9–14	Personal care routines
Items 15–18	Language-reasoning
Items 19–28	Activities
Items 29–33	Interaction
Items 34–37	Programme structure
Items 38–43	Parents and staff

Each item is rated on a 7 point scale (1 = inadequate, 3 = minimal/adequate, 5 = good, 7 = excellent). Completion of the ECERS usually involves approximately one day of observation, as well as talking to the staff about aspects of the routine which were not visible during the observation session (for example, weekly swimming or seasonal outings).

The Early Childhood Environment Rating Scale – Extension (ECERS-E; Sylva et *al.*, 2003)

The new instrument developed for EPPE is the ECERS-Extension (ECERS-E; Sylva *et al.*, 2003). This consists of 18 items on four sub-scales:

Items 1–6	Literacy
Items 7–10	Mathematics
Items 11–15	Science and environment
Items 16–18	Diversity

In the same way as the ECERS-R, analyses were carried out in terms of the total score as well as in terms of the separate sub-scale scores.

Childcare interaction scale (CIS)

The CIS is an observational rating scale of adult–child interaction with 26 items across four sub-scales: Positive Relationship (e.g. 'seems enthusiastic about the children's activities and efforts'), Punitiveness (e.g. 'seems unnecessarily harsh when scolding or prohibiting children'), Permissiveness (e.g. 'expects the children to exercise self-control'), and Detachment (e.g. 'spends considerable time in activity not involving interventions with the children'). On each item the extent to which the statement is characteristic for the caregiver is rated from 1 (not at all) to 4 (very much).

Some detail will be provided about the conceptualisation of the ECERS-E because it was devised according to a pedagogical theory that has influenced education and care around the world. The authors of the ECERS-E turned to the rich literature on 'emerging' literacy, numeracy and understanding of science. They were inspired by the research on ways that adults 'scaffold' learning in young children (Rogoff, 1999), 'extend' their language (Wood *et al.*, 1976) and cater to their individual needs. The literature led to a conceptualisation of the support for learning and development that an Early Childhood centre might offer. This conceptualisation was based on the research literature in developmental psychology and also in Early Childhood. An example of the literature used in creating the Literacy subscale of the ECERS-E is described below.

In conceiving of 'emergent literacy', Whitehurst and Lonigan (1998) defined emergent literacy as the 'skills, knowledge and attitudes that are presumed to be developmental pre-cursors to reading and writing'. Other authors researching along these lines include Sulzby and Teale (1991). Included in the many studies of emergent literacy is consideration of the *social environments* that support the emergence of literacy and these include shared book reading and especially discussion about the text. In this view of emergent literacy, the eventual acquisition of reading is conceptualised as a developmental continuum, with origins early in the life of the child. This is in sharp contrast to consideration of reading as an all-or-none phenomenon that begins when children start school (discussed by Storch and Whitehurst, 2001; Whitehurst and Lonigan, 1998). In the emergent view, there is no clear demarcation between reading and pre-reading, with literacy related behaviours 'emerging' well before entry to school and supported by many different kinds of interactions and texts. Thus, there is a continuum of literacy acquisition that includes all of the pre-school period. The origins of reading, writing, and oral language can be found in the home and in the pre-school setting and especially in the children's exposure to interactions in social contexts with print (for example book reading, 'environmental print') provide the learning context.

The construct of emergent literacy includes children's conceptual knowledge about literacy as well as their procedural knowledge about reading and writing. Here, children's 'pretend reading' and 'invented writing' are important pre-cursors to reading and the formal writing that will take place later in the school years (Senechal *et al.*, 2001; Mason and Stewart, 1990). The authors of the ECERS-E had a vast literature on emergent literacy (and a smaller literature on emergent numeracy and science) to aid them in constructing indicators of the enabling environment they thought would support children's emergent literacy in the pre-school setting.

Quality across the sample of pre-schools

Observations for the EPPE project were made in the period May 1998–June 1999. Researchers spent a full day in each setting, but only after they had visited on several occasions earlier so that children felt comfortable. A score for each sub-scale was calculated for the ECERS-R and the ECERS-E and a total score was created as well.

Some items were not considered to be applicable for the centres; most notably the 'nap/rest' item on the personal care practices sub-scale was not relevant to 114 centres catering for children aged 3 to 5. Only relevant items (i.e. those that were rated) were used in the calculation of sub-scale scores, thus non-relevant items had no effect on the results.

The distribution of the total scores on the ECERS-R and the ECERS-E are shown in Figures 5.1 and 5.2. The mean total score from 141 centres on the ECERS-R was 4.34 (SD: 1.00) and 3.07 (SD: 1.01) on the ECERS-E. The ECERS-R mean score is in the 'adequate to good' range while the ECERS-E indicates 'adequate' quality. A comparison of the mean scores on the two instruments is shown in Figure 5.3.

Distribution of scores and an overview of the sub-scales

The total ECERS-R and total ECERS-E scores were normally distributed (see Figures 5.1 and 5.2 respectively) and met parametric assumptions. Analysis of Variance (ANOVA) tests with Tukey's HSD post hoc tests were employed to compare differences between types of centres for total ECERS-R and ECERS-E scores. Furthermore, with one exception, the mean sub-scale scores were normally distributed and therefore parametric statistical tests were employed in the analysis of the sub-scales. The exception to this is the ECERS-E science and environment sub-scale in which parametric assumptions are not satisfied. Accordingly for this sub-scale, non-parametric tests were used to test the significance of pair-wise comparisons.

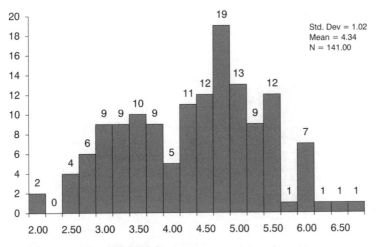

Figure 5.1 Histogram of total ECERS-R score

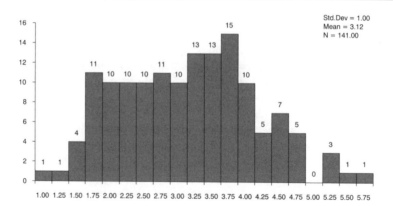

Figure 5.2 Histogram of total ECERS-E scores

Overall the ECERS-R scores of individual settings tend towards the top of the 'adequate' range and sometimes approach 'good'. The ECERS-E scores are lower with provision for mathematics, science and diversity hovering around 'minimal' ratings.

Figure 5.4 breaks down the two scales into their sub-scale components. The highest scores are found in 'social interactions', 'organisation and routines' and 'space and furnishings' while the lowest scores are seen in 'personal care', 'pre-school activities'. Although the ratings averaged across all types of provision are broadly satisfactory, closer inspection within types of provision reveals some striking differences. In this sample many centres were found to be exciting places where children were challenged and supported in their learning and where the interactions between staff and children were sensitive and enabling. Unfortunately, other centres were characterised by poor implementation of the curriculum and overly directed activities.

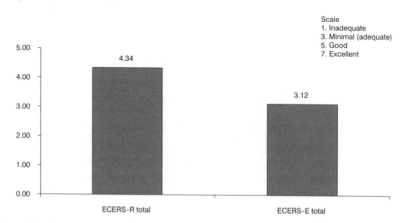

Figure 5.3 Comparison between Mean ECERS-R and ECERS-E Scores

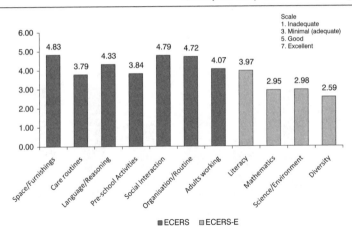

Figure 5.4 ECERS-R and ECERS-E sub-scale scores

A comparison of ECERS-R scores according to type of provision

We turn now to the analyses on differences in the environment according to type of provision. Figure 5.5 shows that the three types of provision managed by the Local Education Authority had significantly higher scores for total ECERS-R when compared to other types of provision. Statistical tests were carried out to identify exactly which pre-school types differed significantly from each other. Local authority day centres, nursery classes, nursery schools and combined centres all had significantly higher scores than playgroups and private day nurseries. Additionally private day nurseries had a significantly higher total ECERS-R

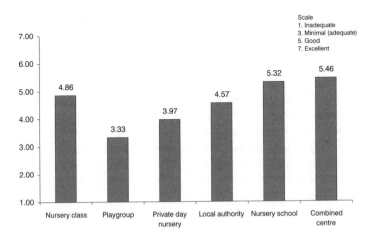

Figure 5.5 Total ECERS-R scores by pre-school type

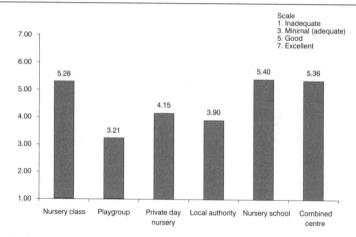

Figure 5.6 Language and reasoning by pre-school type

score than playgroups, and local authority centres had significantly lower total ECERS-R scores than nursery schools and combined centres.

We shall now consider ECERS-R sub-scales which focus specifically on aspects of the educational and care environment experienced by children and staff. Some sub-scales focus more on facilities while others describe pedagogical practices and the ways adults and children interact with one another in a purely social way. The pedagogy is described in terms of the balance between child-initiated activity and adult-led activities. For more detail on pedagogical practices see Chapter 8 and Siraj-Blatchford *et al.*, 2002, 2003).

The trends seen in the ECERS-R total scores are fairly consistent throughout the sub-scale scores. Of the six pre-school types, playgroups had the lowest mean sub-scale score for all 7 sub-scales; private day nurseries had the second lowest mean sub-scale scores for all sub-scales except language and reasoning in which they were rated slightly higher than local authority day nurseries. Nursery classes, nursery schools and combined centres were rated consistently high on all the sub-scales. There were significant pre-school differences for 6 out of the 7 sub-scales. (No significant pre-school differences were found in personal care routines.) Statistical tests show that, in terms of quality measured on ECERS-R, the LEA provision generally scored highest followed by local authority day care, then private day nurseries, and finally playgroups. Although the pattern of significant pair-wise differences varied slightly across the sub-scales, in general *post hoc* tests were similar to the Tukey test results for the total ECERS-R scores.

In general, the maintained provision (nursery schools, classes and combined centres run by the Local Education Authority) had higher quality on the ECERS-R and ECERS-E sub-scales.

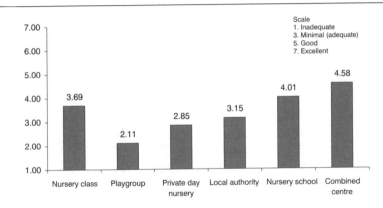

Figure 5.7 Total ECERS-E scores by pre-school type

A comparison of ECERS-E scores according to type of provision

The total ECERS-E scores for the six types of provision show an almost identical trend to the ECERS-R scores (see Figure 5.7). Playgroups and private day nurseries are rated lowest. Nursery schools and nursery schools combining care and education are rated highest on most sub-scales. Total ECERS-E scores were found to differ significantly. The results were almost identical to those found for the ECERS-R: LEA nursery classes, nursery schools and nursery schools combining care and education score most highly, significantly higher than playgroups and private day nurseries. Local authority (day care) centres score significantly more highly than playgroups, *but not* private day nurseries (this difference was significant for total ECERS-R scores); local authority (day care) centres also score significantly lower than *both* nursery schools and nursery schools combining care and education. Additionally, private day nurseries score significantly higher than playgroups, and centres combining care score significantly higher than nursery classes.

Moving away from total scores to sub-scale scores, statistical tests on all four ECERS-E sub-scales showed that there were significant differences according to type of provision. Nursery schools and nursery schools combining care and education are consistently rated more highly than playgroups and private day nurseries (see Figures 5.8–5.10). These figures are included here because they show so clearly the strengths of the maintained sector, especially in provisions for literacy (activities as well as texts and other learning aids).

Summary of results from ECERS-R and ECERS-E

To summarise, the findings on both rating scales showed that nursery schools, combined centres (combining nursery education and care), and to a slightly lesser degree nursery classes, are rated in the 'good' range on both observations

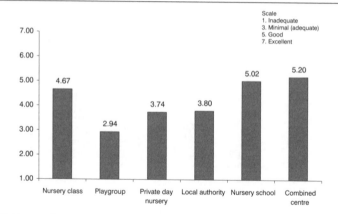

Figure 5.8 Literacy by pre-school type

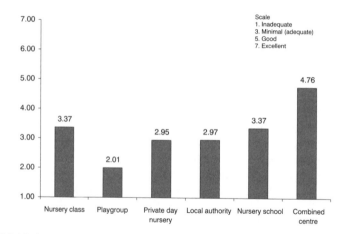

Figure 5.9 Mathematics by pre-school type

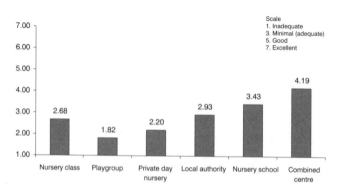

Figure 5.10 Diversity by pre-school type

of scales. Playgroups and private day nurseries are rated with lower 'quality' (minimal/adequate) provision while local authority day care (social service) centres are identified as medium provision. Social service centres combining care and education had significantly lower quality of provision than nursery schools which combine education and care.

Concurrent validity, predictive validity and reliability

Figure 5.11 is a scattergram depicting the relationship between the two ECERS measures. The strong relationship (Pearson product moment correlation = 0.78) is consistent with the view that the different rating scales are both tapping into something akin to 'quality' but that there are small, but perhaps important, differences in what they measure. With the exception of 'personal care routines' most of the sub-scales are moderately correlated with one another. This means that centres high on one sub-scale tend to be high on others.

As expected, the CIS is only modestly related to scores on the two ECERS measures: significant moderate relationships were found between the ECERS-E total and two CIS sub-scales: Positive Relationship (r =0.59, p<.01) and Detachment (r=−0.45, p<.01). The other two sub-scales of the CIS (Punitiveness, Permissiveness) were also significantly related to the ECERS-E total in the expected direction, but these relations were less strong (−18, −.32, p<.05) (Sammons *et al.*, 2002).

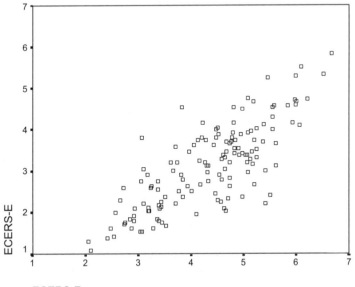

Figure 5.11 Scattergram – ECERS-R (total) and ECERS-E (total)

The strong correlation between the ECERS-E and ECERS-R total scores demonstrates that the scales are picking up similar but not identical aspects of quality. The ECERS-R was designed to detect pre-school quality and we believe it does – although in less detail on pedagogy and curriculum than the English instrument. The lower correlation between the ECERS-E and the CIS is in line with the fact that the CIS focuses strongly on 'relationship' aspects which caregivers establish with the children, while the ECERS-E assesses curriculum as well as relationship. Because the ECERS-E indicators assess the warmth and sensitivity of curriculum activities, it was expected that the ECERS-E would relate moderately with the CIS. Overall these findings support the construct validity of the ECERS-E, with higher correlations with the ECERS-R and lower (but still significant) correlations with the CIS.

Inter-rater reliability was calculated for the two environmental scales on 25 randomly chosen centres throughout the regions (Sylva *et al.*, 1999). It was calculated in two ways: (a) as the percentage of exact agreement between the two observers and (b) as a kappa coefficient (Cohen, 1968). The analysis was done separately for each region and showed that on the ECERS-R, the percentage of exact agreement ranged from 78.2 to 91.4 while the kappas ranged from 0.75 to 0.90. The range of the percentages of exact agreement on the ECERS-E was 85.2 to 97.6 and the range of kappas was 0.83 to 0.97. These results indicate good to excellent inter-observer reliability across centres and regions.

The predictive validity of the ECERS-R and E was established through its relationship with children's developmental progress, as reported in Chapter 6 and summarised at the end of this chapter.

Structural quality in the settings

EPPE also investigated structural measures of quality, especially those related to staff (Taggart *et al.*, 2000) and found that the maintained sector (nursery schools and classes and most of the combined centres) had staff with higher qualifications than staff in the private, voluntary and independent sectors. The managers of nursery schools, classes and combined centres were far more likely to have had level 5 qualifications, which in the vast majority of cases was Qualified Teacher Status (QTS). Table 5.1 shows this clearly with not a single playgroup managed by a teacher.

The managers in the three maintained groups tended to be older as well and their staff members were older also. Finally, there was more staff turnover (see Table 5.2 on turnover) in the playgroups and private day nurseries, another measure of quality related to structure.

Both age of staff and annual turnover are thought to be related to quality. Are the process aspects of quality measured on the ECERS related to structure of settings? The answer is yes; Figure 5.12 shows clearly that the higher the qualifications of the centre manager, the higher the measured process quality of the setting across the first sub-scales of the ECERS-E.

Table 5.1 Managers' highest child care/educational qualification (by pre-school type)

	Nursery class %	Playgroup %	Private day nursery %	LA %	Nursery school %	Combined centre %
Unqualified		8.3	3.6	4.2		
Level 2		41.7	10.7	4.2		
Level 3/4	8.7	50.0	57.1	66.7		33.3
Level 5	91.3		28.6	25.0	100.0	66.7
n	23	36	28	24	20	6

Table 5.2 Staff leaving in last twelve months (by pre school type)

	Nursery class %	Playgroup %	Private day nursery %	LA %	Nursery school %	Combined centre %
None	82.6	47.1	19.4	50.0	42.1	14.3
One	17.4	32.4	29.0	12.5	47.4	42.9
Two		8.8	19.4	20.8	5.3	14.3
Three		5.9	12.9	8.3	5.3	14.3
Four		5.9	3.2	8.3		14.3
Six			12.9			
More than 6			3.2			
Response	23 / 24	34 / 34	31 / 31	24 / 24	19 / 20	7 / 7

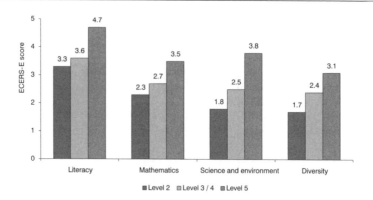

Figure 5.12 ECERS-E sub-scale scores by manager qualification

Relating this study to previous research

The main findings from this large study on the characteristics and quality of pre-school provision are supported by other sources. Research in London by Lera, Owen and Moss (1996) showed higher scores on ECERS for nursery classes, followed by social services day nurseries and then playgroups. In 2008 the Office for Standards in Education (Ofsted) reported more favourably on provision in the maintained sector compared to private and voluntary.

Looking back at Figure 5.4 reveals the sub-scale scores for the entire sample, undivided as to type of provision. Across the sample, the totals and sub-scale scores on ECERS-R range from 4 to 5, just short of 'good' provision. Kwan (1997) summarised comparative data from studies using ECERS in other countries. How does the UK compare? The other countries with sub-scale means similar to the UK include Canada (a small group of 'superior' centres studied in Montreal) and Sweden along with one study from the USA (Head Start). International studies in Germany and New Zealand report sub-scale means of just under 4, while studies in Bermuda report means closer to 3. Hence earlier findings from other 'western' countries indicate that the UK is not too different from Sweden and parts of North America; it appears to be marginally better than Germany and New Zealand (Kwan, 1997; Tietze *et al.*, 1997). A recent US study on quality and sector (Sosinsky *et al.*, 2007) found higher quality in not-for-profit centres. This was a finding similar to EPPE, which found higher quality in the state sector, followed by voluntary, and then private. Another large scale US study by LoCasale-Crouch *et al.* (2007) found quality was lowest in centres attended by the poorest children. All these comparisons must be taken with some caution as they may not be fully representative of the country and only one of the studies reported here had a sample as large as that in the EPPE study.

Profiles found in different types of provision

Although the EPPE results present a picture of satisfactory pre-school environments, centres varied considerably in their ECERS profiles according to type of provision. The traditional nursery schools and LEA nursery-combined-with-care usually had the highest scores, often close to 'excellent', followed by nursery classes. Unfortunately many young children are attending centres where the provision is 'minimal' rather than 'good'. The playgroups and private day care nurseries typically had the lowest scores, with social services day care nurseries somewhere in between. This study shows clearly that well-resourced pre-school centres which had a history of 'education' (including a more substantial number of trained teachers, local authority 'education' training) were providing the highest quality of care and education. The centres from the 'care' tradition, despite their more favourable ratios, were offering a different level of care and education. It is relevant here to mention that care-oriented provision usually offers the lowest salaries to staff, employs workers with the lowest level of qualifications, and has limited access to training and higher staff turnover. We found that provision above the 'minimal' level was concentrated in well-resourced centres.

Appropriateness of ECERS-R and ECERS-E

This chapter on the EPPE centres has concluded that they vary in 'quality' as measured on an international instrument (devised initially in North America) and one devised in the UK based on the Desirable Learning Outcomes, the relevant curriculum at the beginning of the EPPE study. It is necessary to ask whether some types of provision have been 'disadvantaged' by the structure and the content of ECERS-R. For example, it is not easy for a playgroup to provide special facilities for parents or for staff, both of which are required for high ECERS-R ratings on certain items. Brophy *et al.* (1992) have suggested that the focus of playgroups on parental involvement is not adequately assessed through the ECERS. The ECERS-R includes an item on parental involvement but the main data on this topic within the EPPE sample is derived from interviews with centre managers (n = 141) and with parents (n = 2,000+). Thus the EPPE study investigated provision for parents through its case studies, rather than its observational scales.

Conclusion

To conclude, EPPE found that the standard of education and care in pre-school provision (before 2000) was of adequate quality in the vast majority of settings. In the 'educational' (or maintained/state) settings, it was particularly good. The chapters that follow describe the outcomes of such provision in terms of children's cognitive, social and behavioural development. Applying 'value added' analyses of children's outcomes, the EPPE research shows how these observational profiles predict children's longer-term intellectual, social and behavioural progress.

The most important analyses in the EPPE study related to quality were those in which we investigated the effects of quality on children's developmental outcomes throughout their primary schooling. Chapters 6 and 7 report on these analyses, so they will only be summarised here.

1   Children who attended settings that had higher quality scores on the ECERS-E had better academic outcomes (English and Mathematics national tests) when they were aged 7 and also 11. Moreover, quality scores on the ECERS-E in pre-school settings were also related to many positive social-behavioural outcomes at ages 7 and 11 as well.

2   Scores on the ECERS-R were related to positive social-behavioural outcomes at ages 7 and 11. There were some positive cognitive outcomes found at age 7, but by the age of 11 the ECERS-R quality scores were not related to cognitive outcomes in children.

3   By the age of 11, EPPE found that certain children were more susceptible to the positive benefits of quality than others: these included children with multiple disadvantage, and also boys.

Thus, this chapter has shown that it is possible to measure quality in early childhood through structured observations, complemented by interview and inspection of documents. Further, the quality of early childhood provision a child experiences in the period 3–5 years predicts later cognitive outcomes at the age of 11 (for the ECERS-E) and social-behavioural outcomes as well (ECERS-R, ECERS-E).

Since the EPPE study there has been a greater focus on what constitutes 'quality' in early years settings. The introduction of the Early Years Foundation Stage (DCSF, 2008) has gone some way to ensuring an equal entitlement for all children to a broad and balanced educational content. However the debate about how these curriculum guidelines should be delivered is still a matter for considerable debate and is proving a controversial topic amongst both early years academics and practitioners alike. What cannot be disputed is the importance of 'quality'. The EPPE study has been able to establish the links between educational and care processes and children's developmental outcomes (see Chapters 6 and 7). These findings are important for not only national policies which seek to improve the outcomes for all children but also for the day-to-day practices which help to enrich the lives of very young children, especially those from disadvantaged backgrounds and make them good life-long learners.

Table 5.A1 Structure of the Early Childhood Environmental Rating Scale–Revised (Source: Harms, T., Clifford, M. and Cryer, D., 1998)

I	*Space and furnishings*	*III*	*Language-reasoning*
1	Indoor space	15	Books and pictures
2	Furniture for routine care, play and	16	Encouraging children to communicate
	learning	17	Using language to develop reasoning skills
3	Furnishings for relaxation and comfort	18	Informal use of language
4	Room arrangement for play		
5	Space for privacy	*IV*	*Activities*
6	Child related display	19	Fine motor
7	Space for gross motor play	20	Art
8	Gross motor equipment	21	Music/movement
		22	Blocks
II	*Personal care routines*	23	Sand/water
9	Greeting/departing	24	Dramatic play
10	Meals/snacks	25	Nature/science
11	Nap/rest	26	Math/number
12	Toileting/diapering	27	Use of TV, video, and/or computers
13	Health practices	28	Promoting acceptance of diversity
14	Safety practice		

V		*Interaction*
29		Supervision of gross motor activities
30		General supervision of children (other than
		gross motor)
31		Discipline
32		Staff–child interactions
33		Interactions among children
VI		*Programme structure*
34		Schedule
35		Free play
36		Group time
37		Provisions for children with disabilities
VII		*Parents and staff*
38		Provisions for parents
39		Provisions for personal needs of staff
40		Provisions for professional needs of staff
41		Staff interaction and cooperation
42		Supervision and evaluation of staff
43		Opportunities for professional growth

Table 5.A2 Structure of the Early Childhood Environmental Rating Scale–Extension (Source: Sylva, K., Siraj-Blatchford, I., and Taggart, B., 2003)

I	*Literacy*	*II*	*Mathematics*	*III*	*Science and environment*	*IV*	*Diversity*
1	'Environmental print': letters and words	7	Counting and the application of counting	11	Natural materials	16	Planning for individual learning needs
2	Book and literacy areas	8	Reading and writing simple numbers	12	Areas featuring science/ science resources	17	Gender equality and awareness
3	Adult reading with the children	9	Mathematical activities: shape and space (select either 9a or 9b for evidence; choose the one which you observed most)	13	Science activities: science processes: non living (select one of a, b, c for evidence; choose one you observed most)	18	Race equality and awareness
4	Sounds in words	10	Mathematical activities: sorting, matching and comparing	14	Science activities: science processes: living processes and the world around us		
5	Emergent writing/mark making			15	Science activities: science processes: food preparation		
6	Talking and listening						

References

Arnett, J. (1989) *Caregivers in day-care centres, Does training matter? Journal of Applied Developmental Psychology*, 10, 4, 541–552.

Berrueta-Clement, J.R., Schweinhart, L.J., Barnett, W.S.. Epstein, A.S. and Weikart, D.P. (1984) *Changed Lives: The effects of the Perry Pre-School Programme on Youths Through Age 19.* Ypsilanti, MI: The High/Scope Press.

Brophy, J., Statham, J. and Moss, P. (1992) *Playgroups in Practice Self-help and Public Policy*, London: HMSO Department of Health.

Burchinal, M.R., Roberts, J.E., Riggins, R., Zeisel, S.A., Neebe, E. and Briant, D. (2000) Relating quality of centre-based child care to early cognitive and language development longitudinally, *Child Development*, 71, 2, 339–357.

Burchinal, M.R., Howes, C. and Kontos, S. (2002) Structural predictors of child care quality in child care homes, *Early Childhood Research Quarterly*, 17, 1, 87–105.

Cohen, J. (1968) Weighted kappa: nominal scale agreement with provision for scaled agreement or partial credit, *Psychological Bulletin*, 70, 4, 213–220.

Department for Children, Schools and Families (DCSF) (2008) *Early Years Foundation Stage*, London DCSF Publications.

Department for Education and Employment (1996) *Nursery Education: Desirable Learning Outcomes for Children's Learning on Entering Compulsory Education*, London: DfEE/SCAA.

De Kruif, R.E.L., McWilliam, R.A., Ridley, S.M. and Wakely, M.B. (2000) Classification of teachers' interaction behaviours in early childhood classrooms, *Early Childhood Research Quarterly*, 15, 2, 247–268.

Gallagher, P.A. and Lambert, R.G. (2006) Classroom quality, concentration of children with special needs, and child outcomes in head start, *Exceptional Children*, 37, 1, 31–53.

Gilliam, W.S. (2000) *The School Readiness Initiative in South-Central Connecticut: Classroom Quality, Teacher Training, and Service Provision.* Final report of findings for fiscal year 1999. Retrieved December 2nd, 2002 from http://nieer.org/resources/research/CSRI1999.pdf

Harms, T., Clifford, M. and Cryer, D. (1998) *Early Childhood Environment Rating Scale, Revised Edition (ECERS-R)*, Vermont: Teachers College Press.

Jaeger, E. and Funk, S. (2001) *The Philadelphia Child Care Quality Study: An Examination of Quality in Selected Early Education and Care Settings.* A technical report submitted to the Improving School Readiness project of the united way of South-Eastern PA. Retrieved December 2nd, 2002 from http://psych.sju.edu/faculty/Jaeger/JaegerFunk2001.pdf

Katz, L. (1993) Multiple perspectives on the quality of early childhood programmes, *European Early Childhood Education Research Journal*, 1, 2, 5–9.

Kwan, C. (1997) The effects of environmental variations in day care centres on the development of young children in Singapore, PhD thesis, University of London.

Lera, M-J., Owen, C. and Moss. P. (1996) Quality of educational settings for four-year-old children in England, *European Early Childhood Education Research Journal*, 4 (2), 21–33.

LoCasale-Crouch, J., Konold, T., Pianta, R., Howes, C., Burchinal, M., Bryant, D., Clifford, R., Early, D. and Barbarin, O. (2007) Observed classroom quality profiles in state funded pre-kindergarten programmes and assosciations with teacher, programme and classroom characteristics, *Early Childhood Research Quarterly*, 22, 1, 1–160.

Mason, J. M. and Stewart, J.P. (1990) Emergent literacy assessment for instructional use in kindergarten, in L.M. Morrow and L.K. Smith (eds) *Assessment for Instruction in Early Literacy*, Englewood Cliffs, NJ: Prentice-Hall, pp.155–175.

Munton, A.G., Mooney, A. and Rowland, L. (1995) Deconstructing quality: A conceptual framework for the new paradigm in day care provision for the under eights, *Early Child Development and Care*, 114,1, 11–23.

The Office for Standards in Education, Ofsted (2008) *Outcome of the Consultation on Inspecting Provision in the Early Years Foundation Stage from September 2008*, The Office for Standards in Education, London: Ofsted Publication Centre HMI.

OHMCI (1999) *Standards and Quality in the Early Years: Educational Provision for Four Year-Olds in the Maintained and Non-maintained Sectors*, Cardiff: Education Department Inspectorate, Welsh Office.

Osborn, A.F. and Milbank, J.E. (1987) *The Effects of Early Education: A Report from the Child Health and Education Study*, Oxford: Clarendon Press.

Peisner-Feinberg, E.S. and Burchinal, M.R. (1997) Relations between preschool children's child care experiences and concurrent development: the cost, quality and outcomes study, *Merrill-Palmer Quarterly*, 43, 3, 451–477.

Peisner-Feinberg, E.S., Burchinal, M.R., Clifford, R.M., Yazejian, N., Culkin, M.L., Zelazo, J., Howes, C., Byler, P., Kagan, S.L. and Rustici, J. (1999) *The Children of the Cost, Quality, and Outcomes Study go to School: Technical Report*, Chapel Hill, NC: University of North Carolina at Chapel Hill, Frank Porter Graham Child Development Center.

Phillips, D., McCartney, K. and Scarr, S. (1987) Child care quality and children's social development, *Journal of Applied Developmental Psychology*, 23,4, 537–543.

Phillipsen, L.C., Burchinal, M.R., Howes, C. and Cryer, D. (1997) The prediction of process quality from structural features of child care, *Early Childhood Research Quarterly*, 12, 3, 281–303.

Rogoff, B. (1999) Thinking and learning in a social context, in J. Lave (ed.) *Everyday Cognition: Development in Social Context*, Cambridge, MA: Harvard University Press, pp. 1–8.

Sammons, P., Sylva, K., Melhuish, E.C., Siraj-Blatchford, I., Taggart, B. and Elliot, K. (2002) *The Effective Provision of Pre-school Education Project (EPPE), Technical Paper 8a: Measuring the Impact of Pre-school on Children's Cognitive Progress over the Pre-school Period*, London: DfES/Institute of Education, University of London.

Sammons, P., Sylva, K., Melhuish, E., Siraj-Blatchford, I., Taggart, B. and Hunt, S. (2008a) *Effective Pre-School and Primary Education 3–11 Project (EPPE 3–11) Influences on Children's Attainment and Progress in Key Stage 2: Cognitive Outcomes in Year 6*. Research report No. DCSF-RR048, Nottingham: DCSF Publications.

Sammons, P., Sylva, K., Melhuish, E., Siraj-Blatchford, I., Taggart, B. and Hunt, S. (2008b) *Effective Pre-School and Primary Education 3–11 Project (EPPE 3–11) Influences on Children's Development and Progress in Key Stage 2: Social/Behavioural Outcomes in Year 6*. Research report No. DCSF-RR049, Nottingham: DCSF Publications.

Schweinhart, L.J. and Weikart, D.P. (1997) *Lasting Differences, The High/Scope Preschool Curriculum Comparison Through Age 23*, Ypsilanti, MI: High/Scope Press.

Senechal, M., Lefevre, J., Smith-Chant, B.L., and Colton, K.V. (2001) On refining theoretical models of emergent literacy: the role of empirical evidence, *Journal of School Psychology*, 39, 5. 439–460.

Sheridan, S., Giota, J., You-Me, H. and Jeong-Yoon, K. (2009) A cross-cultural study of preschool quality in South Korea and Sweden: ECERS evaluations, *Early Childhood Research Quarterly*, 24.

Siraj-Blatchford, I. and Wong, Y. (1999) Defining and evaluating 'quality' early childhood education in an international context: dilemmas and possibilities. Early years, *International Journal of Research and Development*, 20, 1, 7–18.

Siraj-Blatchford, I., Sylva, K., Muttock, S., Gilden, R. and Bell, D. (2002) *Researching Effective Pedagogy in the Early Years*. DfES Research Report 356, London: DfES.

Siraj-Blatchford, I., Sylva, K., Taggart, B., Sammons, P. and Melhuish, E. (2003) *The EPPE Case Studies Technical Paper 10*, London: University of London, Institute of Education/ DfEE.

Sosinsky, L.S., Lord, H. Zigler, E. (2007) For profit/nonprofit differences in center based child care quality: results from the National Institute of Child Health and Human Development Study of Early Child Care and Youth Development, *Journal of Applied Developmental Psychology*, 28, 390–410.

Soucacou, E.P. and Sylva, K. (in press) Developing instruments for assessing 'difficult to measure' aspects of quality in early childhood practice, in E. Tucker, G. Walford and M. Viswanathan (eds) *The Sage Handbook of Measurement: How Social Scientists Generate, Modify, and Validate Indicators and Scales*, Thousand Oaks, CA: Sage Publications.

Storch, S.A. and Whitehurst, G.J. (2001) The role of family and home on the literacy development of children from low-income backgrounds, *New Directions for Child and Adolescent Development*, 92, 52–72.

Sulzby, E. and Teale, W. (1991) Emergent literacy, in R. Barr, M. Kamil, P. Mosenthal and P. D. Pearson (eds), *Handbook of Reading Research*, Vol. 2, New York: Longman.

Sylva, K., Siraj-Blatchford, I. and Taggart, B. (2003) *Assessing Quality in the Early Years: Early Childhood Environment Rating Scale-Extension (ECERS-E): Four Curricular Subscales*, Stoke-on Trent: Trentham Books.

Sylva, K., Sammons, P., Melhuish, E., Siraj-Blatchford, I. and Taggart, B. (1999) *The Effective Provision of Pre-School Education (EPPE) Project. Technical Paper 1 – An Introduction to the EPPE Project.*, London: University of London, Institute of Education/DfEE.

Sylva, K., Melhuish, E., Sammons, P., Siraj-Blatchford, I. and Taggart, B. (2004) *The Effective Provision of Pre-School Education (EPPE) Project: Final Report*, London: DfES/ Institute of Education, University of London.

Taggart, B., Sylva, K., Siraj-Blatchford, I., Melhuish, E., Sammons, P. and Walker-Hall, J. (2000) *Technical Paper 5: Characteristics of the Centres in the EPPE Sample: Interviews*. London: DfES/Institute of Education, University of London.

Tietze, W., Hundertmark-Mayser, J. and Rossbach, H-G. (1997) European Child Care and Education Study: Cross-national analyses of the quality and effects of early childhood programmes on children's development. European Union DG XII: Science, Research and Developmental RTD Action: Targeted Socio-Economic Research Final Report.2, 142–156.

Whitebook, M., Howes, C. and Phillips, D. (1989) *Who Cares? Child Care Teachers and the Quality of Care in America*. Final report of the National Child Care Staffing Study. Oakland, CA: Child Care Employee Project.

Whitehurst, G. J. and Lonigan, C. J. (1998) Child development and emergent literacy, *Child Development*, 69, 3, 848–872.

Wood, D.J., Bruner, J.S. and Ross, G. (1976) The role of tutoring in problem solving, *Journal of Child Psychology and Psychiatry*, 17, 89–100.

Chapter 6

Does pre-school make a difference?

Identifying the impact of pre-school on children's cognitive and social behavioural development at different ages

Pam Sammons

This chapter summarises the key findings on the impact of pre-school identified over the pre-school period. It highlights the importance of various features of young children's pre-school experience, including duration and quality, and identifies the effects of individual centres. The results help to explain why some pre-school settings do better than others in providing children with a better start to primary school.

Introduction

The EPPE study was designed to explore several 'big' questions. First, we wanted to know whether attending a pre-school centre makes a difference to young children's intellectual and social/behavioural development. In other words do children who attend a pre-school have better outcomes and so are better prepared when they start primary school than those children who do not attend a pre-school? Second, we wanted to know whether the effects of pre-school last. In other words do the effects continue in terms of better child outcomes throughout Key Stage 1 (ages 6 and 7 years) and on to the end of Key Stage 2 (age 11 years)? We also wanted to find out whether certain features of pre-school experience are of special importance. We were especially interested to find out the answer to the superficially straightforward question of whether any kind of pre-school is beneficial. (Does going to a pre-school rather than not going have measurable benefits in later child outcomes?) We also wanted to establish whether the type of pre-school attended matters, and we collected data for children attending a range of different types of provision to explore this. In addition, we thought that other measures, particularly the duration in months that a child attends a pre-school, the mode of attendance (part or full time), the quality of the pre-school experience, and other factors such as staff qualifications or staff child ratios might be important influences too, and so we collected extra information about these aspects to test the various potential features of provision that may shape pre-school experience.

All pre-schools are not the same, even if notionally of the same type (e.g. there is much variation between individual playgroups in staffing set up and ethos, for example). We know that individual pre-schools vary in a range of ways (forms of leadership, nature of pedagogy, etc.) as our case studies in Chapter 8 will illustrate. Another important question for our research therefore was: Are some individual pre-schools more effective (foster better child outcomes) than others? To address this question we designed our study to enable us to identify individual pre-school centre effects.

In total we had eight broad aims that guided our analyses of children's cognitive and social behavioural development and progress and the study of pre-school impact. These were:

1 To produce a detailed description of the 'career paths' of a large sample of children and their families between entry into pre-school education and completion (or near completion) of Key Stage 1.

2 To compare and contrast the developmental progress of 3,000+ children from a wide range of social and cultural backgrounds who had differing pre-school experiences.

3 To separate out the effects of pre-school experience from the effects of primary schooling.

4 To establish whether some pre-school centres are more effective than others in promoting children's cognitive and social/behavioural development.

5 To identify the individual characteristics (structural and process) of pre-school education in those centres found to be most effective.

6 To investigate differences in the progress of different groups of children, e.g. children who do not have English as their first language, children from disadvantaged backgrounds and both genders.

7 To investigate the medium-term effects of pre-school education on educational performance at Key Stage 1 in a way which will allow the possibility of longitudinal follow-up at later ages to establish long-term effects, if any.

8 To investigate the role of pre-school provision in combating social disadvantage and exclusion.

In Chapter 3 we discussed the EPPE mixed methods research design adopted to shed light on the research aims described above. Here we present some of the main results from multilevel statistical analyses of a wide range of child outcomes at different ages. Due to the wealth of data collected we can only illustrate our findings briefly and the interested reader may want to consult our Technical Papers (see website http://eppe.ioe.ac.uk or Appendix 3). We have also provided more detailed accounts in several journal articles (Sammons et al., 2004, 2008; Taggart et al., 2006).

This chapter first presents a summary of our key findings over the first two important phases we studied: pre-school (ages 3+ to rising 5 years) and Key Stage

1 (ages 5 to 7 years). We then go on to unpack some of these findings in more detail. In the next chapter we focus on the results in Key Stage 2 based on the longer term follow up of the child sample to age 11, the end of primary schooling.

Key findings over the pre-school period

Impact of attending a pre-school

- Pre-school experience, compared to none, enhances all-round development in children.
- Duration of attendance (in months) is also important; an earlier start (under age 3 years) is related to significantly better intellectual development by the time children start primary school especially for language outcomes.
- Full time attendance leads to no better gains for children than part-time provision.
- Disadvantaged children benefit significantly from good quality pre-school experiences, especially where they attend centres with a mixture of children from different social backgrounds.
- Overall, disadvantaged children tend to attend pre-school for fewer months on average than those from more advantaged backgrounds (around 4–6 months less on average) and this shorter time in pre-school acts as an additional disadvantage for such vulnerable children.

Does type of pre-school matter?

- There are significant differences between individual pre-school settings in their impact on children; some settings are significantly more effective than others in promoting positive child outcomes.
- Good quality can be found across all types of early years settings; however in this study quality was higher overall in settings integrating care and education and in nursery schools (see Chapter 5).

Effects of quality and specific 'practices' in pre-school

- High quality pre-schooling is related to better intellectual and social/behavioural development for children.
- Settings that have staff with higher qualifications have higher quality scores and their children make more progress.

Does it matter which individual pre-school a child attends?

- There were significant variations between our 141 pre-school centres in their effectiveness in terms of accounting for variation in children's outcomes, taking account of their prior development and background. Some centres fostered better outcomes in particular areas of children's development by the time they started at primary school. We identified a number of more effective 'outlier' centres (and some that were significantly less effective too). We discuss the features of some of these more effective centres in Chapter 8 through our intensive case studies.

The importance of home learning

- For all children, the quality of the early home learning environment (HLE) is more important for intellectual and social development than parental occupation, education or income. What parents do is more important than who parents are, as we discussed earlier in Chapter 4 in relation to early home learning influences. The quality of pre-school experience is particularly important for children who experience a poor early HLE because it can help to ameliorate this disadvantage by providing a stimulating environment and wider range of experiences.

Key findings at the end of Key Stage I

Lasting effects

- The beneficial effects of pre-school on children's outcomes remained evident throughout Key Stage 1, although the longer term boost given to some outcomes was not as strong as it had been found to be at primary school entry.

Duration and quality

- The number of months a child attended pre-school continues to have an effect on their attainment and progress throughout Key Stage 1, although this effect is found to be stronger for academic skills than for social behavioural development. Children who had spent a longer time in pre-school (related to an earlier start) continue to show better developmental outcomes at age 7 indicating that primary school experiences do not 'wash out' those of pre-school.
- Pre-school quality is also still significantly related to children's scores for Reading and Mathematics at age 6. By the time children are age 7 the relationship between quality and academic attainment is somewhat weaker but remains evident, although at this point the effects of quality on social behavioural development are no longer statistically significant.
- High quality pre-school provision combined with longer duration has the strongest overall effect on development. Children who had experienced this combination show better outcomes in several important areas of development.

Effective settings

- Individual pre-schools varied in their 'effectiveness' in terms of influencing particular measures of children's development. The developmental advantages for a child of attending a particularly 'effective' pre-school centre also persists up to age 7. This does not mean that experiences at primary school have no impact on children's outcomes – however the individual pre-school attended continues to influence children's developmental trajectories during Key Stage 1 over and above the effects of the particular primary school they attend.

Vulnerable children

- A small group of children continued to be identified 'at risk' of developing special educational needs (SEN), both cognitive and social/behavioural, with more of the 'home' children falling into this group even after taking into account the influence of background factors. Pre-school experience, especially of high quality, helps reduce the risk of a child later being identified by teachers as showing a SEN during KS1. High quality pre-school may be seen as an effective intervention that reduces the risk of SEN.
- Multiple disadvantage continued to depress children's intellectual and social development up to the end of Key Stage 1. However, the negative impact of English as an additional language (EAL) on outcomes is much reduced at age 7, compared to the strength of the effect of this factor when children were ages 3 and 5.

Home learning environment

- The positive effects of the early HLE continues to be strongly evident in children's developmental profiles at the end of Key Stage 1. This confirms the crucial importance of learning in the early years and the role of parents and other care givers in providing a rich and stimulating environment for young children.

What features of pre-school experiences make a difference in children's development?

Having outlined our overall 'headline' key findings this chapter unpacks and elaborates these in more detail.

Attending or not attending pre-school

Our results clearly show that at entry to primary school (average age 4 years 9 months) there are significant benefits for children who had attended a pre-school compared with those who had not (the home group) across a range of outcomes.

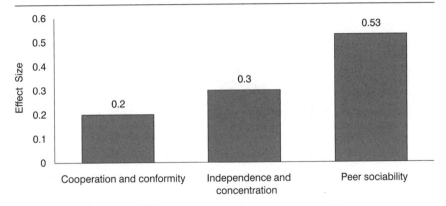

Figure 6.1 Effect sizes for attending pre-school versus not attending for children's social behavioural outcomes at entry to primary school

Figure 6.1 shows the differences for three social behavioural outcomes in terms of net effect sizes. Effect sizes are a measure of the strength of the pre-school influence after taking into account child, family and HLE influences. The effects are especially strong for Peer sociability. Mixing with other children in pre-school has important benefits in promoting young children's social skills and abilities to interact positively with other children. It also benefits children's Independence and concentration which is closely linked with their learning behaviours and is significantly correlated with children's cognitive outcomes. Cooperation and conformity reflects children's abilities to follow classroom procedures and it also shows a boost although more modest. There were no significant pre-school effects found for the fourth measure of behaviour, Anti Social/worried upset, related to attending or not attending a preschool centre.

However the measure of just attending pre-school, or not, showed somewhat less impact on social behaviour outcomes when we followed-up the children at ages 6 and 7, when school and peer group influences are likely to be more powerful.

We now turn to differences in cognitive attainment at entry to primary school. There were significant benefits especially large for children's Language development, followed by Early number concepts and Pre-reading skills when we compare results for children having attended a pre-school versus not attending even after taking account of child and family and HLE backgrounds effects. Figure 6.2 shows net effect sizes for Pre-reading/Reading and Early number concepts/Mathematics at three time points. The effect on Language was only assessed at ages 3+ at entry to the study and again at entry to primary school (rising 5 years). It can be seen that the pre-school influence is strongest for Early number concepts when children start primary school but reduces for Mathematics attainment over Years 1 and 2. For Pre-reading the effects are

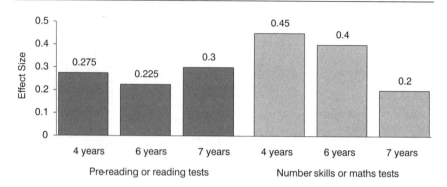

Figure 6.2 Effect sizes for attending pre-school versus not attending for children's cognitive outcomes at entry to primary school and across Key Stage I (Year I and Year 2)

more modest, but the impact shows less decline across Key Stage 1.[1] It appears from our results across Key Stage 1 that the pre-school impact lasts longer for attainment in Reading and Mathematics than in social behaviour (although in Chapter 7 we show that the benefits for Peer sociability continue to be evident at ages 10 and 11 years).

Duration of pre-school and timing of entry

The multilevel analyses show that duration (a child's time at pre-school in months) was related to gains in terms of three important cognitive skills (Language, Pre-reading and Early number concepts) at school entry. The effects of duration were especially marked on Language development (vocabulary and comprehension of English) and this is likely to reflect the benefits of children mixing with a wider group of children and adults that exposes them to a broader and richer range of Language experiences. Perhaps, unsurprisingly, we found that children for whom English is an additional language show particularly strong improvement in Language development over the pre-school period, compared with EAL children who did not attend a pre-school. This has important implications in enabling them to make a better start at primary school, and is particularly relevant to policy makers and practitioners because we found that significantly more of the home children were from ethnic minority groups and did not use English as their first language (around 38 per cent of the home group compared with only around 14 per cent of the main EPPE pre-school sample were EAL children). The duration

---

1   The method of calculating effect sizes is described in Technical Papers 8a and 8b. In Technical Papers 9 and 11 further information is given in relation to duration of attendance. It should be noted that the average time in pre-school was around 22 months (sd 11 months) and the majority attended part time rather than full time. For comparison children attended primary school full time for between 2–3 years by the end of Key Stage 1.

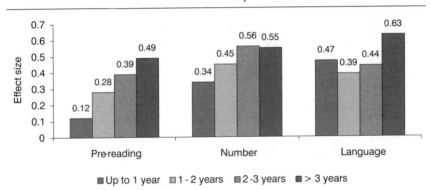

Figure 6.3 Effect sizes for amount of pre-school experience compared with none on cognitive attainment at entry to primary school

of time in pre-school continued to predict better attainment in both Reading and Mathematics when children were in Year 1 at age 6 years and Key Stage 1 results in both English and Mathematics when children were age 7. Duration of pre-school therefore seems to provide a significant cognitive boost that lasts for several years into primary school.

Figure 6.3 summarises the findings in terms of effect sizes, which shows the relative strength of the impact of different periods of time in a target pre-school across different outcomes. In general, the longer a child was in a target pre-school centre, the stronger the positive impact on attainment. Effect sizes for those with 2 to 3 years or 3+ years in pre-school compared with none (the home group) tend to be larger (ranging from 0.44 to 0.63 for Language, 0.54 to 0.55 for early number and 0.38 to 0.48 for Pre-reading). The effect sizes for 2–3 years, or 3+ years in pre-school are similar to those attributable to a mother having a degree versus none. For comparison, a mother having a degree versus no qualification showed an ES of 0.39 for early number, 0.45 for Pre-reading, 0.62 for Language outcomes at entry to primary school.

The change in effect size for duration (in months) over the early years of primary school for two outcomes is illustrated in Table 6.1.

Comparisons with the home group also indicate that one year of pre-school centre experience has relatively less impact on Pre-reading (ES 0.12) than on either language (ES 0.47) or early number concepts (ES 0.33).

As we might expect, the age a child starts pre-school is closely linked with the duration of pre-school attendance. An early start at pre-school (when children were between 2 and 3 years old) is linked to better intellectual attainment and being more sociable with other children (from our teacher ratings of Peer sociability) when children enter primary school.

The benefits of this early start continue to be evident up to the end of Key Stage 1. Our results provide clear evidence that an early start in group settings enhances young children's social skills and that this enhanced sociability remains

Table 6.1 Effect of duration at entry to school and end of Year 1

Duration	Pre-reading/reading		Early number concepts/mathematics	
	Entry to school	End of Year 1	Entry to school	End of Year 1
Up to 1 year	0.12	0.26	0.34	0.32
1–2 years	0.28	0.17	0.45	0.36
2–3 years	0.39	0.26	0.56	0.46
> 3	0.49	0.35	0.55	0.52

evident up to age 7. However, there were indications that a very early start in group care, before the age of 2, is a predictor of higher scores on measures of behaviour problems for a small group of children when they were 3 and again at 5. There was no evidence of this effect lasting up to age 7. The effects of group care in the first 3 years are discussed in Chapter 4. Nonetheless, we should point out that the vast majority (over 90 per cent) of such children who were very early starters continue to show good behaviour.

Although we found that the effects of time in pre-school (in months) remain significant and positive for several child outcomes at age 7, there was no evidence that full-day attendance led to better development than half-day attendance. Thus it appears that the benefits to young children of pre-school apply equally to full-time and part-time attendance. Of course there may be economic benefits to families and society associated with full-time provision in allowing parents to work full time and so increase earnings, reduce the incidence of families relying on benefit income or allowing parents to undertake further education or training. But our data show that there are no extra benefits, nor indeed disadvantages, to children arising from full time pre-school attendance in terms of later cognitive or social behavioural outcomes.

Pre-school effects on different groups of children

The EPPE research also explored whether pre-school differed in its impact on the progress of different groups of children. While pre-school is beneficial for all children, pre-school is particularly beneficial for children from more disadvantaged backgrounds. Our initial assessments showed that one in three children were identified as 'at risk' of developing learning difficulties at the start of pre-school; however, this proportion fell to one in five by the time they started school[2]. This indicates that the boost to learning provided by pre-school helps to reduce the numbers of children with very low cognitive skills who are most likely to struggle when they start primary school. Our findings therefore suggest that pre-school (particularly high quality pre-school) can be an effective intervention

---

2   See the Early Transition and Special Education Needs (EYTSEN) Institute of Education for more detail on SEN in the early years.

for the reduction of special educational needs (SEN), especially for the most disadvantaged and vulnerable children (see Chapter 9). It thus has a valuable role to play in narrowing the achievement gap and so may help combat social exclusion (which is strongly linked with poor educational outcomes at older ages) in the longer term.

Different groups of children have different learning needs. Disadvantaged children are more likely to have adverse social profiles at age 3 and at school entry. Our results suggest that specialised support in pre-schools, especially for Language and Pre-reading skills development, can benefit children from disadvantaged backgrounds and those for whom English is an additional language.

It is also interesting to note that from the start of the study girls generally show better cognitive and social development than boys. Our results suggest that boys show particular benefits from high quality pre-school, because they seem to be more sensitive to the impact of quality pre-school. This may link with the finding that there were significant differences in the early years HLE experienced by girls and boys. On average we found (from parents' own reports) that proportionately more boys than girls experienced less stimulating learning opportunities at home. Thus higher quality pre-school may be of particular value for boys in providing a greater range of stimulating experiences.

Our results also indicate that children's likelihood of showing Anti-social behaviour can be reduced by high quality pre-school in the period 3–5 years.

Overall, our results lead us to conclude that, while not eliminating the adverse impact of social disadvantage, pre-school can help to ameliorate its effects by providing vulnerable children with a better start to primary school which provides the bedrock for better educational outcomes at age 7. Therefore investing in pre-school provision can be an effective policy tool for combating intergenerational cycles of disadvantage.

The quality of the pre-school attended

An important question for the EPPE research was whether higher quality pre-school provision makes a difference to the intellectual and social behavioural development of young children. If so, what is essential in ensuring quality? We have already discussed in Chapter 5 the quality measures (ECERS-R, ECERS-E and the CIS instruments) used to study pre-schools and shown that there were significant variations between individual centres and between types of provider (or sector). Our data showed a significant link between higher quality and better intellectual and social/behavioural outcomes for children at entry to school. For example, children who attended high quality centres show more independence and reduced anti-social/worried behaviour by the time they enter primary school. The quality of the interactions between children and staff were particularly important; where staff showed warmth and were responsive to the individual needs of children, children made more progress.

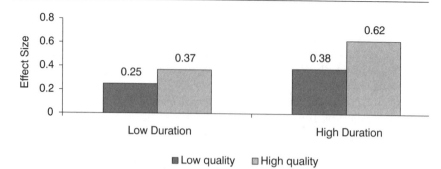

Figure 6.4 Effect sizes for different combinations of quality and duration of pre-school experience on young children's attainment in pre-reading at entry to primary school

One of the quality rating scales (ECERS–E) measured four of the developmental domains in the Foundation Stage Curriculum. Centres that put particular emphasis on literacy, mathematics, science/environment and children's 'diversity' (catering to children of different genders, cultural backgrounds and abilities or interests) promote better outcomes for children especially in Reading and Mathematics at age 6. Pre-school centres that are strong on the intellectual aspects of the curriculum tended to be strong on the social-emotional side as well. Centres that scored higher on the ECERS-E measure tended to promote both better social behavioural as well as cognitive outcomes. Thus high quality pre-school promotes better *all round development*, a point we elaborate in our detailed case studies of more effective pre-school centres in Chapter 8.

Pre-school quality was significantly related to children's scores on Reading and Mathematics at age 6. At age 7 the relationship between quality and academic attainment was somewhat weaker but still evident. We find that high quality pre-school provision combined with longer duration has the strongest effect on development.

Our results showed that the combination of duration and quality predicted better development for cognitive outcomes in particular.

Figure 6.4 groups the data comparing two categories, high versus low duration and high versus low quality, and shows the impact measured in effect sizes on children's Pre-reading attainment measured at entry to primary school. The baseline comparison is with the 'no pre-school' group. It can be seen that pre-school effects are mediated by quality and duration. Although even the combination of low quality and low duration at pre-school is better than no pre-school experience at all, the impact is relatively modest. Higher quality and longer duration both show positive benefits, the most favourable combination being high quality, and high duration.

Ratios and staff qualification

Adult–child ratios can be measured in several ways. Statutory minimum levels vary by type of provision. However many settings operate with more generous ratios than those statutorily required. Observed ratios (with and without volunteers) were used to provide indicators of staffing levels normally experienced by children aged 3–5 years in individual centres. Statutory, reported (by centre managers) and observed ratios were all tested for links with children's cognitive progress. We found no statistically significant relationships between observed or statutory ratios and young children's cognitive progress or their social/behavioural developmental gains over the pre-school period. This may be because of the way ratios varied for different types of provision. Moreover ratios could vary day to day in different centres in relation to variations in children's attendance, and the presence of parent helpers in some centres, particularly playgroups, may also affect practice and climate.

Centre managers' qualifications and the proportion of staff hours at different qualification levels also show significant variation between centres and by type of provision. Centre managers' qualifications are significantly associated with the observed quality profiles of centres. Centres where managers reported they had Level 5 qualifications (e.g. trained teachers[3]) exhibited higher quality (as shown in Chapter 6). Findings from the associated Researching Effective Pedagogy in the Early Years study (REPEY, see Siraj-Blatchford *et al.*, 2002) also indicate that the observed behaviour of other staff is positively influenced by working alongside, in the same room, a member of staff with Level 5 qualifications (see Chapter 8).

The multilevel analyses of children's progress found a significant positive relationship between the proportion of staff who had Level 5 qualification and young children's progress in Pre-reading. This suggests a link between more highly qualified (i.e. qualified teacher) staff and better child outcomes in Pre-reading, although this link may operate indirectly through an impact on centre quality. There was also a significant positive relationship between higher proportions of Level 5 staff and young children's social/behavioural developmental gains in Co-operation and Conformity as well as reductions in Anti-social/Worried behaviour.

Children make more progress in pre-school centres where staff had higher qualifications, particularly if the manager is highly qualified. Having trained teachers working with children in pre-school settings (for a substantial proportion of time, and most importantly as the curriculum leader) has the greatest impact on quality, and is linked specifically with better child outcomes in Pre-reading and social development at age 5.

Given the complex inter-relationships between ratios, staff qualifications, quality and type of provision, plus the extent of variation between individual centres of the same type, these influences on children's outcomes may be confounded (although the significant relationship between proportions of staff at Level 5 and young children's progress in Pre-reading indicates that staff qualifications are important

---

3   For further details of classifications, see EPPE Technical Paper 5.

in this complex of influences). It may be more relevant for policy makers and practitioners to consider the impacts of *packages* of provision, rather than to try to separate the impact of particular features in isolation, and to recognise that quality of provision and qualifications of staff are predictors of better child outcomes.

Type of pre-school

Even after taking account of a child's background and prior attainment, our results reveal that the type of pre-school a child attends has an important effect on their developmental progress. Integrated centres that fully combine education with care and have a high proportion of trained teachers, along with nursery schools, tend to promote better intellectual outcomes for children. Similarly, integrated centres and nursery classes tend to promote better social development even after taking account of children's backgrounds and prior social behaviour.

Good quality pre-school education can be found in all kinds of settings, however the EPPE data indicates that, at the time the pre-school element of our research was conducted (1997–2001), integrated centres and nursery school provision had the highest quality, while playgroups, private day nurseries and local authority day nurseries had lower quality (see Chapter 5). The integrated centres in the EPPE sample were all registered as nursery schools but had extended their provision to include flexible hours for childcare along with substantial health and family support services (see Chapter 2).

We conducted further analyses to see if the effects of type of provision were partly due to differences in quality. Our results reveal that, when account is taken of variation in quality of centre environments, the impact of type of provision is reduced. This indicates that the impact of type of provision is likely to be, at least in part, attributed to variations in environmental quality and adult–child interactions. In interpreting the findings on type of provision, it is important to acknowledge the very different resourcing levels typical of different types of provision at the time, which have implications for staffing, training and facilities. The maintained sector differs quite markedly in this respect from voluntary provision, particularly playgroups which, in the past, have had little access to resources in England and often few staff with higher levels of relevant qualifications.

Individual centre effects

The value added multilevel analyses of children's progress show that the individual pre-school centre attended by a child also has an impact on cognitive progress.[4] In some centres children make significantly greater gains than in others. Centre effects are larger for Pre-reading followed by early number concepts, possibly reflecting different emphases between individual settings in curriculum provision

---

4   Significant centre-level variance in children's cognitive progress remains, even when account is taken of prior attainment and other intake differences (in terms of child, parent and HLE characteristics).

and the priority accorded to different types of activities. A number of centres were identified – some more effective in terms of child outcomes and some less effective. Just over one in five centres (22.0 per cent) were found to be statistical *outliers* (performing *significantly above or significantly below* what would be expected from the characteristics of their children at entry to pre-school).

Value added multilevel analyses show the individual pre-school centre attended by a child also has an impact on children's social/behavioural gains.[5] In some centres children showed better (positive outliers) or, by contrast, poorer social/behavioural developmental gains than predicted (negative outliers), given their prior social/behaviour and background. Just over one in 10 centres (12.8 per cent) were found to be statistical outliers (performing significantly above or below expectation for one or more social/behavioural area).

Social mix of child intakes in centres

Overall we found that young children from disadvantaged families make more cognitive progress if they attend pre-school settings with a mixture of children from different social backgrounds rather than in settings catering mostly to children from disadvantaged families (e.g. Melhuish *et al.*, 2001, 2008b). This contextual effect was fairly modest, however, in comparison with the influence of a child's own background characteristics, but does have implications for the locating of pre-school centres in areas of social disadvantage. Our results suggest that locating centres in neighbourhoods that will have a social mix, where possible, is likely to be most beneficial. However this may be difficult to achieve in practice, given many parents' preferences for centres close to home, and the extent that social and ethnic groups cluster in some neighbourhoods.

Multiple disadvantage and children 'at risk' of SEN

Few large-scale research studies have explored the relationship between pre-school experience and concepts of 'at risk' status and definitions of SEN at different ages. The EPPE project developed an index of multiple disadvantage, and sought to establish whether this shows good prediction of 'at risk' status. The following shows factors considered within the index.

Overall, child and parental factors were more strongly associated with children's cognitive outcomes than with social/behavioural development. Multiple disadvantage is strongly associated with low cognitive scores amongst young children at age 3 years plus. Children scoring highly in terms of multiple disadvantage were much more likely to be identified in the '*strong* cognitive risk' category than others.

---

5   Significant centre level variance in children's social/behavioural developmental gains remains even when account is taken of prior social/behavioural development and other intake differences (in terms of child, family and HLE characteristics).

Table 6.2 Factors in the index of multiple disadvantage

Child characteristics	Disadvantage indicator
First language	English not first language
Large family	Three or more siblings
Premature/low birth weight	Premature or below 2,500 grams
Parent characteristic	
Mother's highest qualification	No qualifications
Social class of father's occupation	Semi-skilled, unskilled, never worked, absent father
Father's employment status	Not employed
Young mother	Age 13–17 at birth of EPPE child
Lone parent	Single parent
Mother's employment status	Unemployed
Home environment characteristics	
Home environment scale	Bottom quartile

Our findings in Chapter 4 illustrate that there are important differences in young children's cognitive and social/behavioural attainments related to specific child, parent and home environment characteristics at entry to the study (age 3 years plus) and our multilevel analyses show that such background influences remain powerful at subsequent follow ups. Background influences tend to be stronger predictors of cognitive than social behaviour outcomes. The continued effect of multiple disadvantage on children's cognitive outcomes is illustrated in Table 6.3.

Table 6.3 Percentage of children identified as 'at risk' of SEN using multiple disadvantage indicators at entry to primary school

IMD	Pre-school sample children			'Home' children		
Number of indicators	General cognitive ability	Pre-reading 'risk'	Early number concepts 'risk'	General cognitive ability	Pre-reading 'risk'	Early number concepts 'risk'
0	6.6	7.2	9.4	33.3*	22.2*	22.2*
1–2	13.1	16.8	14.8	35.5	37.5	33.3
3–4	34.5	28.5	34.3	51.0	38.7	45.3
5+	54.7	44.0	55.8	70.8	46.7	69.0
n	2582	2567	2560	185	185	184

Note:
* Less than 10 pupils

We conducted additional analyses for the sub-group of children identified as 'at risk' of special education needs (SEN), defined as those showing very low cognitive scores at entry to the study. Our results reveal that children who are multiply disadvantaged (in terms of a range of child, family and home learning environment characteristics) show much better attainment than similarly disadvantaged children in the home sample at the start of primary school (age rising 5 years). Again this finding points to the positive impact of pre-school experience on cognitive development for particularly vulnerable groups of young children.

The impact of pre-school on 'at risk' status for Special Educational Needs (SEN)

Four questions relevant to the impact of pre-school on young children were explored:

1 Do children who have not attended a pre-school centre differ in 'risk' for SEN, taking account of child, family and home environment characteristics?

The 'home' children (those with little or no experience of pre-school) were significantly more likely to be identified as 'at risk' for all measures of cognitive development at entry to primary school and more were also 'at risk' of poor social/ behavioural development in terms of Peer sociability. 'Home' children were also more likely to be multiply disadvantaged than those who had attended pre-school. These differences remained evident at the end of Year 1. Overall, around 44 per cent of 'home' children were 'at risk' in relation to national norms for Reading, and 37 per cent for Mathematics.

2 Does risk reduce as a result of pre-school experience?

One-third of the pre-school sample can be considered 'at risk' of SEN at the start of the study. By the start of primary school the proportion of children had reduced to one in five (21 per cent). This suggests a positive impact of pre-school on young children's cognitive development, which remained evident until at least the end of Year 1.

3 Does an early start in pre-school influence 'risk' for SEN, taking other factors into account?

Those children who made an earlier start (between 2 and 3 years) at pre-school had higher cognitive attainments than other children at age 3+, even when controlling for the impact of child, family and home environment influences. This cognitive advantage remains evident at entry to primary school. On average, children identified as 'at risk' in the cognitive assessments at entry to pre-school were likely to have started pre-school at a later age. However, a very early start (i.e. below 2 years) at pre-school was weakly associated with increased 'risk' for Anti-social/worried/upset behaviour.

4 Does the amount of time (number of months) children attend a pre-school centre relate to risk of SEN over the pre-school period?

Children's progress indicated that longer attendance at pre-school (months of pre-school) has a significant positive impact on cognitive attainment and thus may reduce the 'risk' of SEN.

Do pre-school effects last? The continued impact of pre-school – duration, quality and effectiveness

Our analyses explored cognitive attainment at the end of Year 2 (age 7 years) and whether this relates to duration (number of months), quality and effectiveness of pre-school experience. In all comparisons the attainment of the 'home' group is significantly poorer than that of children who had attended a pre-school centre. It is not possible to fully separate the influence of quality, duration and effectiveness of pre-school attended in comparisons of the pre-school and 'home' sample, since, in practice, pre-school is experienced as a 'package' combining these different features. However, the findings support the conclusion that these three features generally remain predictors of better cognitive attainment during Key Stage 1. Also, measures of the effectiveness of the pre-school attended continue to show a significant positive impact on young children's subsequent attainments at the end of Key Stage 1.

In terms of progress in primary school, there is no indication that pre-school children made greater gains than the 'home' children. The absolute attainment scores of the pre-school children remains significantly higher than the attainment of the 'home' children at the end of Key Stage 1, although there has been a modest narrowing of the gap from the 'home' children's lower starting point.

The results suggest that, overall, attending a pre-school rather than none has a positive impact. In addition, experiencing a longer duration, higher quality and attending a more effective pre-school centre all have significant benefits in preparing young children for a better start to school and fostering better outcomes later on in primary school. The Year 2 analyses suggest that such children continue to show better Reading and Mathematics attainment in national assessments at the end of Key Stage 1. The lessening of effect sizes over time has been mentioned earlier in light of two explanations: the rise of the 'primary school effect', and also the use of national assessments as outcome measures at age 7 rather than standardised tests at age 6 and at school entry. National assessment measures are more closely

Table 6.4 Comparison of the effects of duration of pre-school attendance on children's cognitive attainments at end of Year 1 and end of Year 2

| Duration | Effect of duration at end of Year 1 and end of Year 2 | | | |
| | Reading | | Mathematics | |
	End of Year 1	End of Year 2	End of Year 1	End of Year 2
Up to 1 year	0.26	0.29	0.32	0.21
1–2 years	0.17	0.27	0.36	0.18
2–3 years	0.26	0.29	0.46	0.22
> 3	0.35	0.36	0.52	0.29

related to children's curriculum experiences in Key Stage 1 and are likely to be more sensitive to teaching and primary school effects (a topic we examine in more detail in the next chapter, that explores the influence of the primary school as well as continuing pre-school effects across Key Stage 2. The changes in effects over the school period vary by outcome and are illustrated in Table 6.4.

The impact of duration of pre-school upon Reading is maintained in approximately equal magnitude right through to the end of Key Stage 1. However, the impact of duration of pre-school upon Mathematics is reduced by about 40–50 per cent at the end of Year 2 as compared with the end of Year 1. This indicates that primary school influences on Mathematics is starting to reduce the impact of pre-school. This could be related to the curriculum emphasis on mathematics evident with the introduction of the National Numeracy Strategy.

The importance of pre-school effects compared with family income on children's attainment at age 5

Many researchers argue that family income is paramount in determining children's outcomes and few other influences matter. However while we recognise that poverty is influential in shaping children's life chances, the EPPE research shows that pre-school effects can be substantial and very important in providing a better start to school and that such influences tend to be stronger than those attributable to income.

We conducted further analysis of the impact of family income on young children's cognitive attainment when they entered primary school, and made comparisons with the impact of both quality and duration of pre-school to help policy makers identify the relative strength of pre-school influences and to inform decisions about additional investment in and expansion of pre-school provision in England during the first phase of the research. These analyses focused in the main on two child outcomes collected at entry to primary school. Pre-reading and Language attainment were chosen because they show stronger relationships with child and family background in our main multilevel analyses (Sammons *et* al., 2002, 2003). We have already described the positive impact of pre-school on Early number concepts and different measures of social behaviour, especially Peer sociability earlier in this chapter in the main EPPE pre-school results section.

EPPE is the first study of pre-school effectiveness to explore the size of pre-school effects compared to those of family income or parents' employment status. Such analyses are of particular policy relevance for those concerned with narrowing the attainment gap and enhancing children's educational prospects and future life chances. Investment in the expansion of early years provision especially for disadvantaged children can be justified by such evidence which shows that pre-school effects are comparable or larger in size than those of family income.

Our analyses showed that the effects of pre-school on young children's Language outcomes are moderately strong and much larger than those of parents' income level at 5 years, when children started primary school. For example, the effects of duration of pre-school attendance for three years reached ES=0.59. Family income effects were strongest for children's Pre-reading outcomes and only weak for Language and Early number concepts. For Pre-reading, the effects of duration reached ES=0.36 to 0.40 for 2–3 years or 3 years plus of pre-school attendance. By comparison the effect of higher family earned income compared with none (i.e. those on benefit) ranged from ES=0.32 to 0.50. When comparisons were made of the combination of pre-school experience of both high quality and high duration, the ES on Language was very marked (ES=1.01) and also moderately strong (ES=0.62) for Pre-reading. These effect sizes are both larger than the equivalent effects of higher family income on these two outcomes. We show further details of these comparisons of family income and parents' employment effects with pre-school influences in Appendix 6.

The EPPE findings in the context of other research studies

The EPPE findings are similar to other research studies and this increases confidence in its conclusions.

Related studies have shown:

- Short-term, positive effects of pre-school education have been shown conclusively in the US, Sweden, Norway, Germany, Canada, Northern Ireland and New Zealand (see Tymms et al., 1997; Melhuish, 2004) and have influenced policy in many countries (see Melhuish and Petrogiannis, 2006).
- The effects of greater staff training and qualifications have been shown in the U.S. (Peisner-Feinberg and Burchinal, 1997) and in Northern Ireland (Melhuish et al., 2006).
- The contribution of quality to children's developmental progress has been shown in many studies, often using the ECERS observational scale (Melhuish, 2004).

- The US National Institute of Child Health and Development Study (NICHD) found that family characteristics have a greater impact on outcomes for children than pre-school factors. However, the effect of attending pre-school (versus not) on developmental progress is greater than the effect of social disadvantage. In addition, for children attending pre-school, the effect of attending a specific centre is about half that of all social background factors (NICHD, 2002).
- Early day care was found in EPPE to relate to increased cognitive outcomes better Independence and Peer sociability at 5 years but also to some increased scores for Anti-social behaviour but only in the short term. These findings are similar to those in the US and Northern Ireland (NICHD, 2002; Melhuish et al., 2001, 2002).
- The findings on the impact of disadvantage are mirrored elsewhere (see Sammons et al., 1983, 2002; Sammons, 1995; Sammons and Smees, 1998; Sammons et al., 2002; Melhuish, 2004) and are the basis for many compensatory policy initiatives all over the world (Young, 1996).
- EPPE is one of few studies (the only in the UK) to demonstrate the role of pre-school education as an effective means of early intervention in reducing the likelihood of SEN (Sammons et al., 2002; Sammons et al., 2008; Taggart et al., 2006).
- EPPE is the first large-scale multi-level modelling study to show convincingly that individual pre-school centres have lasting effects on children's development.

In this chapter we have discussed the findings about the influence of pre-school on young children's cognitive attainments and progress and their social behavioural outcomes at ages 5, the start of primary school, and up to age 7 years (end of Key Stage 1) in primary school. Our results show that pre-school can play an important part in combating social exclusion and promoting inclusion by offering disadvantaged children, in particular, a better start to primary school. The findings indicate that pre-school has a positive impact on children's developmental progress over and above important family background influences. The quality of the pre-school setting experience as well as the quantity (more months but not necessarily more hours per day) are both influential.

The results also show that all pre-school experience is not the same. Individual pre-school centres vary in their effectiveness in promoting intellectual progress over the pre-school period, and on social behavioural development too. They indicate that, at the time we conducted this study, better outcomes were associated with certain forms of provision. Likewise, the research points to the separate and significant influence of the home learning environment (Melhuish et al., 2008a, 2008b). These aspects (quality and quantity of pre-school and home learning environment) can be seen as more susceptible to change through policy and practitioner initiatives than other child or family background characteristics, such as SES.

For social/behavioural outcomes in Year 2 there is less evidence of the positive impact of duration and quality of pre-school, in contrast to results for Reading and Mathematics at this age. Individual pre-schools differed in the benefits for children's development that they provided. Where pre-schools provided greater developmental benefit, they were regarded as more 'effective'. Hence the effectiveness (children showing more/less progress than expected given their initial profile and background characteristics) of a pre-school is a measure of the total benefit associated with the characteristics of that pre-school. The effectiveness of the pre-school centre attended in promoting better social/behavioural and cognitive outcomes continues to show a positive impact for the pre-school sample up to the end of Year 2.

Having shown that pre-school has important benefits for children in the short to mid-term, in the next chapter we move on to discuss the important question of how lasting these effects are. Does the pre-school influence just provide children with an initial boost in the short term, proving a better start to primary school but later fade away as primary school and family influences take over? Or do the benefits continue to show in terms of better outcomes in the longer term across Key Stage 2 and up to age 11 years?

References

Peisner-Feinberg, E.S. and Burchinal, M.R. (1997) Relations between preschool children's childcare experiences and concurrent development: The cost, quality, and outcomes study, *Merrill-Palmer Quarterly*, 43, 451–477.

Melhuish, E. (2004) *A Literature Review of the Impact of Early Years Provision Upon Young Children with Emphasis Given to Children from Disadvantaged Backgrounds: Report to the Controller and Auditor General*, London: National Audit Office.

Melhuish, E. and Petrogiannis, K. (eds) (2006) *Early Childhood Care and Education: International Perspective on Policy and Research*, London: Routledge.

Melhuish, E., Sylva, K., Sammons, P., Siraj-Blatchford, I. and Taggart. B. (2001) *The Effective Provision of Pre-school Education Project, Technical Paper 7: Social/behavioural and Cognitive Development at 3–4 Years in Relation to Family Background*, London: London Institute of Education/DfES.

Melhuish, E., Quinn, L., Sylva, K., Sammons, P., Siraj-Blatchford, I., Taggart, B. and Shields, C. (2002) *The Effective Pre-school Provision in Northern Ireland Project, Technical Paper 5: Preschool Experience and Cognitive Development at the Start of Primary School*, Belfast, N. Ireland: Stranmillis University Press.

Melhuish, E., Quinn, L., Sylva, K., Sammons, P., Siraj-Blatchford, I. and Taggart. B. (2006) *The Effective Pre-school Provision in Northern Ireland Project, Summary Report*, Belfast: Stranmillis University Press, http://www.deni.gov.uk/researchreport4.1.pdf

Melhuish, E., Sylva, K., Sammons, P., Siraj-Blatchford, I., Taggart, B. and Phan, M. (2008a) Effects of the home learning environment and pre-school center experience upon literacy and numeracy development in early primary school, *Journal of Social Issues*, 64(1), 95–114.

Melhuish, E., Sylva, K., Sammons, P., Siraj-Blatchford, I., Taggart. B., Phan, M. and Malin, A. (2008b) Pre-school's influences on mathematics achievement, *Science*, 321, 1161–1162.

National Institute of Child Health and Human Development Early Child Care Research Network (2002) Early child care and children's development prior to school entry: Results from the NICHD Study of Early Child Care, *American Educational Research Journal*, 39(1), 133–164.

Sammons, P. (1995) Gender, ethnic and socio-economic differences in attainment and progress: A longitudinal analysis of student achievement over nine years, *British Educational Research Journal*, 21(4), 465–485.

Sammons, P. and Smees, R (1998) Measuring pupil progress at Key Stage 1: using baseline assessment to investigate value added, *School Leadership and Management*, 18, 3, 389–407.

Sammons, P., Kysel, F. and Mortimore, P. (1983) Educational priority indices – a new perspective, *British Educational Research Journal*, 9(1), 27–40.

Sammons, P., Sylva, K., Melhuish, E.C., Siraj-Blatchford, I., Taggart, B. and Elliot, K. (2002) *The Effective Provision of Pre-school Education Project (EPPE), Technical Paper 8a: Measuring the Impact of Pre-School on Children's Cognitive Progress Over the Pre-School Period*, London: DfES/Institute of Education, University of London.

Sammons, P., Sylva, K., Melhuish, E.C., Siraj-Blatchford, I., Taggart, B. and Elliot, K. (2003) *The Effective Provision of Pre-School Education (EPPE) Project: Technical Paper 8b: Measuring the Impact of Pre-School on Children's Social/Behavioural Development over the Pre-School Period*. London: DfES/Institute of Education, University of London.

Sammons, P., Elliot, K., Sylva, K., Melhuish, E., Siraj-Blatchford, I., Taggart, B. and Smees, R. (2004) The impact of pre-school on young children's cognitive attainments at entry to reception, *British Educational Research Journal*, 30(5), 691–712.

Sammons, P., Anders, Y., Sylva, K., Melhuish, E., Siraj-Blatchford, I., Taggart, B. and Barreau, S. (2008) Children's cognitive attainment and progress in English primary schools during Key Stage 2: investigating the potential continuing influences of pre-school education, *Zeitschrift für Erziehungswissenschaften*, 10. Jahrg., Special Issue (Sonderheft) 11/2008, 179–198.

Taggart, B., Sammons, P., Smees, R., Sylva, K., Melhuish, E., Siraj-Blatchford, I., Elliot, K. and Lunt, I. (2006) Early identification of special needs and the definition of 'at risk'. The early years transition and special educational needs (EYTSEN) project, *British Journal of Special Education*, 33,(1), 40–45.

Tymms, P., Merrell, C. and Henderson, B. (1997) The first year at school: a quantitative investigation of the attainment and progress of pupils, *Educational Research and Evaluation* 3(2), 101–118.

Young, M. E. (1996) *Early Child Development: Investing in the Future*, Washington DC: The World Bank.

Chapter 7

Do the benefits of pre-school last?

Investigating pupil outcomes to the end of Key Stage 2 (aged 11)

Pam Sammons

This chapter examines the longer term effects of pre-school on children's academic and social behavioural outcomes across Key Stage 2 up to age 11 years in primary school. It investigates the lasting impact of different features of pre-school experience including quality and duration and also explores the influence of primary school using measures of primary school academic effectiveness. It shows how the influences of pre-school and primary school in combination can help to mediate the effects of disadvantage.

Introduction

In Chapter 6 we presented some of the key findings on the impact of pre-school on young children's cognitive and social behavioural development up to age 7 years. We made comparisons of children's progress and development from age 3-plus to the point they entered primary school (rising 5 years). In addition, we made comparisons between our pre-school sample and a group of 'home' children recruited at primary school entry who had not attended pre-school. We followed up both these groups of children to the end of Key Stage 1 and found that the positive impact of pre-school continued to be evident, although, unsurprisingly, the effects were somewhat weaker at age 7 than when children first started at primary school.

Now we address the important question of whether these positive effects last over the longer term. We want to know whether the pre-school effects merely act to provide an initial boost, giving children a better start to primary school and in the first couple of years in school, or whether the positive effects remain evident in the longer term across Key Stage 2 (age 7–11), after children had experienced 6 years in full-time primary education. As we discussed in Chapter 1, some early research in the US had suggested that pre-school influences do not 'last' as children move through primary school, that they are 'washed out' by more powerful school and family influences, although much longer term follow up suggested they could re-emerge at later ages promoting better adult outcomes and improving life chances (as has been shown in the High Scope follow up by Schweinhart and Weickart, 1997a and b).

We know from educational effectiveness research that school and teacher effects are also significant predictors of children's educational outcomes. Some primary schools are more effective at promoting academic achievement and make a difference to progress and so to later attainment levels over and above pupils' own background characteristics (see reviews by Scheerens and Bosker, 1997; Teddlie and Reynolds, 2000; Sammons *et al.*, 2008a). We know that children spend a lot of their waking lives in school (over 7,000 hours) in their six-plus years of primary education. By contrast, for the EPPE sample the average experience was 18 months' part time duration of attendance in pre-school, roughly only 900 hours' experience (though some children had considerably longer, and duration in months attended was important as shown in the previous chapter). So it is of real interest to see whether pre-school experiences still show any impact on later attainment, progress and development.

We need to adopt an analysis strategy that allows us to identify and separate pre-school and primary influences as well as taking into account the important impact of a range of child, family and home learning environment influences that we also know predict children's outcomes at different times and their developmental trajectories, as we have shown in Chapter 4 and also followed up further in Chapter 9. We adopt a view that children are located in the centre of a series of nested circles of influences that shape their development. First they are surrounded and influenced by their parents and family circle, then the community (which includes pre-schools and later schools), and finally the national and cultural framework within which each family and school is embedded. EPPE began with the child at the centre of its research focus, and then studied the influences that shaped them. We identified six overarching domains of influences and seek to measure their effects on cognitive and social behavioural development at different ages. The domains of influence include:

1   individual characteristics associated with the child, e.g. gender or birth weight
2   family characteristics, e.g. parental education, home language
3   home learning environment (HLE), i.e. learning opportunities in the home
4   neighbourhood/community characteristics
5   pre-school attendance and experiences
6   primary school experiences.

In addition to investigating the separate effects of all these influences, the EPPE 3–11 follow up attempted to discover how these factors interact with each other to shape children's development during Key Stage 2. This was made possible by the large scale and longitudinal nature of the study, and the rich and varied data collected on children, families, pre-schools and schools.

In this chapter we start by providing a summary of the main headline results of our analyses of children's cognitive and social/behavioural development for the EPPE 3–11 sample up to age 11. The study investigates the long term impact of child, family, the Early years Home Learning Environment (HLE) and pre-school on children's English and Mathematics attainments at age 11 as well as focusing on four dimensions of social/behavioural development: Self-regulation, 'Pro-social' behaviour, 'Hyperactivity' and 'Anti-social' behaviour measured by teacher assessments. In addition, we explore the influence of the pre-school, and the influence that is attributable to the academic effectiveness of the primary school attended, and then examine the *combined* impact of pre-school and primary school on children's developmental outcomes.

Our main aims for the Key Stage 2 analyses were as follows:

- to establish the relative importance of different sources of influence (child, family, home learning environment, neighbourhood, pre-school and school on children's outcomes at age 11;
- to establish how far educational influences can help to combat disadvantage and narrow the achievement gap for vulnerable groups of children.

We addressed the following questions:

- Does the effect of pre-school remain evident as a predictor of better child outcomes at age 11?
- What features of pre-school are important (examining three key indicators: attendance or not, duration of attendance, and quality of provision)?
- What is the impact of primary school, measured by the indicator of academic effectiveness?
- What is the size of the pre-school effect compared with that of the primary school?
- What is the combined effect of pre-school and primary school influences on children's outcomes?
- How far can educational influences (pre-school and primary school) combat the effects of disadvantage and reduce the equity gap?

Key findings across Key Stage 2

First we provide a short summary of our key findings grouped under a number of headings before presenting more details about our analyses and discussing and illustrating the results in more depth. Inevitably given the size and scope of our large research programme we are only able to cover some of our rich data and findings. The interested reader can consult our various reports and papers listed in Appendix 3 for a lengthier account and discussion of the findings and research details.

Child and family background characteristics

- The most important background predictors of English and Mathematics attainment and Self-regulation in Year 6 are: the Early years HLE measured at age 3–4, mothers' highest qualification levels, and continued need for support with English as an Additional Language (EAL) in upper primary. (Note it is important to recognise that most EAL children did not show poorer outcomes at age 11, only the small minority identified by their teachers as still in need of support related to their EAL status.)

- Gender has a strong effect on both 'Pro-social' behaviour and 'Hyperactivity', a moderate effect on Anti-social behaviour (girls have more favourable scores on all) but weaker effects on English (girls have higher attainment) and Mathematics (boys have higher attainment).
- Background factors are generally more important for academic than social/behavioural outcomes. Taken together, the combined influence of child, family and background factors on children's outcomes are weaker at age 11 than we found it to be at younger ages.
- The influence of neighbourhood disadvantage as a predictor of children's cognitive and social behavioural outcomes is weak and smaller than that of pre-school or primary school effects in contrast to the importance of individual pupil background factors. The effect of neighbourhood disadvantage is no longer statistically significant after taking into account child and family characteristics, particularly HLE.

Continuing pre-school effects

- Pre-school quality and effectiveness remain statistically significant predictors of children's attainment and social/behavioural outcomes in Year 6 and of progress across Key Stage 2, after the influence of background factors has been taken into account.
- Children gained most benefit from having attended high quality pre-school provision, but medium quality provision also led to better Mathematics and social behavioural outcomes in Year 6 compared to either low quality or no pre-school (the 'home' group).
- Children who had attended low quality pre-school did no better in Mathematics and English than those who had not attended a pre-school, and showed slightly higher levels of Hyperactivity in Year 6, whereas children who had not attended pre-school continued to show poorer Pro-social behaviour compared to those who had gone to pre-school.
- Although having attended any pre-school versus none shows benefits for a range of educational outcomes in Year 6, the impact is carried mainly by the pre-school quality and effectiveness effects except for Pro-social behaviour where having attended any pre-school provision still shows sustained benefits compared with none.
- For academic outcomes, particularly Mathematics, and for all social/behavioural outcomes, having attended a high quality pre-school is found to be of particular benefit for boys, children with special educational needs (SEN) and disadvantaged children. While higher quality pre-school benefits all children, the benefits are greater for these groups. The difference between

attending a high quality or high effectiveness pre-school and attending a low quality or effectiveness pre-school is larger for children who come from more disadvantaged backgrounds than the difference of attending high versus low quality or effectiveness pre-school for children who come from less disadvantaged backgrounds. Pre-school thus helps to reduce the attainment gap.

Primary school academic effectiveness

- Attending a more academically effective primary school (measured by independent value-added indicators[1]) had a significant positive influence on EPPE children's English and particularly their Mathematics attainment in Year 6. The impact of attending a highly academically effective school versus a low one is on a par with the impact of family income for English and as strong as that found for the Early years HLE for Mathematics.
- By contrast, the academic effectiveness of the primary school did not show a statistically significant relationship with social/behavioural outcomes overall. However it was important for particular sub-groups of children; those identified as having SEN in primary school, and those with mothers who had low qualification levels showed better Self-regulation and reduced scores for Anti-social behaviour if they attended highly academically effective primary schools.
- Early HLE and support with EAL are twice as strong as the influence of pre-school quality and primary school effects on English attainment, and mother's highest qualification (degree versus none) is twice as strong as the influence of pre-school quality for Mathematics and Self-regulation.
- Although pre-school and primary school effects are moderate when studied separately, further analyses of their combined influence show stronger positive effects on a range of child outcomes showing that the combination of good educational influences is important.

Combined pre-school quality and primary school academic effectiveness

- For cognitive attainment (particularly for Mathematics) and Self-regulation, the earlier experience of high quality pre-school continues to provide some protection against the disadvantage of later attending a less academically effective primary school. Similarly, attending a highly academically effective primary school helps to compensate for the disadvantage of not attending pre-school or attending a low quality pre-school in terms of later cognitive

---

1   The contextualised value-added analyses have been undertaken independently of the EPPE 3–11 research for three full cohorts of pupils (2002 – 2004) in all primary schools in England, in order to create a value-added measure of academic effectiveness for every school attended by an EPPE child (Melhuish *et al.*, 2006).

attainment and Self-regulation. Moreover, both the experience of high quality pre-school and high academically effective primary schools offer similar degrees of protection in terms of promoting better outcomes in Year 6 individually, and in combination for academic outcomes and Self-regulation.

Academic and social behavioural progress over Key Stage 2

- EPPE also measures progress over Key Stage 2. Pupils' academic and social/behavioural progress over KS2 is also influenced by background factors such as gender, mother's qualifications and Early years HLE, although the effects are much weaker than those found for attainment.
- Educational influences related to pre-school quality and primary school academic effectiveness show a stronger impact on cognitive progress over Key Stage 2 than most background factors. The impact of attending a high academically effective primary school versus a low effective primary is on a par with the effect of a mother having a degree versus no qualification (slightly stronger for Mathematics, slightly weaker for English). The influence of pre-school quality on children's progress across KS2 is also still evident, although not as strong as that of the primary school academic effectiveness. The effect of a high quality experience versus none is on a par with the influence of a child's eligibility (or not) for free school meals.
- High quality and highly effective pre-schools have a similar positive impact on social/behavioural progress across Key Stage 2 as they do on developmental levels at age 11 in Year 6. The effect of having had a high quality pre-school experience versus none is comparable with the effect of a child's eligibility (or not) for free school meals for all social/behavioural outcomes, except for Pro-social behaviour, for which there was no FSM effect, but for which pre-school quality remains significant. However primary school academic effectiveness had no statistically significant influence on social/behavioural progress, just as it showed no significant effect for social/behavioural development outcomes in Year 6.

Studying the various influences on children's educational outcomes at age 11

We provide a brief account of the numbers of children and schools involved in our Key Stage 2 analyses, and illustrate our approach to the analysis before discussing in more detail each of the main findings summarised above. This gives the reader an indication of the evidence base for our conclusions and illustrates the strength of the research.

The child sample

Over 2,800 children were recruited around the age of 3+ at their pre-school settings together with over 300 'home' children without pre-school experience who were recruited at the start of school (see Sammons *et al.*, 1999). During the primary school phase of the study there were over 2,500 children still in the study.

The primary school sample

From all primary schools that contain EPPE 3–11 children (800+ schools approximately 100 local authorities and 2,500 children), using all data on the longitudinal sample of EPPE 3–11 children, and their pre-schools and schools, the contribution of background, pre-school and school factors has been estimated.

Cognitive outcomes

Taking account of developmental change, the study uses different cognitive assessments:

- Year 1: NFER-Nelson Primary Reading Level 1 and Mathematics 6 tests
- Year 2: Key Stage 1 National Assessments: Reading and Mathematics
- Year 5: NFER-Nelson Primary Reading Level 2 and Mathematics 10 tests
- Year 6: Key Stage 2 National Assessments: Mathematics and English – a combined measure of Writing, Spelling and Reading (via comprehension).

Social/behavioural outcomes

Beginning at age 6 we used an extended version of the Strengths and Difficulties Questionnaire (Goodman, 1997) to measure different features of children's social/behavioural development in Years 1, 2, 5 and 6. The social/behavioural child profile was completed by a teacher who knew the EPPE 3–11 child well. Principal component analysis and confirmatory factor analysis were used to identify the main underlying dimensions of social behaviour in Year 6 and to see if the social behavioural factors were similar to Year 5 results (see Sammons *et al.*, 2007b). The Year 5 findings were replicated at Year 6 in defining the main four aspects of social behaviour: Self-regulation, 'Pro-social' behaviour, 'Hyperactivity' and 'Anti-social' behaviour. For specific items associated with the social/behavioural dimensions at different time points see Appendix 4.

Higher scores indicate better behaviour for Self-regulation and 'Pro-social' behaviour; lower scores indicate better behaviour (lower incidence from teacher ratings) for 'Hyperactivity' and 'Anti-social' behaviour. We found that scores on all social/behavioural measures are skewed towards the more desirable end of the scale indicating that most children showed positive behavioural profiles in their teachers' ratings. This is especially important for the more negative aspects of social behaviour where raised scores indicate potential maladaptive behaviour. It is important to recognise that such negative behaviours were only evident for a very small minority of children in the sample (only 3.9 per cent for 'Anti-social' behaviour and 7.4 per cent for 'Hyperactivity'). Similarly, under 10 per cent (9.8 per cent) of children show extremely low levels of 'Pro-social' behaviour and just under 12 per cent (11.5 per cent) of children show very low levels of Self-regulation in Year 6. Very few (only 1.9 per cent) children had extreme scores on both 'Hyperactivity' and 'Anti-social' behaviour, and even fewer (only 1.2 per cent) had extreme scores on all four aspects of social behaviour. Most children are rated positively for these features of social behaviour, in line with findings from other research and with the skewed distribution of scores found for EPPE children at younger ages.

Information about the 'influences' on children's developmental trajectories

Individual children and their families: data were collected about child and family characteristics that may influence children's attainment, development and progress (see Chapter 4).

The early years HLE: the pre-school parent interview collected information on the Early years HLE (reading with children, number/letter activities, etc.), and other activities such as bedtime, TV viewing, etc. In addition, information on the KS1 HLE was collected through a questionnaire towards the end of KS1 (ages 6/7). We also collected information on 'other learning' activities at the end of KS2, including computer access and use at home, homework and out of school learning opportunities. The Early years HLE is used extensively in KS2 analyses because it is a stronger predictor of outcomes at age 11 than the KS1 HLE.

The neighbourhood: parental perceptions of their neighbourhood were studied via the parental questionnaires in KS1. Postcode information was also used to derive a measure of area deprivation from administrative databases.

The primary schools: in analyses, measures of child, family, HLE and pre-school from the earlier EPPE work up to the end of KS1 (age 7 years) are included (see Sammons *et al.*, 2002, 2003). However differences between the schools attended by EPPE children in KS2 are also taken into account. To this end EPPE set about establishing measures of primary school academic effectiveness, and also classroom and school processes as described below.

To identify primary school academic effectiveness we analysed government national data sets based on pupil results for all primary schools in England (16,000 schools, 600,000 children, see Melhuish *et al.*, 2006).

EPPE used KS1 and KS2 national assessment scores for every child in England, grouped by the schools they attended. This enabled the research team to locate in each primary school an EPPE pupil who attended on a scale of 'academic effectiveness', after controlling for prior attainment and the demographic characteristics of each school's intake. We estimated each school's contextualised 'value added' to children's academic attainment using data from all state primary schools, and all their pupils. Multilevel modelling was employed to estimate the effectiveness of each school in England for English, Mathematics and Science as well as average attainment based on three successive national cohorts (2002–2004). Within this database it was possible to create an overall 'academic effectiveness' score for each school that EPPE children attended based on three years of data, taking account of background factors and prior attainment (see Melhuish *et al.*, 2006 for technical details).

Full details of data collection procedures, instruments and response rates are contained in the technical reports associated with each phase of the study (see http://eppe.ioe.ac.uk/ or http://www.dcsf.gov.uk/research/programmeofresearch/index.cfm?type=5).

Analytical strategy

As with the analyses reported in Chapters 4 and 6 we employed a range of statistical techniques including multilevel (hierarchical) regression methods to examine the way child, family and home characteristics influence children's cognitive attainment and progress up to the end of KS2. In these analyses we also establish the effects associated with both pre-school and school characteristics. However this can only be adequately achieved if we first take account of the influence of a range of background factors that also affect children's development as shown in the diagram below (Figure 7.1). In the statistical analyses, multilevel modelling is used as it capitalises on the hierarchical structure of the data (i.e. pupils clustered within schools, Goldstein, 1995), and therefore produces more accurate estimates of the net effects of different factors.

The analyses are based, in the main, on establishing the 'value added' contribution to children's development of pre-schools, primary schools, families

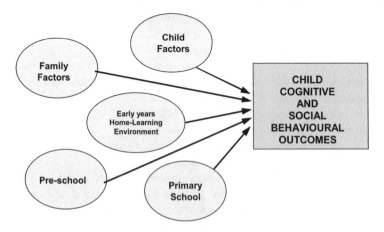

Figure 7.1 Different influences on child outcomes

and communities. They explore whether the effects of pre-school continue through to Key Stage 2 and how pre-school influences interact with those of the primary school in shaping children's development.

EPPE investigated whether these early benefits remain apparent for both cognitive and social/behavioural development at the end of primary school. This part of the research is particularly concerned with establishing whether the influence of attending a more effective pre-school, or one of higher rather than lower quality, is maintained or reduced for those who attend less effective primary schools. Likewise, do those who had no pre-school experience, or only limited or poor quality pre-school experience 'catch up' if they attended a more effective primary, indicating to what extent later 'good' school experience can compensate for early lack of or poor pre-school experience? Similarly, did those children who attend both a more effective pre-school and a more academically effective primary obtain a greater benefit? This is of particular policy relevance for promoting better outcomes for disadvantaged pupils and thus addressing the equity gap. Our initial results on the short term effects of pre-schools described in Chapter 6 indicate that pre-school, especially high quality pre-school, could be viewed as an effective intervention for vulnerable groups, but does this continue through Key Stage 2?

Our analyses document the enduring impact of pre-school on children's outcomes towards the end of primary education, after controlling for child and family characteristics along with HLE. This is one of the few studies in the international literature to attempt such educational effectiveness design and to explore individual pre-school effects longitudinally (see Sammons *et al.*, 2008a, 2008c; Melhuish *et al.*, 2008).

Studying the influence of background factors

The EPPE project has considered how a wide range of factors may influence children's development. For example when looking at a child's attainment in English, analyses considered whether child, family, neighbourhood, pre-school and school were influential. When progress is considered, the child's prior attainment is added into the statistical model. The large sample size and the statistical methods allow the separate influence of each of the predictors to be estimated, so that when an effect for pre-school is shown it is after allowing for all the relevant background factors.

We report here briefly on the way we controlled for the important influence of background factors upon children's development, in particular the child, family and HLE influences. For more details of the way such factors affect different outcomes see Chapter 4.

Child characteristics

EPPE has measures related to the child on a range of characteristics that are tested for significant associations with child outcomes. These are:

Age	Gender
Ethnicity	English as an additional language (EAL)
Birth weight	Birth order
Perinatal health difficulties	Early developmental problems
Early behaviour problems	Early health problems

In addition when considering progress over a particular period the child's attainment at the start of that period is included. Not all of these factors were found to show significant effects and only those that do show significant effects upon children's outcomes are discussed here.

Children's attainment and progress in English (and Reading) and Mathematics at the end of primary school in Year 5 and Year 6 (ages 10 and 11) has been analysed. The results are similar for both ages 10 and 11 years. For English (and Reading), gender, birth weight, ethnicity, the need of EAL support and early developmental problems are all found to have statistically significant effects that are distinct from the effects of all other characteristics considered. For Mathematics the following child characteristics are found to have a significant net effect: birth weight, early health problems, gender and ethnicity.

Parental, family and home characteristics

A range of measures of the parents, family, and home characteristics have been derived from the parental interview at the start of the study and parental questionnaires during Key Stage 1 (KS1) and Key Stage 2 (KS2). These measures, shown below, have been tested for their effects upon children's development.

1 Parental characteristics

Socio-economic status (SES) taken from the highest occupational status of either parent:

Family earned income (from KS1 parental questionnaire)
Poverty (child eligible for free school meals or not – FSM)
Marital status

Mother's level of employment	Father's level of employment
Mother's education	Father's education
Mother's age	Father's age

2 Family characteristics

Lone parent	Number of siblings	Life events

3 Home characteristics

- The Early years HLE in the pre-school period
- The KS1 HLE

For a list of all HLE items, see Appendix 2.

Identifying continued pre-school effects

In this section of the chapter we examine our findings in relation to our three important indicators of pre-school experience that we found were important in predicting children's outcomes at younger ages in Chapter 6. These are: attending any pre-school versus none; duration of months of attendance at pre-school and quality of pre-school.

We compared differences in the attainments of children who attended pre-school with the 'home' group at ages 7 and 11 years.

Cognitive outcomes

As we showed in the last chapter, the beneficial effects of pre-school remained evident throughout Key Stage 1 (first three years of primary school), although effects for some outcomes were not as strong as they had been at school entry, probably because of the increasingly powerful influence of the primary school on children's development. By the end of Year 2 most children had been at their primary school for up to three years (including time in the reception year) while the typical child had only been in pre-school for 18 months part time. By the end of Key Stage 2 most children had 6 to 7 years' experience of primary education.

Figure 7.2a shows the difference in attainment levels for children's National Assessments in Reading at age 7, classified by their family SES and by whether they had attended a pre-school or not. Average reading scores are higher for the children in the higher social groupings. However, at each social class level it is clear that the pre-school children have higher Reading scores than those who had not attended a pre-school. It is evident that the scores of disadvantaged children (from semi/unskilled manual backgrounds in terms of family SES) who did not attend pre-school fall below Level 2, the watershed for skills needed to progress on to Key Stage 2 school work (and the national expected level for children of this age). A similar pattern is found for Mathematics results at age 7 (Figure 7.2b).

We then compared the same child groupings for National Assessment attainments at the end of Key Stage 2 at age 11 (see Figures 7.3a and b). The pattern remained remarkably similar and consistent to that found at age 7 years. This shows that attainment differences related to attending a pre-school remain evident, suggesting that pre-school effects persist and that the home group does not catch up over Key Stage 2.

Further analyses tested the existence of pre-school effects more rigorously using multilevel models that control simultaneously for a wide range of child, family, and home learning influences.

Continuing effects of pre-school were considered in terms of pre-school versus no pre-school, and also whether there were any significant effects associated with pre-school quality or pre-school effectiveness.

Pre-school attendance or not

In Year 6, there are significant net effects on attainment in English and Mathematics for the most basic indicator of pre-school influence: attendance at pre-school compared to no pre-school (ES=0.22 and ES=0.26, respectively) which is consistent with earlier findings for Year 2. We also found that attending a pre-school compared with not attending (the 'home' group) still showed a positive effect on children's 'Pro-social' behaviour (ES=0.19) at the end of Year 6, although there were no statistically significant differences for other aspects of social behaviour.

These effects are relatively modest but nonetheless represent a significant long term boost. Moreover, the size of the effect is comparable to that found for a child's eligibility for free school meals a basic indicator of disadvantage (where the FSM ES=0.23 in the analyses of English outcomes but was somewhat weaker for Mathematics at ES=0.15). They are slightly weaker than the gender effect on English (ES=0.29 in favour of girls) but stronger than the gender effect for

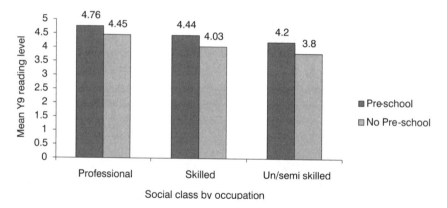

Figure 7.2a Reading at age 7 by SES and pre-school experience

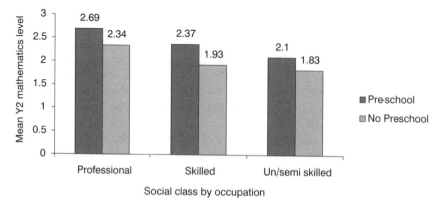

Figure 7.2b Mathematics at age 7 by SES and pre-school experience

Mathematics (ES=0.19 in favour of boys). We can conclude therefore that going to pre-school does have a lasting and positive impact on cognitive attainment, but also on some aspects of social behaviour, being significant for peer sociability throughout primary school.

Pre-school quality

However, as we have shown in Chapter 5, children's pre-school experiences differ because individual pre-schools have been shown to vary in their observed quality. This feature predicted better child progress and development over the pre-school period and better outcomes at age 5 and age 7 years.

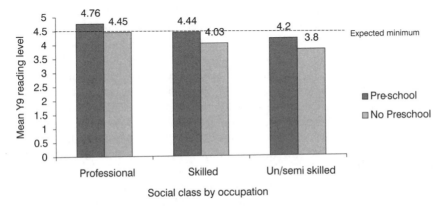

Figure 7.3a Reading at age 11 by SES and pre-school experience

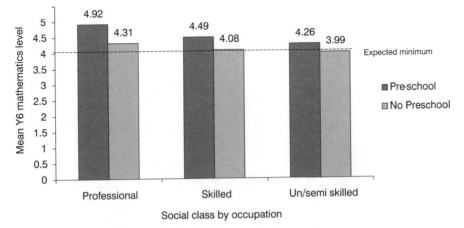

Figure 7.3b Mathematics at age 11 by SES and pre-school experience

Does quality still make a difference at the end of Key Stage 2?

We divided the sample into groups of children with different experiences to test this.

1 no pre-school experience (i.e. the 'home' group, 10 per cent of sample);
2 low quality pre-school (15 per cent);
3 medium quality pre-school (52 per cent);
4 high quality pre-school (23 per cent).

These groupings were based on pre-school ECERS-E scores. After adjusting for background factors the effects associated with each of these groups can be seen in Figure 7.4 for effects on cognitive attainment, where the no pre-school ('home' children) group is used as the comparison or baseline group (effect size=0).

Our results show a clear gradient whereby the attainment of each of the pre-school groups increases compared to the no pre-school group as pre-school quality increases. The low quality group scores more highly on English and Mathematics than the no pre-school group (ES=0.12); however the differences do not reach statistical significance. For both the medium and high quality groups, their advantage over the no pre-school group does reach statistical significance. In addition, the high quality group scores better than the low quality group for English (ES=0.17) and Mathematics (ES=0.21). The advantage of the medium quality group over the low quality group reaches statistical significance for Mathematics (ES=0.14) but not for English. The effect of high quality versus none is most noticeable for Mathematics (ES=0.34) but still clear for English (ES=0.29).

We can conclude that pre-school quality is a significant predictor of children's later Key Stage 2 attainment in both English and Mathematics outcomes at age 11. Also medium and high quality pre-school is associated with significantly enhanced

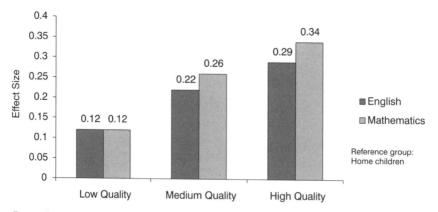

Figure 7.4 The impact of pre-school quality (ECERS-E) on English and Mathematics attainment in Year 6

attainment compared to no pre-school or low quality pre-school, and the effects are comparable in size to the difference between boys and girls in attainment.

Social/behavioural outcomes

Two measures of pre-school quality both had a statistically significant impact on all four social/behavioural outcomes at age 11, with ECERS-R having a slightly stronger impact on later 'Pro-social' and 'Anti-social' behaviour than ECERS-E (see Figures 7.5 to 7.8). Children who had attended medium and high quality pre-schools showed higher levels of Self-regulation in Year 6 than others (ES=0.24 for ECERS-R and ES=0.25 for ECERS-E). Moreover, 'home' children were rated by teachers as displaying less 'Pro-social' behaviour relative to children who had attended pre-school, although the difference is most marked for those who attended high quality (ES=0.28 for ECERS-R and ES=0.23 for ECERS-E). All these effects are 'net' of the background influences included in our models and listed earlier.

In terms of negative social/behavioural outcomes, for the 'home' (no pre-school) group and the high quality pre-school group, children were rated by teachers as displaying significantly less 'Hyperactivity' in Year 6 than children who had attended low quality (ES=0.22 for both ECERS-R and ECERS-E) and medium quality pre-school (ES=0.17 for ECERS-R and ES=0.14 for ECERS-E). This finding is in line with the findings for Year 5 (Sammons *et al.*, 2007b). The impact of pre-school quality on 'Anti-social' behaviour had a similar effect as for Self-regulation and 'Pro-social' behaviour and indicates that children who had previously attended high quality pre-schools had lower 'Anti-social' behaviour in Year 6 than 'home' children (ES=–0.23 for ECERS-R and ES=–0.22 for ECERS-E).

Overall our findings reveal that attending a high or medium quality pre-school has a lasting effect in promoting or sustaining better social/behavioural outcomes in the longer term, in terms of increased Self-regulation, higher 'Pro-social' behaviour and lower 'Anti-social' behaviour levels at age 11. However, our results

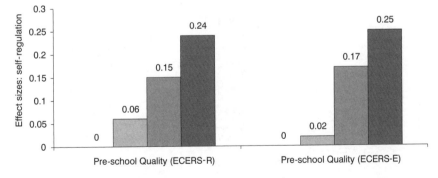

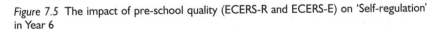

Figure 7.5 The impact of pre-school quality (ECERS-R and ECERS-E) on 'Self-regulation' in Year 6

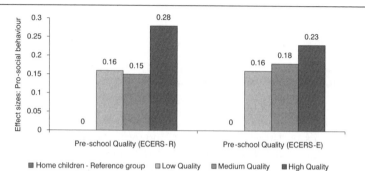

Figure 7.6 The impact of pre-school quality (ECERS-R and ECERS-E) on 'Pro-social' behaviour in Year 6

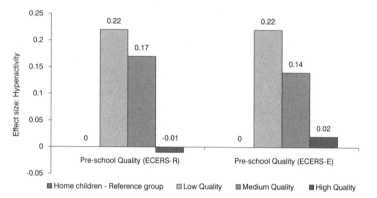

Figure 7.7 The impact of pre-school quality (ECERS-R and ECERS-E) on reducing 'Hyperactivity' in Year 6

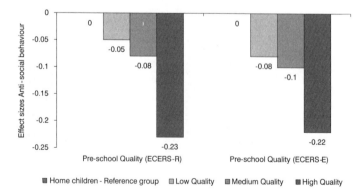

Figure 7.8 The impact of pre-school quality (ECERS-R and ECERS-E) on reducing 'Anti-social' behaviour in Year 6

indicate that the no pre-school group and the high quality pre-school group both show less 'Hyperactivity' than the low and medium quality pre-school groups.

Differential effects of quality for particular subgroups of children

We conducted further analyses to explore whether there are differential effects of pre-school quality for certain groups of children. Differential effects of pre-school quality were tested for gender, FSM in Year 6, early behavioural problems (as reported by parents at the start of the study), and low versus high levels of mother's qualifications. Our analyses also explored the potential differential impact of pre-school quality for children who were identified for special educational needs (SEN) versus children who were never identified for SEN during primary school. We tested interaction effects between each of these variables and the pre-school quality measure as defined by ECERS-E.

Controlling for significant background characteristics, differential effects were evident only for gender (boys vs. girls) and SEN (children identified as SEN vs. never identified as SEN). Our findings indicate that boys benefit more from attending a higher quality pre-school than girls in terms of increased levels of teacher-rated Self-regulation (ES=0.32 for boys versus ES=0.18 for girls) and especially 'Pro-social' behaviour (ES=0.45 for boys versus ES=0.02 for girls), and lower levels of 'Hyperactivity' (ES=−0.28 for boys versus ES=−0.10 for girls) and 'Anti-social' behaviour (ES=−0.34 for boys versus ES=−0.11 for girls) in Year 6. Overall, girls have much better scores on all four social/behavioural outcomes than boys; however, boys who previously attended a higher quality pre-school show greater long term benefit relative to girls. In other words, girls tend to have similar levels of social/behavioural outcomes in Year 6 regardless of earlier pre-school quality, the exception being for Self-regulation where girls who had previously attended high quality pre-school tended to have higher Self-regulation in Year 6 than girls who had attended low quality pre-school or no pre-school. In particular, boys gain more than girls in terms of improved Self-regulation if they had experienced higher quality pre-school. High quality pre-school therefore may be seen as a valuable intervention that can narrow the gender gap in educational outcomes that is widely prevalent in many systems.

Children identified as having a SEN during primary school also gained more from attending a higher quality pre-school centre in terms of increased Self-regulation (ES=0.36 for SEN group versus ES=0.04 for non-SEN group) and 'Pro-social' behaviour (ES=0.23 for SEN group versus ES=0.17 for non-SEN group), and lower 'Hyperactivity' (ES=−0.32 for SEN group versus ES=−0.08 for non-SEN group) and 'Anti-social' behaviour (ES=−0.39 for SEN group versus ES=−0.03 for non-SEN group) in Year 6. Overall, children who were never identified as having a SEN have better scores on all four social/behavioural outcomes than children who were identified as having a SEN during primary school as might be expected. However, children identified as having a SEN show significantly better outcomes if they attended a higher quality pre-school than other children (i.e. children never identified as having a SEN tend to have similar levels of social/ behavioural outcomes in Year 6 regardless of pre-school quality). This suggests that medium and especially high quality pre-school can serve as a protective factor for children identified as having a SEN and benefit their all-round social/ behavioural development throughout their years in primary school.

Analyses also tested if there was a differential effect of attending pre-school for children with low versus high multiple disadvantage. Our multiple disadvantage index is a summary measure (see Appendix 5) based on various child, family, and Early years HLE predictors, such as low birth weight or living in a family with low socio-economic status (SES), which are associated with an increased risk for lower attainment and poor social/behavioural outcomes. The findings suggest that children from a high multiple disadvantage background benefit more from attending a high quality pre-school than children from low multiple disadvantage backgrounds. Overall children with low multiple disadvantage have better scores on 'Hyperactivity' and 'Anti-social' behaviour outcomes than children with high multiple disadvantage; however, children with high multiple disadvantage showed better outcomes at the end of Key Stage 2 if they previously attended a high quality pre-school than children with low risk do (for Hyperactivity, ES=−0.29 for high multiple disadvantage group versus ES=−0.13 for low disadvantage group; for Anti-social behaviour, ES=−0.34 for high multiple disadvantage group versus ES=−0.06 for low disadvantage group). These findings are also in line with other recent studies in the USA, which suggest that children who come from a high family risk level benefit more from pre-school than children coming from low family risk level (Niles *et al.*, 2008), although such studies did not explore the interaction with quality of pre-school centre.

Pre-school centre effectiveness

Cognitive outcomes

As described earlier we were able to produce measures of pre-school centre effectiveness (see Sammons *et al.*, 2002, 2003).

We tested whether pre-school centre effectiveness (in terms of promoting children's progress in Pre-reading) predicted better English attainment later in Key Stage 2, and also whether pre-school centre effectiveness (in terms of promoting children's progress in Early number concepts) predicted better Mathematics attainment in Key Stage 2 National Assessments.

Controlling for child, family and HLE influences, pre-school effectiveness showed a positive net impact on children's attainment in both English and Mathematics at Year 6 (see Figures 7.9 and 7.10). Our analyses reveal that children who had attended a more effective pre-school setting also show significantly better attainment than children who had attended no or only a low effective pre-school

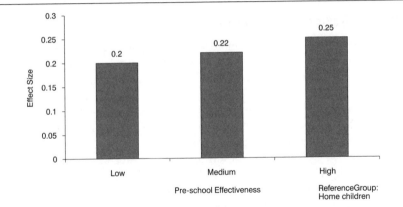

Figure 7.9 The impact of pre-school effectiveness (Pre-reading) on attainment in English at Year 6

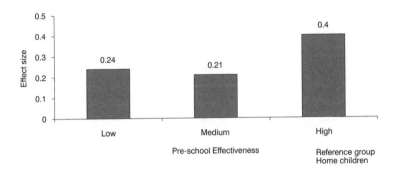

Figure 7.10 The impact of pre-school effectiveness (Early numbers concepts) on attainment in Mathematics at Year 6

setting, although the gradient is less strong than for our quality measure discussed earlier.

In terms of English attainment, compared to 'no pre-school', children who went to low, medium, or high effective pre-schools still have significantly higher attainment six years later at age 11.

For Mathematics attainment the picture is similar, compared to 'no pre-school'; children who went to low, medium, or high effective pre-school defined by its impact on promoting early number concepts still have significantly higher attainment. In addition, those who attended high effective pre-schools did significantly better than those who had attended low or medium effective pre-schools. The effect of attending a high effective pre-school is moderately strong and on a par with the mother having an A level qualification versus no qualification.

Social/behavioural outcomes

Children who had attended a more effective pre-school setting still showed significantly better social/behavioural development six years later. More specifically, pre-school academic effectiveness had a positive impact on children's later Self-regulation and 'Pro-social' behaviour (see Figures 7.11 and 7.12). The findings reveal that children who attended a more effective pre-school show higher levels of Self-regulation (ES=0.29) and 'Pro-social' behaviour (ES=0.27) in Year 6.

All four indicators of pre-school effectiveness related to social/behavioural development were significant predictors for better Self-regulation and 'Pro-social' behaviour at age 11 (see Figures 7.13 and 7.14). Overall, children who have attended a medium or high effectiveness pre-school show better Self-regulation and more 'Pro-social' behaviour than the 'home' group. Also, children who have attended medium and high effective pre-schools were rated by their teachers as showing better

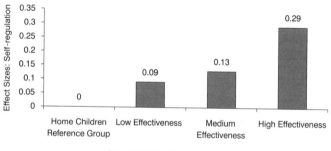

Figure 7.11 The impact of pre-school effectiveness (Early number concepts) on 'Self-regulation' in Year 6

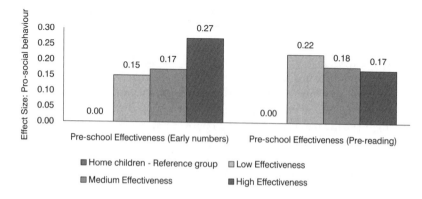

Figure 7.12 The impact of pre-school effectiveness (Early number concepts and Pre-reading) on 'Pro-social' behaviour in Year 6

Self-regulation (ES=0.12 to ES=0.24) and more 'Pro-social' behaviour (ES=0.17 to ES=0.38) than children from low effectiveness pre-schools. The difference for Pro-social behaviour between the high effective and low group is largest (ES=0.38).

Pre-school effectiveness was a significant predictor for lower 'Hyperactivity' and 'Anti-social' behaviour at age 11 (Figures 7.15 and 7.16). Children who had attended a low effectiveness pre-school in terms of 'Independence and concentration' and 'Peer Sociability' were found to have higher levels of 'Hyperactivity' in Year 6 than others, especially the 'home' group. Similarly, children who attended a high effectiveness pre-school in terms of reducing 'Anti-social' behaviour were found to have lower levels of 'Anti-social' behaviour in Year 6 than others. Nonetheless 'home' children still showed good outcomes for 'Hyperactivity' in Year 6 in contrast to the other three social/behavioural outcomes, and significantly better outcomes than those who attended low effective pre-school settings.

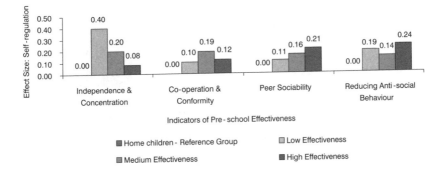

Figure 7.13 The impact of pre-school effectiveness (Social behaviour) on 'Self-regulation' in Year 6

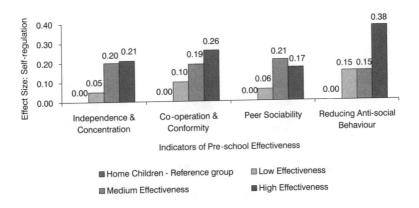

Figure 7.14 The impact of pre-school effectiveness (Social behaviour) on 'Pro-social' behaviour in Year 6

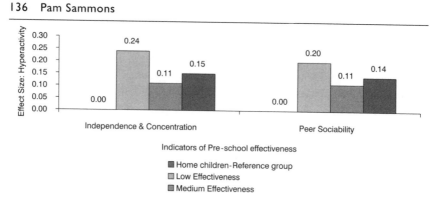

Figure 7.15 The impact of pre-school effectiveness ('Independence and Concentration' and 'Peer Sociability') on 'Hyperactivity' in Year 6

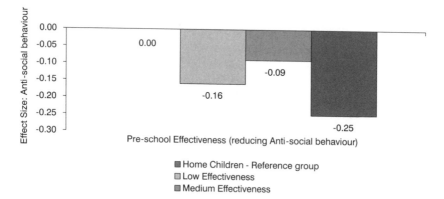

Figure 7.16 The impact of pre-school effectiveness ('Anti-social' behaviour) on 'Anti-social' behaviour in Year 6

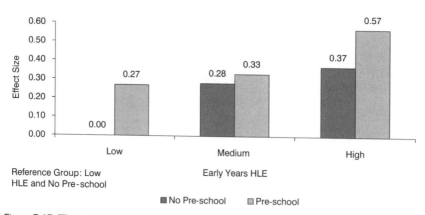

Figure 7.17 The combined impact of Early years HLE and pre-school on English attainment at Year 6

The combined effect of the home learning environment (HLE) and pre-school

Given that the analyses described above have already demonstrated modest effects for the quality and effectiveness of pre-school experience and strong effects for the Early years HLE on child outcomes, their joint effects were investigated. For this analysis the Early years HLE index was regrouped into three categories representing low, medium and high Early years HLE.

Figure 7.17 shows the combined effect of Early years HLE and pre-school attendance, the reference group for these analyses is 'no pre-school and low Early years HLE'.

We can also see that, for English, the positive effect of a good Early years HLE for the 'home' children is evident. Children who did not go to pre-school and who had a medium or high score on the Early years HLE index show a benefit, ES=0.29 and ES=0.37 respectively, compared to the 'home' children (no pre-school) with low Early years HLE.

However, when comparing these two groups of 'home' children with either high or medium Early HLE to the equivalent groups of pre-school children (those with medium and high Early years HLE scores), the benefits of attending pre-school are clearly apparent; the pre-school children with medium and high Early years scores have effects sizes of 0.33 and 0.57 respectively. Furthermore, children with low Early years HLE tend to benefit especially from pre-school attendance (ES=0.27) compared to 'home' children. Children with high Early years HLE and pre-school experience show the largest positive effects, ES=0.57. Interestingly the difference in ES between the low Early years HLE group who did or did not go to pre-school (ES=0.27) is slightly larger than the difference in ES between the high Early years HLE group who did or did not attend pre-school (ES difference 0.20). This again points to the potential ability of pre-school to help narrow the attainment gap for vulnerable groups.

For Mathematics the pattern is similar to that for English. The Early years HLE has a fairly strong positive influence on attainment in Year 6, controlling for background factors such as SES or the qualification level of parents. For Mathematics, the group of children with low Early years HLE receive a distinct advantage from attending a pre-school compared to 'home' children with a low Early years HLE (ES=0.29). For children who had medium Early years HLE scores, pre-school attendance makes some difference (ES=0.25 no pre-school versus 0.34 pre-school). The group of children with high Early years HLE not only get a boost through Early years HLE, but also an additional advantage from going to pre-school (ES=0.24: the difference between the two groups' effect sizes, and the difference between the effect of pre-school and no pre-school). Again the relative advantage of attending pre-school versus not attending for those children who had a low Early years HLE (ES=0.29) is slightly stronger than that for high HLE children (ES=0.24) who attended pre-school compared to the high Early HLE group who did not. Taken together the results support the view that both children who had a low Early years HLE and those who had a high Early years HLE show a significant benefit from pre-school attendance. The positive pre-school impact is likely to be particularly important for children who had lower Early years HLE given the boost others gain from a more favourable Early years HLE and is larger than the effect of FSM.

Early years home learning environment (HLE) and the quality of the pre-school

We conducted further analyses investigating the quality of the pre-school centre attended and any joint effects with the Early years HLE. The reference group in these analyses is again the 'low Early years HLE and no pre-school' group. Children who had a low Early years HLE gained an advantage from attending any pre-school, but particularly from high quality pre-schools (ES=0.44). Children who had medium Early years HLE scores received an additional benefit from attending higher quality pre-school, though the extra boost (in ES) for the 'high quality' pre-school group who had a high Early years HLE is not as great as the boost found for children who had a low Early years HLE but went to a high quality pre-school.

Cognitive outcomes

Children who had a high Early years HLE and went to a medium or high quality pre-school have the strongest benefit in English attainment at the end of Year 6 (ES=0.61 and 0.58 respectively). Again the 'home' children and those attending low quality provision also benefit from high Early years HLE, with a comparable net effect size (ES=0.37 for both respectively). However their boost is not as great as that for low Early years HLE children who went to high quality pre-school.

Children who went to low quality pre-school who had high Early years HLE (ES=0.37) are still doing better than those children who went to low quality pre-school and had low (ES=0.33) or medium (ES=0.25) Early years HLE. These findings underline the importance of the quality of the pre-school centre for promoting English attainment and also the importance of Early years HLE.

For the most disadvantaged (in terms of Early years HLE); any pre-school makes a positive difference but especially high quality. Here the net effect is slightly stronger than that found for a mother having an A-level qualification compared to having no qualification.

Figure 7.18 shows that for Mathematics the pattern of results is similar to that for English, indicating significant positive effects. Children who had low Early years HLE are doing best at the end of Year 6 if they previously attended a high quality pre-school and the effect is moderately strong (ES=0.51) compared to the 'low Early years HLE and no pre-school' combination. Children with medium Early years HLE show smaller, but significant effects of pre-school, with the effect sizes increasing gently in a linear fashion as the quality of the pre-school improves

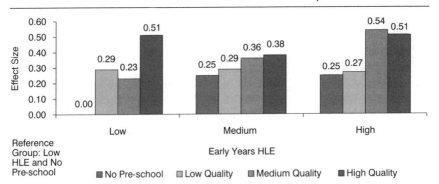

Figure 7.18 The combined impact of Early years HLE and quality of pre-school on attainment in Mathematics at Year 6

compared to 'low Early years HLE and no pre-school' (ES=0.29 for low, ES=0.36 for medium and ES=0.38 for high quality pre-school).

For children who did not go to pre-school, those who had a medium Early years HLE show better Mathematics results at Year 6 than children who had experienced a low Early years HLE (ES=0.25). In contrast, children who had a high Early years HLE show greater benefit from medium and high quality pre-school for later Mathematics results (ES=0.54 for medium quality, ES=0.51 for high quality compared to ES=0.25 for 'high Early years HLE and no pre-school') when compared to the 'low Early years HLE and no pre-school'. The impact of high quality pre-school versus none is strongest for children who had a low Early years HLE (0.51) compared with children who had a high Early years HLE where the ES difference is 0.26 (0.51–0.25).

The interactions suggest that the benefits of the pre-school experience are mediated by the quality of Early years HLE experienced by children and that high quality pre-school is particularly important for children who had a low Early years HLE.

Social/behavioural outcomes

Self-regulation was the only social/behavioural outcome that showed significant results when we explored interactions between Early years HLE and pre-school quality.

Self-regulation

As can be seen in Figure 7.19, 'home' children with high Early years HLE scores (ES=0.29) have a higher Self-regulation level in Year 6 relative to 'home' children with low (reference group) and medium (ES=–0.02) Early years HLE scores. On the other end, children with low Early years HLE who previously attended a high quality pre-school have significantly better Self-regulation in Year 6 (ES=0.42)

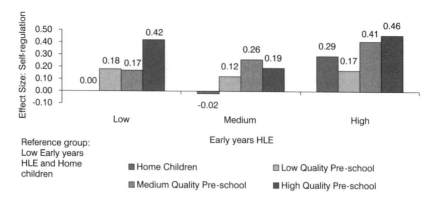

Figure 7.19 The combined impact of Early years HLE and Pre-school quality (ECERS-E) on 'Self-regulation'

relative to children with low Early years HLE but no pre-school experience (i.e. 'home' children). As expected, Self-regulation benefits from the combined effect of medium or high pre-school quality and high Early years HLE (ES=0.41 for medium and ES=0.46 for high quality).

There is a strong combined impact of Early years HLE and pre-school quality on later Self-regulation. Controlling for other background characteristics, a combination of high Early years HLE and attendance at a medium or high quality pre-school is a strong predictor of higher Self-regulation levels at the end of Key Stage 2. In addition, high Early years HLE seems to act as a protective factor for children who do not attend pre-school, helping them achieve higher levels of Self-regulation in primary school (ES=0.29). Similarly, attending high quality pre-school seems to protect against the disadvantage of a low Early years HLE and promotes children's later Self-regulation and this boost (ES=0.42) is stronger than the influence of FSM or SES.

Early years home learning environment (HLE) and pre-school effectiveness

We also investigated the interaction of Early years HLE and pre-school centre effectiveness for cognitive outcomes and found similar patterns to the results for quality described above. Results for English show a clear trend: compared to low Early years HLE and no pre-school, all other combinations show a sustained benefit on later attainment in Year 6; the effect sizes tend to increase in terms of both Early years HLE score and pre-school effectiveness.

Figure 7.20 shows the results for Mathematics, which is similar to those for English, although the differences tend to be even more pronounced. Overall, the beneficial effects tend to increase in terms of both Early years HLE score and pre-school effectiveness.

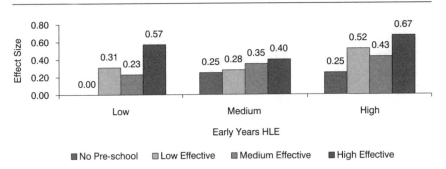

Figure 7.20 The combined impact of Early years HLE and effectiveness of pre-school (in terms of Numeracy) on attainment in Mathematics at Year 6

Children who had a low Early years HLE obtain most advantage from attending pre-schools that were highly effective in promoting young children's numeracy (ES=0.57), as opposed to medium effective (ES=0.23) or low effective pre-schools (ES=0.31). For children who had a medium Early years HLE, attainment also shows a steady if modest increase along with the effectiveness of the pre-school. The children who show the greatest attainment boost are those children who had a high Early years HLE compared to those who had a lower Early years HLE but who attend pre-schools of equivalent effectiveness. Consistent with this, the children that do best had both a high Early years HLE and attended a highly effective pre-school (ES=0.67). These children not only benefit from the high level of their Early years HLE but get an additional boost from attending a more effective pre-school.

For English and Mathematics these findings are in accord with those for pre-school quality. Nonetheless, the boost from a highly effective pre-school is most marked for those children who had a low Early years HLE (ES=0.57) compared with the difference between no pre-school and highly effective pre-school for those children who had a high Early years HLE (0.67–0.25=0.42). Again this points to the long term benefits of effective pre-school in narrowing the attainment gap for vulnerable groups of children.

Primary school academic effectiveness

We wanted to study primary school influences as well as the continued impact of pre-school. The academic effectiveness of the primary school EPPE 3–11 children went on to attend had a significant influence on their later attainment in English and Mathematics in Year 6, taking account of the influence of background influences. For English, attending a high academically effective primary school was associated with a significant boost to attainment (ES=0.24). Moreover, results show that previously attending a high quality pre-school still offered some compensation/protection for those who went on to attend an academically less effective primary school. Also, for Mathematics the quality and effectiveness of the pre-school still predicted later attainment controlling for other factors. However, the academic effectiveness of the primary school was a more important predictor of Mathematics (ES=0.38) in Year 6, which appears to be more sensitive to the academic effectiveness of the primary school than English in Year 6. This is in line with earlier school effectiveness research indicating that school effects tend to be stronger for Mathematics and Science.

Attending a highly academically effective primary school is a predictor of better educational attainment particularly for disadvantaged pupils. In English the effectiveness of the primary school is relatively more important for the more disadvantaged than the less disadvantaged, where disadvantage is measured in terms of multiple disadvantage index (see Appendix 5). The more disadvantaged children, children who score two or above on the multiple disadvantage index, show higher attainment when they go to a highly effective primary school (ES=0.25) compared to those attending a low effective primary school. The more disadvantaged children also show higher attainment in Mathematics when they attend a highly effective primary school (ES=0.43), or even a medium effective primary school (ES=0.24) compared to a low effective primary school.

The effectiveness of the primary school attended is also a predictor of better Mathematics outcomes for children with low qualified parents. Children with low qualified parents have significantly better scores in Mathematics if they attend a medium (ES=0.35) or high (ES=0.44) academically effective primary school. In addition, attending a highly academically effective primary school is a predictor of increased Self-regulation and reduced 'Anti-social' behaviour for children identified as having a SEN in primary school (ES=0.32 for Self-regulation and ES=0.37 for 'Anti-social' behaviour outcome) and those with mothers who had a low qualification level (ES=0.33 for 'Anti-social' behaviour outcome only).

The combined impact of pre-school experience and primary school effectiveness

Given that pre-school experience and primary school academic effectiveness both predict later cognitive attainments, their joint effects were investigated. We sought to establish whether going to a high quality or more effective pre-school had a protective influence if a child went on to a less effective primary school, and whether 'home' children, or those who went to a less effective or low quality pre-school, did better later if they went to a more effective primary school. We combined the two measures of pre-school quality (according to the ECERS-E score of the pre-school) and primary school academic effectiveness and incorporated them in the same model to explore any joint effects of pre-school and primary school. Due to smaller numbers, medium and highly effective primary schools were grouped together, and the reference group is no pre-school ('home' children) and low effective primary school.

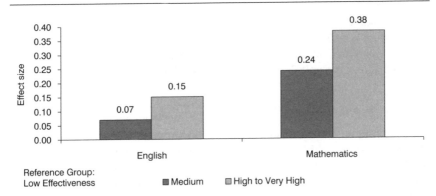

Figure 7.21 The impact of primary school academic effectiveness on English and Mathematics at Year 6

The pattern of results for English was less clear than for Mathematics, although the combined impact of attending a high quality pre-school followed by an academically effective primary had the most positive impact. The pattern of results for Mathematics was stronger, the better the quality of pre-school the higher the attainment in Mathematics, and the more academically effective the primary school the higher the Mathematics attainment in Year 6. Importantly, our results reveal that 'home' children who did not attend pre-school gain a particularly strong benefit from attending a more academically effective primary school (ES=0.43). Children who went to a low or medium quality pre-school centre and low effective primary school later on are still doing better than those children who did not have any pre-school experience and went to a low effective primary school (ES=0.29). Children who went to high quality pre-school are doing particularly well, even if they then moved on to a low effective primary school later on (again indicative of an apparent compensatory effect). For children who went to a high quality pre-school centre and a medium/high effective primary school, we find an additive effect. These children show the greatest boost in attainment at the end of Year 6 controlling for the influence of all other background factors (ES=0.67), so for those who went to a high quality pre-school the effectiveness of the primary school had less impact than it did for those who did not go to pre-school or attended a low quality pre-school.

The combined impact of pre-school effectiveness and primary school effectiveness

In addition to the analyses of the individual impact of pre-school and primary school academic effectiveness, these two measures were taken together and incorporated in the same model so that the combined effects could be studied. We sought to establish whether going to a more effective pre-school had a protective influence if a child went on to a less effective primary school, and whether 'home' children or those who went to a less effective pre-school centre did better later if they went to a more effective primary school. The reference group for these analyses are children with no pre-school experience ('home' children) who attended a low academically effective primary school.

Cognitive outcomes

For both English and Mathematics where children had previously attended high effective pre-schools, they have comparable levels of attainment regardless of the academic effectiveness of the primary school they attend. This, however, does not hold for children who attended lower effective pre-schools: in such cases there is a clear gradation of attainment by primary school academic effectiveness. The pattern of results for Mathematics is particularly striking for those who went to no pre-school where those who attended a high academically effective primary school show a significant boost (ES=0.65), which is almost twice as strong as the effect of SES. The difference for those who went to low effective pre-school related to primary school academic effectiveness is also large (ES difference 0.9–0.4=0.5). Therefore the effectiveness of the primary school attended is particularly important for children who attend a less effective pre-school, or have not attended pre-school.

Social behavioural outcomes: Self-regulation

Primary school academic effectiveness was not a significant predictor of social/behavioural dimensions on its own. We sought to establish whether primary school academic effectiveness might be significant in combination with pre-school quality as was found in analyses of children's academic outcomes.

At age 11 the only significant interaction was between pre-school quality and primary school academic effectiveness (in terms of Mathematics) related to children's Self-regulation. Children who attend low or even medium academically effective primary school but who previously attended a high quality pre-school show significantly better Self-regulation at the end of Key Stage 2. Similarly, attending a high academically effective primary school will benefit those children who either did not attend any pre-school or those who attended only a low quality pre-school in terms of higher levels of Self-regulation at age 11. As expected, children who either did not attend pre-school or went to low quality pre-school and afterwards to a low academically effective primary school had the lowest Self-regulation levels at the end of Key Stage 2.

These findings suggest that pre-school and primary school effects interact and may be additive and, therefore, the 'masking' of pre-school effects may be bi-directional. Thus, primary school academic influences may not only mask earlier pre-school effects but may also be masked by the positive or negative effects of the pre-schools that children had attended, such that high quality pre-schools may attenuate negative effects of primary schools and low quality pre-schools may reduce positive effects. It appears that Self-regulation is the only social/behavioural outcome for which we find evidence of a clear and significant pattern of influences related to academic effectiveness of the primary school. This is likely to reflect stronger links at child level between Self-regulation and academic attainment.

Pupils' progress across Key Stage 2 (KS2)

We conducted further analyses to study children's progress over Key Stage 2 by controlling for their prior attainment at age 7 (Key Stage 1 national assessment results).

We did this because we wanted to know whether pre-school influences subsequent learning besides giving a boost to attainment or social behaviour. We found that the quality and effectiveness of the pre-school also predicted pupils' progress from Key Stage 1 to Key Stage 2 (pre-school quality for English ES=0.23; Mathematics ES=0.20; pre-school effectiveness for English ES=0.28; Mathematics ES=0.22). This shows that attending a better pre-school not only provides an initial boost to attainment levels that lasts up to age 11, but it also helps promote later progress (possibly by fostering children's capacity to learn, and their motivation may be via increasing their Self-regulation). Similarly children attending more academically effective primary schools make significantly more progress during KS2 and it is important to note that the impact on progress is larger than that of most child or family background factors especially for Mathematics (English ES=0.37; Mathematics ES=0.52).

The boost to children's progress over KS2 given by attending an academically more effective primary school is stronger than that of the pre-school, as might be expected given the length of time children spend in primary school (over 6 years). This again confirms the importance of the primary school as an influential factor for children's educational progress as well as their attainment levels, net of background factors and prior attainment. Again as with attainment, the school effects are stronger for progress in Mathematics than English (in line with findings in other educational effectiveness studies, see Teddlie and Reynolds, 2000).

Summary

These findings based on analysing EPPE children's National Assessment outcomes at the end of primary school (Year 6) are broadly in line with those we identified when children were age 10 (Sammons *et al.*, 2007a, 2007b), where standardised assessments (NFER tests) were adopted to measure children's attainments in Reading and Mathematics. In both years, teachers' assessments of social behaviour were also collected. The consistency in our findings for academic and social/behavioural outcomes in these two years provides greater confidence in the robustness of the results (since Year 5 was not a National Assessment year and therefore there was less likelihood of any possible bias that might be introduced through the possible impact of high stakes assessment on teachers' behaviour/test preparation on children's Year 6 outcomes).

Our data suggest that low quality and less effective pre-school has only a fairly small benefit on children's longer term outcomes at age 11 in comparison with the 'home' (no pre-school) group and was associated with some poorer social outcomes, although not for 'Pro-social' behaviour where a significant benefit remains evident. Conversely, medium (the common experience for our sample) and particularly high quality pre-school shows significant benefits for children's cognitive and social/behavioural outcomes at age 11. It also has the power to boost children's progress over KS2. 'Home' children do less well on most outcomes compared to those who attended medium or higher quality pre-school even when we take account of influence of a wide range of background influences. They do not 'catch' up with other children even after six years in primary school. They also show a continued disadvantage in terms of 'Pro-social' behaviour but reduced scores for 'Hyperactivity'.

Taken together, the findings also confirm that high scores on the Early years HLE seem to be a protective factor for children who did not attend pre-school, promoting better Self-regulation in Key Stage 2. Similarly, previous experience of attending high quality pre-school ameliorates the negative impact for a child of experiencing a less stimulating home environment as measured by a low Early years HLE, by fostering relatively better Self-regulation in the longer term at age 11.

Attending an academically more effective primary school also boosts children's academic outcomes in English and particularly in Mathematics; there are also benefits for improved Self-regulation which is itself associated with learning outcomes, while there is no evidence of a negative influence on other social/behavioural outcomes. This has important implications for the Every Child Matters agenda in England by showing that promoting better academic outcomes does not seem to compete with fostering better social/behavioural development for children in primary school. Our data reveal that the value added measure of primary school academic effectiveness is a particularly significant influence for those children who did not have the advantage of attending a pre-school, many of whom came from families with low levels of education. This finding is very relevant to policy aims to encourage social inclusion as well as raising standards.

Conclusion

Overall, these follow up results confirm that pre-school effects remain evident as significant influences on children's outcomes in the mid- to longer term even after six years in primary school. Our findings suggest that the combination of different influences at home and in education (of a high Early years HLE along with a higher quality, more effective pre-school and a more academically effective primary school) can give a significant boost to children's outcomes at age 11 years.

These findings also add to the debate about reducing the achievement gap for disadvantaged groups which we will discuss in more detail in subsequent chapters. Concerted action to improve the Early years HLE, and both pre-school and primary school experiences (reducing variation in quality and effectiveness) will be needed to make a difference to outcomes for the most disadvantaged children. In addition, the present findings suggest that there will still be a need for specially targeted interventions for children who are identified as well behind their peers in cognitive and social/behavioural profiles at the start of primary school, particularly if these children have not had the benefit of a good pre-school experience or a good Early years HLE. This may go some way to narrowing the achievement gap during KS1 and KS2 since early intervention has a better chance of improving such pupils' learning trajectories (Sammons *et al.*, 2004; Hurry and Sylva, 2007; Sylva *et al.*, 2008).

References

Goldstein, H. (1995) *Multilevel Statistical Models*, London: Arnold.

Goodman, R. (1997) The strengths and difficulties questionnaire: a research note, *Journal of Child Psychology and Psychiatry*, 38, 581–586.

Hurry, J. and Sylva, K. (2007) Long term outcomes of reading interventions, *Journal of Research in Reading*, 30(2), 1–22.

Melhuish, E., Romaniuk, H., Sammons, P., Sylva, K., Siraj-Blatchford, I. and Taggart, B. (2006) *Effective Pre-school and Primary Education 3–11 Project (EPPE 3–11): The Effectiveness of Primary Schools in England in Key Stage 2 for 2002, 2003 and 2004. Full Report*. London: Institute of Education, University of London. http://eppe.ioe.ac.uk

Melhuish, E.C., Sylva, K., Sammons, P., Siraj-Blatchford, I., Taggart, B., Phan, M. and Malin, A. (2008) Preschool influences on mathematics achievement, *Science*, 321, 1161–1162.

Niles, M.D., Reynolds, A.J. and Roe-Sepowitz, D (2008) Early childhood intervention and early adolescent social and emotional competence: second-generation evaluation evidence from the Chicago Longitudinal Study, *Educational Research*, 50 (1), 55–73.

Sammons, P., Sylva, K., Melhuish, E.C., Siraj-Blatchford, I., Taggart, B. and Elliot, K. (2002) *The Effective Provision of Pre-School Education (EPPE) Project: Technical Paper 8a – Measuring the Impact of Pre-School on Children's Cognitive Progress over the Pre-School Period*. London: DfES/Institute of Education, University of London.

Sammons, P., Sylva, K., Melhuish, E.C., Siraj-Blatchford, I., Taggart, B. and Elliot, K. (2003) *The Effective Provision of Pre-School Education (EPPE) Project: Technical Paper 8b – Measuring the Impact of Pre-School on Children's Social/Behavioural Development over the Pre-School Period*, London: DfES / Institute of Education, University of London.

Sammons, P., Sylva, K., Melhuish, E., Siraj-Blatchford, I., Taggart, B. and Hunt, S. (2008) *Influences on Children's Attainment and Progress in Key Stage 2: Cognitive Outcomes in Year 6*. DCSF Research Report RR-048, Nottingham: DCSF.

Sammons, P., Sylva, K., Melhuish, E.C., Siraj-Blatchford, I., Taggart, B., Elliot, K. and Marsh, A. (2004) *The Effective Provision of Pre-School Education (EPPE) Project: Technical Paper 11 – Report on the Continuing Effects of Pre-School Education at Age 7*, London: DfES/Institute of Education, University of London.

Sammons, P., Sylva, K., Melhuish, E., Siraj-Blatchford, I., Taggart, B., Grabbe, Y. and Barreau, S. (2007a) *Effective Pre-school and Primary Education 3–11 Project (EPPE 3–11): Summary Report: Influences on Children's Attainment and Progress in Key Stage 2: Cognitive Outcomes in Year 5*. Research Report No. RR828, Nottingham: DfES Publications.

Sammons, P., Sylva, K., Melhuish, E., Siraj-Blatchford, I., Taggart, B., Barreau, S. and Grabbe, Y. (2007b) *Effective Pre-school and Primary Education 3–11 Project (EPPE 3–11): Influences on Children's Development and Progress in Key Stage 2: Social/behavioural Outcomes in Year 5*. Research Report No. DCSF-RR007. Nottingham: DfES Publications.

Sammons, P., Sylva, K., Melhuish, E., Siraj-Blatchford, I., Taggart, B., Hunt, S. and Jelicic, H. (2008a) *Effective Pre-school and Primary Education 3–11 Project (EPPE 3–11): Influences on Children's Development and Progress in Key Stage 2: Social/behavioural Outcomes in Year 6*. DCSF Research Report, DCSF-RR-49 Nottingham: DCSF.

Sammons, P., Sylva, K., Melhuish, E., Siraj-Blatchford, I., Taggart, B., Jelicic, H., Barreau, S., Grabbe, Y. and Smees, R. (2008b) *Effective Pre-school and Primary Education 3–11 Project (EPPE 3–11): Relationships Between Pupil Self-perceptions, Views of Primary School and their Development in Year 5*. http://eppe.ioe.ac.uk/.

Sammons, P., Sylva, K., Melhuish, E., Siraj-Blatchford, I., Taggart, B., Hunt, S. and Jelicic, H. (2008c) *Effective Pre-School and Primary Education 3–11 Project (EPPE 3–11): Influences on Children's Cognitive and Social Behaviour (Attainment, Progress and Development) to the End of Primary School (Year 6)*. DCSF Research Brief DCSF-RB048-049, Nottingham; DCSF.

Sammons, P., Sylva, K., Melhuish, E.C., Siraj-Blatchford, I., Taggart, B., Smees, R., Dobson, A., Jeavons, M., Lewis, K., Morahan, M. and Sadler, S. (1999) *The Effective Provision of Pre-School Education (EPPE) Project: Technical Paper 2 – Characteristics of the Effective Provision of Pre-School (EPPE) Project Sample at Entry to the Study*, London: DfEE/ Institute of Education, University of London.

Scheerens, J. and Bosker, R. (1997) *The Foundations of Educational Effectiveness*, Oxford, Pergamon.

Schweinhart, L.J. and Weikart, D.P. (1997a) The high/scope pre-school curriculum comparison study through age 23, *Early Childhood Research Quarterly*, 12(2), 117–143.

Schweinhart, L.J. and Weikart, D.P. (1997b) *Lasting Differences: The High/Scope Pre-school Curriculum Comparison Study Through Age 23*. High/Scope Educational Research Foundation Monograph No. 121, Ypsilanti, MI High/Scope Press.

Sylva, K., Melhuish, E., Sammons, P., Siraj-Blatchford, I. and Taggart, B. (2008) *Effective Pre-school and Primary Education 3–11 Project (EPPE 3–11). Final Report from the Primary Phase: Pre-school, School and Family Influences on Children's Development during Key Stage 2 (Age 7–11)*, Department for Children, Families and Schools (DCSF), Research Report DCSF-RR 061, Nottingham: DCSF.

Teddlie, C. and Reynolds, D. (2000) *The International Handbook of School Effectiveness Research*, London: RoutledgeFalmer.

Chapter 8

A focus on pedagogy
Case studies of effective practice

Iram Siraj-Blatchford

This chapter describes the day-to-day experiences in early years settings that lead to better outcomes for children through a focus on pedagogy. In addition to investigating the effects of pre-school provision on young children's development, EPPE explored the characteristics of effective practice (and the pedagogies which underpin them) through collecting intensive, detailed qualitative and quantitative data from twelve case studies of settings with good to excellent child developmental outcomes. This chapter provides working definitions of pedagogy and curriculum before reflecting on some current tensions which currently exist in European discourses around these areas. The chapter goes on to explain the methods used for this part of the study and discusses the key findings.

What is pedagogy?

Different definitions of the term 'pedagogy' have often been applied in the UK and in continental Europe and this has led to some confusion in the use of the term 'curriculum' in UK early childhood contexts. At times this has resulted in accounts where pedagogy and curriculum are applied synonymously or appear indistinguishable. The easiest way to understand the concept of 'pedagogy' is therefore to begin by first differentiating it from what is generally understood by the term 'curriculum'. It is extremely unfortunate that both of these terms have been applied loosely in the past, and, as we shall see, this may have led some significant contemporary writers to present false dichotomies between 'schoolification' and 'socio-pedagogy'.

The definition of pedagogy that we adopted in the EPPE project was based on the work of Gage (1985), who argued for a 'scientific basis for the art of teaching'. Gage argued that we should distinguish between knowledge that is general (nomothetic knowledge), and knowledge that applies to the understanding of particular events or individuals (ideographic knowledge). He argued that teachers creatively apply their nomothetic knowledge to the ideographic problems posed by the unique groups of children that they are faced with; with all of their specific needs, socio-cultural status and cognitive and affective demands.

Pedagogy was therefore defined broadly to refer to the full set of instructional techniques and strategies that enabled learning to take place in early childhood that provided opportunities for the acquisition of knowledge, skills, attitudes and dispositions. This definition was considered wide enough to take in such indirect teacher behaviours as the provision of 'discovery' learning environments, and the encouragement of parental involvement.

So what is curriculum?

In New Zealand the *Te Whāriki* defines curriculum broadly as 'the sum total of the experiences, activities and events, whether direct or indirect, which occur within an environment designed to foster children's learning and development' (New Zealand Ministry of Education, 1996, p. 10). Such a broad definition seems particularly apt in the case of early childhood education although it may sometimes be important to recognise that some sort of learning and development happens whether we consciously design the environment for that purpose or not. Young children are learning all the time, and however implicit or hidden it may be in some settings, the content of this learning (the 'curriculum') is *always* determined by the adults who care for them. The notion of a totally 'free' play environment may therefore be considered a myth. The material resources (toys, furniture, and props), the activities, the social interactions, and the environments that we offer children, define both the opportunities and the limitations for their learning. The linguistic and cultural context that they are immersed in, even more fundamentally, influences what it is that they learn. Practitioners are therefore faced with the option of simply acknowledging all of these influences, or making the choice of actively managing them. In the UK today, most professional early childhood educators choose the latter option, they apply their knowledge and skill to the best of their ability in passing on all those capabilities, knowledge, understandings, and attitudes that they consider to be especially shared and valued by our multicultural society.

The bulk of the EPPE qualitative data was collected in 2000, which was the first year of implementation of the *Curriculum Guidance for the Foundation Stage* (CGFS) (QCA/DfEE, 2000) for 3–5 year olds in England. The following short account of the CGFS is therefore provided to clarify the context within which the case studies were conducted, and in an engagement with Bennett's (2004) account of the two broad 'approaches' to early childhood education that are allegedly applied across Europe; a 'social pedagogy' approach where the curriculum is developed at a centre level, and an 'infant school' approach where the curriculum is provided by a central authority. This is an argument that is extended by Bennett in the *Starting Strong II* report (Bennett and Tayler, 2006).

The CGFS has been particularly significant in defining the role of the early childhood practitioner explicitly in terms of 'teaching'. While the importance of *supporting and extending children's play was* re-emphasised, for the first time, practitioners were encouraged to draw upon 'a range of teaching and care strategies'.

Practitioners need to plan learning experiences of the highest quality, considering both children's needs and achievements and the range of learning experiences that will help them make progress.

(p.7)

The main 'principles for early years education' that were identified by the CGFS included the need to provide for 'parent partnership', 'planned and free play' and for 'practitioner intervention' in achieving a range of *Early Learning Goals (ELGs)*. The ELGs covered six curriculum areas: Personal, Social and Emotional Development; Communication, Language and Literacy; Mathematical Development; Creative Development, Physical Development and Knowledge and Understanding of the World. Most of the statements of 'what the practitioner needs to do' in the CGFS referred to curriculum, where practitioners were advised to encourage or provide specific experiences and activities, but many of the statements were pedagogically ambiguous. A few recommendations in these sections suggested that practitioners should 'recognise', 'be aware' or 'know' things. Many more referred to the importance of 'helping' or 'supporting' children in unspecified ways, 'enabling', 'giving time' or 'promoting' particular understandings.

But systematic analysis showed that the direct teaching emphasis of the CGFS was predominantly in subject areas involving practical *skill* development and/or safe practices, there was also an emphasis on questioning in 'mathematics', and on external visits in the area of 'knowledge and understanding of the world'. Throughout the Guidance document an emphasis on practitioner modelling was striking, which suggested a general acceptance of the 'emergent' learning philosophy in all six areas of the Early Learning Goals (Siraj-Blatchford and Siraj-Blatchford, 2001).

Socio-pedagogy

In most Northern European contexts, child-care was originally family oriented and concerned with promoting the ideology of the family, which may be contrasted with more educationally oriented approaches, e.g. Robert Owen's (1824) 'Infant school', Froebel's (1826) 'Kindergarten', and Montessori's (1909) 'case di bambini' (children's houses). But, as Bennett (2004) has suggested, the social pedagogy approach has been particularly influential in recent years throughout northern European countries and in eastern Europe. In Sweden the social pedagogy tradition can be traced back to a seminar led by Alva Myrdal in 1935; the *Socialpedagogiska Seminariet* (Social Pedagogy Seminar) (Myrdal, 1945, p. 396). Rather than specifying any pre-defined knowledge, skills or attitudes that children would require to achieve success in everyday life, the central aim of social pedagogy has been to empower children as active citizens, so that they can act to change their own lives. In practice this has generally been seen to focus attention on the nurture of children's identity and self-esteem. Similar approaches have also been popular in the UK where a diverse range of approaches has historically been developed to satisfy perceived needs for either 'care' or 'education'. This has been a dichotomy *encouraged by the development of separate state pre-school provisions administered by the social services 'care' sector, and by local authority education departments. It has also stimulated ongoing controversies* over the relative merits of 'child centred' and 'progressive' or 'traditional' methods of teaching in primary education. But recent years have seen a significant moderation of extreme positions and a growing consensus regarding the need to adopt a more balanced approach (often expressed in terms of a commitment to 'educate').

Yet in Starting Strong II, Bennett contrasts the English Foundation Stage (FS) with the social pedagogical approach. He argues that it provides an example of an 'early education' approach (also referred to by Bennett, 2004, as an 'infant school', and Bennett, 2006, as a 'schoolification' approach) because it has a central specification of curriculum, it underplays the role of parents and the community, and because it focuses upon cognitive development and school readiness. From the curriculum guidance details presented above, this might always have been an exaggeration, and in the context of the revised Early Years Foundation Stage (EYFS) introduced throughout England in 2008, it is demonstrably incorrect.

The EYFS principles

The EYFS is organised around four broad principles related to: the Unique Child, Positive Relationships, Enabling Environments, and Learning and Development. While the EYFS does include 69 Early Learning Goals, only 30 (43 per cent) actually relate to knowledge content, and only 7 (10 per cent) are concretely specified, the rest being of a very general nature, e.g. *'Extend their vocabulary, exploring the meanings and sounds of new words'* – *'Begin to know about their own cultures and beliefs and those of other people.'* Even where the goals do define very specific knowledge content it is often clear that they would in any event be prioritised in *most* emergent literacy or numeracy curriculum contexts, e.g. *'Know(ing) that print carries meaning and, in English, is read from left to right and top to bottom'* – *'Use language such as "greater", "smaller", "heavier" or "lighter" to compare quantities.'* In fact it could be argued that it would be hard to imagine *any* (socio-pedagogic) early childhood curriculum failing to include most or even all the learning goals directly specifying content, e.g. *'Recognise the importance of keeping healthy, and those things which contribute to this'*.

The Early Learning Goals may also be seen as, in many respects, similar to the objectives (four basic competencies and five broad learning areas) identified by Bennett in the Norwegian national curriculum, and those included in the six areas of the Danish 2004 curriculum. In any event, as Bennett accepts:

> Research suggests that a more unified approach to learning should be adopted in both the early childhood education and the primary school systems, and that attention should be given to transition challenges faced by young children as they enter school.
>
> (Bennett and Tayler, 2006, p. 13)

The challenge is to provide a transition that stimulates growth and development while avoiding any risk of regression or failure. This is widely recognised by researchers and by policy makers. Efforts are therefore being made throughout Europe to develop better transition between nurseries, kindergartens and schools. According to Oberhuemer (2004) in Germany, following the publication of disappointing results in the 2001 OECD-PISA International Student Assessment of 15 year olds, there has been wide recognition that the long tradition of social pedagogy in kindergarten must be reconciled with the emerging demands for school readiness. In Denmark, according to Brostrom (2006), an Act on Educational Curricula was passed in August, 2004. This requires each preschool to implement six dimensions of aims and content which are expressed as general themes: (a) personal competencies, (b) social competencies, (c) language, (d) body and movement, (e) nature and nature phenomena, and (f) cultural ways of expression and values (Socialministeriet, 2004):

> ... the introduction of the concept of learning and the six curriculum themes are understood as a signal to move away from an extreme child-centered practice towards a practice where the child-care workers play a more active role.
>
> (p. 393)

In focusing equally upon cognitive and affective socio-behavioural outcomes, the EPPE project may be seen as entirely consistent with a mainstream social-pedagogic position strengthened by an awareness and concern for transition which has been emerging throughout Europe.

Whilst this report describes the pedagogy that we found applied in effective Foundation Stage settings, more detailed information on reception class practices, childminders and the Foundation Stage curriculum is reported in the Researching Effective Pedagogy in the Early Years (REPEY) Project report (see Siraj-Blatchford *et al.*, 2002).

The EPPE case studies

The aim of the intensive case study analyses was to tease out the specific pedagogical and any other practices that were associated with achieving 'excellent' outcomes compared to those centres with 'good' or more 'average' outcomes. The case study analysis provided explanations for many of the patterns and associations identified between particular practices as measured by the Early Childhood Environment Rating Scales R and E (see Sylva *et al.*, 1999, 2006) and the analysis of developmental outcomes (see Sammons *et al.*, 2002, 2003, 2004).

EPPE controlled for the influence of the family and child characteristics and was able to establish the 'effectiveness' of each of the 141 early years settings in its sample. The analysis showed that none of the settings performed statistically significantly either above or below expectations across all of the outcomes.

But some settings were found to have particular strengths and others areas of apparent weakness. A stratified random sample of 12 settings was therefore selected to include those classified by EPPE as having 'good' (above 68 per cent confidence level) to 'excellent' (95 per cent confidence level) practice in terms of the children's developmental progress in one or more cognitive (Pre-reading, Non-verbal reasoning, Language, Number concepts), or Social/behavioural outcomes (Independence and concentration, Cooperation and conformity, Less anti-social, worried and upset, Peer sociability). The sample thus provided a number of contrasting profiles and a good basis for in-depth comparison.

It was considered important to include the full range of pre-school providers. The 12 pre-school settings therefore included: one playgroup, one local authority day care setting, three private day nurseries, two nursery schools run by the local education authority (LEA), three nursery classes attached to primary schools, and two early excellence centres/combined centres. The selection of centres was made by a member of the EPPE central team who was not involved in the fieldwork or the qualitative analysis. This allowed the researchers to go in 'blind', without knowing the developmental outcomes of the children in any particular setting. Since the EPPE children had left the centres by the time the case studies were conducted, we also needed to adopt criteria for the selection of centres to ensure that they had not changed too much in the intervening period. All the centres were therefore selected for in-depth case study only after we had reassured ourselves that:

1 no significant change in management had taken place since the EPPE children attended;
2 there was a similar or better score in the Early Childhood Environment Rating Scale: Extension (ECERS-E), assessed previously in EPPE;
3 there were no difficult circumstances (e.g. pending/recent Office for Standards in Education (Ofsted) inspection).

In order to identify the pedagogical practices that were being employed to achieve the specific learning outcomes that had been identified, documentary analysis of inspection reports, policy statements, etc., systematic and naturalistic observations of children and staff, staff and parent interviews, and focus group discussions were carried out within each of the case study settings (Siraj-Blatchford et al., 2003). Data was therefore collected from 12 effective pre-school centres, reflecting good child outcomes, (cognitive and social behavioural) and these were then analysed to reveal the unique 'stories' of each centre.

In conducting the case studies, trained researchers, who were already familiar with the centres, spent two weeks conducting the naturalistic observations in each centre. This was followed by a further week of systematic target child observations. Data from policy documents was triangulated with manager and parent interviews, extensive naturalistic observations of staff (over 400 hours) and systematic focal child observations of children (254 target child observations).

Some of the data for the case studies were collected prior to the announcement of a Foundation Stage (FS) in late 1999 and during 2000 and some information from all the centres of the FS during 2001/2 when further funding was made available for the REPEY study.

Every effort was made to collect comparable data across the case studies and to provide a framework for analysis allowing comparison across centres. The case studies were compared in terms of their key quality characteristics, for example the pedagogy they employed, the curriculum on offer, and the ethos, and the management and organisational strategies applied.

As well as the patterns emerging above around management, ethos, etc., four patterns of association within the quantitative data were identified for special attention and closer analysis of the data from systematic observations suggested that each of the following practices should be investigated further:

- adult–child verbal interactions
- differentiation and formative assessment
- discipline and adult support in talking through conflicts
- parental partnership with settings and the home education environment.

The REPEY analytical process was initially 'grounded', as the process began with induction, and this was only followed later by stages of deduction and verification (Strauss, 1987, pp. 11–12; Siraj-Blatchford et al., 2006). Constant comparison was applied to compare each new interaction with the next, and as the theoretical framework emerged, the data served to continually test, moderate and transform that framework. The emergent theory at first took the form of simple links between coding categories, and as core categories were identified the conceptual hierarchies and relationships were defined. As previously suggested. all of this initial work was carried out blind in the sense that that the researcher was unaware of the learning outcomes achieved by the settings and identified by EPPE. Theoretical sampling was carried out in seeking the corroboration or refutation of emergent patterns in alternative data sources. Observation data were then cross checked with setting manager, teacher/nursery nurse and parent interviews. To take two concrete examples from the analysis, it was in this way that the category a) 'sustained shared thinking' (Siraj-Blatchford et al., 2003; 2004) was first formulated. and b) instructional techniques' were at first coded with a multitude of subcategories that included 'Questioning', 'Demonstrating', 'Telling', and 'Dialogue'. The re-classification of some of the 'Dialogue' as 'Sustained Shared thinking' with subcategories of 'Child initiated' or 'Adult Initiated' only took place after the following data were revealed:

Context: Children engaged in water play.

BOY 8 (4:1) (who has been watching various items floating on water), 'Look at the fir cone. There's bubbles of air coming out.'

NURSERY OFFICER 'It's spinning round.'

BOY 8 (4:1) 'That's 'cos it's got air in it.'

NURSERY OFFICER 1 (picks up the fir cone and shows the CHILDREN how the scales go round the fir cone in a spiral, turning the fir cone round with a winding action), 'When the air comes out in bubbles it makes the fir cone spin around.'

GIRL 2E (4:9) (uses a plastic tube to blow into the water), 'Look bubbles.'

NURSERY OFFICER 'What are you putting into the water to make bubbles?... What's coming out of the tube?'

GIRL 2E (4:9) 'Air'.

(Document 421 NS)

Context: the children had been learning about water

We've had the children do a lot of work on the rain and drains and things. As an adult, we could have just said, 'There are no crocodiles down that drain.' But instead you say, 'What makes you think there's crocodiles down the drain? Perhaps there are.' They actually dug a hole in the garden because they were looking for crocodiles but actually, in digging this hole in the garden, they found all sorts of bits of pottery, little pearl buttons, 1901 pennies, and they've been down to the museum. Now that's extending and all because a child said, 'I think there's crocodiles down the drain!'

(421 interview head, para 64)

The analytical process was continued further through theoretical sampling informed by an analysis of the EPPE multi-level outcomes data and the (at that point fully validated) centre quality ratings of the ECERS-R and ECERS-E environmental rating scales. The Pre-Reading and Early Number child outcomes of the full cohort of 141 EPPE settings were found to be positively correlated with the ECERS-E literacy sub-scale ($r=0.17$. $p < 0.05$). Early Number outcomes were also correlated with the ECERS-R interaction sub-scale ($r=0.26$, $p < 0.005$). High scores on the ECERS-R Interaction subscale were also found to be correlated with 'Co-operation and conformity' ($r=0.25$, $p < 0.005$), and 'Independence and concentration' ($r=0.19$, $p < 0.05$). At this point it was possible to develop an explanatory hypothesis regarding the effectiveness of particular practices. Setting 421 (referred to above) was found to have achieved 'excellent' (95 per cent confidence level) practice in terms of the children's developmental progress according to their 'non-verbal' and 'number concepts' assessments. Performance in 'Language' was also found to be good' (above 68 per cent confidence level).

Further analysis soon revealed a general pattern of high cognitive outcomes associated with sustained adult-child verbal interaction along with a paucity of such interactions in those settings achieving less well. In the same way sustained shared thinking (SST) was used as a category in the iterative process of analysing our structured observations. When we analysed the 250+ target child observations (Sylva, 1997) a number of pre-defined categories when 'collapsed' fitted the SST definition, e.g. where adults were observed extending children's thinking and recorded under categories such as adult models or questions. SST thus came to be defined as an effective pedagogic interaction in both the qualitative observations of adults with children and the quantitative, structured observations, of children. We defined this as instances where two or more individuals 'work together' in an intellectual way to solve a problem, clarify a concept, evaluate activities, or extend a narrative. 'Sustained shared thinking' was subsequently found to most commonly occur in 1:1 adult/child interactions.

Face to face interactions with children

The 'excellent' settings were thus found to encourage 'sustained shared thinking', a concept that came to be defined as any episode in which two or more individuals 'worked together' in an intellectual way to solve a problem, clarify a concept, evaluate activities, extend a narrative, etc. To count as sustained shared thinking, both parties had to be contributing to the thinking and it had to be shown to develop and extend thinking. The research found that this did not happen very frequently. In 'excellent' settings there were significantly more 'sustained shared thinking' interactions occurring between staff and children than in the 'good' settings. When it did occur, it extended children's thinking. Our investigations of adult–child interaction suggest that periods of 'sustained shared thinking' are a necessary prerequisite for excellence in early years practice, and it is especially powerful when it is also encouraged in the home by parents.

In the 'excellent' case study settings, the importance of staff members extending child-initiated interactions was also clearly identified. In fact, the target child observation analysis showed that almost half of all of the child-initiated episodes which contained intellectual challenge included interventions from a staff member to extend the child's thinking. The evidence also suggested that adult 'modelling'[1] often combined with sustained periods of shared thinking, and open-ended questioning, was associated with better cognitive achievement. However, open-ended questions were found to make up only 5.1 per cent of the questioning used in the case study settings. This analysis was later extended in a study that showed that out of a total of 5,808 questions recorded, only 5.5 per cent were open-ended questions. The open ended questioning encouraged children to speculate and to learn by trial and error, and it also often provided an initial stimulus for sustained shared thinking. A full account of the analysis and coding of the seven categories of closed questions, and four categories of open-ended questions most commonly asked by early years staff may be found in Siraj-Blatchford and Manni (2008).

In the 'excellent' settings, two-thirds of the activities were found to be child initiated, and about the same proportion of activities were extended by the adults. Half of the child-initiated activities were therefore identified as extended by

---

1   The process where early years educators provide a 'model' in terms of their language, behaviours, skills and/or attitudes for young children to imitate.

the staff. Cognitive challenge was provided by the staff without dominating the activities. The REPEY study found that children in reception classes experienced a different balance of initiation, with a much greater proportion of staff-initiated episodes. In all of the case study settings, children spent most of their time in small groups. But observations show that 'sustained shared thinking' was most likely to occur when children were interacting 1:1 with an adult or with a single peer partner. Freely chosen play activities often provided the best opportunities for adults to extend children's thinking. Adults need, therefore, to create opportunities to extend child-initiated play as well as teacher-initiated group work, as both of these have been found to be important vehicles for promoting learning.

The findings showed that the level 5 qualified staff (almost all trained teachers) provided children with more experience of academic activities (especially language and mathematics) and they encouraged children to engage in activities with higher cognitive challenge. While the most highly qualified staff also provided the most direct teaching (instruction through demonstration, explanation, questioning, modelling, etc.) they were the most effective in their interactions with the children, using the most sustained shared thinking. Furthermore, less well qualified staff were significantly better pedagogues when they worked alongside qualified teachers.

The excellent settings adopted discipline/behaviour policies that involved staff in supporting children in rationalising and talking through their conflicts. In other words, a more problem solving approach was taken. Three settings with very positive social and behavioural outcomes had this practical approach supported by a strong behaviour management policy with which all the staff were familiar. In settings that were less effective in this respect, observations showed that there was often no follow up on children's misbehaviour or conflicts and, on many occasions, children were 'distracted' or simply told to stop.

Planning for learning

The analysis of teacher observations suggested a positive association between curriculum differentiation, formative assessment, the process of selecting activities to provide the optimum cognitive challenge, and sustained 'shared thinking'. The best case study settings kept good records and engaged with parents about their child's progress on a weekly or monthly basis. However, there was little evidence of detailed formative feedback to children during tasks.

The case studies reveal great variation in the conditions and the service provided to children and families. For instance opening times and sessions varied greatly from children attending half-day sessions a few times a week to extended day care and education being provided full time for 48–50 weeks of the year. There was similar variation apparent in the salaries paid to staff. The salary range for the playgroup was under £3,000 to £7,000 per annum; while the maintained sector was £15,000–£32,000 and the private sector £11,000–£24,000. The number of children also tended to vary from 20 or so in playgroup and nursery classes to

100–200 in nursery schools, local authority day care and fully integrated centres. The staff numbers reflect the numbers of children and the extent of the services on offer to families and other early years practitioners, e.g. training support.

Most nursery classes and playgroups are small with two or three members of staff. Most private nurseries are medium sized with 3–8 or more staff, and nursery schools with up to 12 staff. The more complex fully integrated 'combined' and 'early excellence' centres (see Chapter 2) and local authority daycare centres have large numbers of staff due to larger numbers of children on roll and their outreach work to parents, their role as trainers and their dissemination work. For example, in one case study centre, which catered for 200 children and had Early Excellence Centre (EEC) status, the staff total was 55.

EPPE identified good to excellent settings from all types of providers. However, there were many fewer settings whose children had better outcomes amongst playgroups and local authority daycare. Given the variation in staff pay, training and development this isn't really unsurprising. There *is* no level playing field. In spite of this, each of the case study centres was able to portray some (sometimes a good deal of) quality characteristics in terms of ethos:

1 All case study centres had a warm, caring, safe, secure and supportive approach to their children. All the settings engaged children in a range of different groupings, individual and group play, group focused table top activities, interest areas and class snack and story times.

2 All the case study settings appeared very welcoming. The displays on the whole reflected the children's work. The centres were warm and inviting places and the children were generally treated with respect. Staff appeared calm and engaged well with the children. All of these centres had fairly good resources and, although not always ideal, they had sufficient indoor space. However the outdoor play environments varied greatly.

The case studies showed that the practitioners' knowledge and understanding of the particular curriculum area that was being addressed was vital. A good grasp of the appropriate 'pedagogical content knowledge' was found to be a vital component of pedagogy, and just as important in the early years as at any later stage of education. Even in these 'good' and 'effective' settings, there were examples of inadequate knowledge and understanding of curriculum areas, especially in the teaching of phonological skills and science. Educators who demonstrated good 'pedagogical content knowledge' displayed a firm knowledge and understanding of their curriculum content, but crucially, the most 'effective' educators also demonstrated a knowledge and understanding of what part of that content was most significant and relevant to the needs of the children that they were teaching. They were able to draw upon knowledge of the pedagogical strategies found to be most effective in teaching any particular content.

Managing staff

The data reveal that all of the case study pre-school settings had strong leadership and long serving staff. Most of the managers and staff had been in the settings over three years. While we found that there was generally a high turnover of staff in the private sector (Taggart *et al.*, 2000), the private nurseries in the case study sample had stability of staffing with retention between 3–9 years. In the other settings, staff, especially senior management had been in post even longer and 10 to 20 years was not at all uncommon.

All the managers took a strong lead, especially in curriculum and planning. In most of the settings the strong leadership was characterised by a strong philosophy for the setting that was shared by everyone working in the setting. The managers of the excellent centres also had a strong educational focus, valued the importance of adult–child interaction, and supported their staff to develop better ways of engaging children. Further analysis of the case study data has now provided evidence that *contextual literacy*, a commitment to *collaboration* and to the *improvement of children's learning outcomes* may be considered to provide fundamental requirements for *Leadership for Learning* (Siraj-Blatchford and Manni, 2008).

In excellent centres, all the staff were encouraged to attend staff development sessions, although there was a great deal of variation in the training offered and what staff were able to access. Recent developments that have enabled local authorities to offer training to personnel from all the pre-school sectors have shown a positive way forward. However the research indicated that training needed to be more sensitive to the needs of staff from different backgrounds. Discussions with local authority personnel and staff in the case study centres revealed that there were wide variations in training backgrounds. Where there were trained teachers, a stronger educational emphasis was found, with the teachers playing a lead role in curriculum planning and offering positive pedagogical role modelling to less well-qualified staff (see Siraj-Blatchford *et al.*, 2007).

Working with parents

The case studies indicated that where a special relationship in terms of shared educational aims had been developed with parents, and pedagogic efforts were being made by parents at home to support children, sound learning took place even in the absence of consistently good pedagogic practice in the pre-school setting. The excellent settings shared child-related information between parents and staff, and parents were often involved in decision making about their child's learning programme. This level of communication was particularly the case in the private day nurseries. While the settings providing for the needs of children from higher socio-economic groups benefited especially from this, the potential benefit of adopting a combined approach with good pedagogic practice within the setting, and support for the home learning environment, was also clear in more disadvantaged areas.

In more disadvantaged areas, staff in settings had to be proactive in influencing and supporting the home education environment in order to support children's learning. The evidence suggested that the 'excellent' settings in disadvantaged areas recognised the importance of, and made significant efforts to encourage strong parental involvement in the educational process. They made an effort to share their curriculum, pedagogical strategies and educational aims with parents and they offered parents advice on how they could complement this within the home learning environment and explained how this would impact on their child's development.

Summary

In summary, effective pedagogy in the early years was found to involve both the kind of interaction traditionally associated with the term 'teaching', and also the provision of instructive learning environments and routines. The 'excellent' case study settings provided both teacher-initiated group work and freely chosen yet potentially instructive play activities. Children's cognitive outcomes appeared to be directly related to the quantity and quality of the teacher/adult planned and initiated focused group work for supporting children's learning. The research findings supported the general approach taken in Curriculum Guidance for the Foundation Stage (QCA, 2000) and strongly informed the development of the Early Years Foundation Stage (EYFS) in its promotion of 'Sustained Shared Thinking'. The settings that viewed cognitive and social development as complementary managed to achieve the best outcomes for children. Trained teachers were most effective in their interactions with children using the most sustained shared thinking interactions, and less well-qualified staff were better pedagogues when qualified teachers supported them.

The findings showed that good outcomes for children were linked to early years settings that:

- Viewed cognitive and social development of children as complementary and did not prioritise one over the other.
- Had strong leadership and long-serving staff (three years plus, this was the case even in the private daycare settings where the turnover of staff is normally the highest).
- Provided a strong educational focus with trained teachers working alongside and supporting less qualified staff.
- Provided children with a mixture of practitioner initiated group work and learning through freely chosen play.
- Provided adult–child interactions that involve 'sustained shared thinking' and open-ended questioning to extend children's thinking.
- Had practitioners with good curriculum knowledge combined with knowledge and understanding of how young children learn.
- Had strong parental involvement, especially in terms of shared educational aims with parents.

- Provided formative feedback to children during activities and provide regular reporting and discussion with parents about their child's progress.
- Ensured behaviour policies in which staff supported children in rationalising and talking through their conflicts.
- Provided differentiated learning opportunities that met the needs of particular individuals and groups of children, e.g. bilingual, special needs, girls/boys, etc.

Concluding comments

As Oberhuemer (2004) has argued, a special concern in Germany has been that a disproportionate number of students with the lowest level of skills and competence identified by the PISA study were from socially disadvantaged and migrant family backgrounds. The English EYFS initiative was developed to address similar concerns at a young age and, in combination with a range of school initiatives, to improve the outcomes of the most disadvantaged groups. The EPPE 3–11 findings (outlined in Chapter 7) now show that effective pre-school practice has a particularly significant impact on the achievements of disadvantaged children right up to the age of 11 years. It is also notable that the quality of the Home Learning Environment (HLE) in the early years continues to have a strong effect on educational outcomes at age 11. Cross-cultural comparisons of the sort identified at the start of this chapter may be especially misleading when other significant factors are ignored, and one of the most significant of these for the Nordic countries may be the much stronger tradition of pre-primary educational support for children provided by families in the home.

To understand the significance of 'Sustained Shared Thinking' (SST) as a pedagogy for early childhood it is important to recognise that it emerged as an analytic node or 'condensation' symbol in the process of our qualitative research. It was defined in this way because respondents and observers specifically referred to the sharing of thinking, and to the particularly sustained nature of some of the interactions. What is novel and important here is the evidential basis for SST; it is not the concept of SST that should be considered especially original. Arguably, many other researchers engaged in the study of other educational contexts and sectors have adopted similar terms, and describe essentially the same pedagogic practice. The strongest theoretical resonance is with Vygotsky (1978) who described a process where an educator supports children's learning within their 'zone of proximal development'. Interactions of this sort have also been described as 'guided participation' (Rogoff et al., 1993) and as 'scaffolding' (Wood, Bruner and Ross, 1976). 'Participation' and 'interaction' also characterise 'dialogic teaching' (Wells, 1999; Mercer and Littleton, 2007; Alexander, 2008).

These findings have been extremely influential (Siraj-Blatchford et al., 2008). The English EYFS guidance promotes a pedagogy which involves negotiating and co-constructing the curriculum through playful processes of 'sustained shared thinking' (SST) that may be initiated by either the adult or the child. In fact the question of who initiates this SST may be seen as irrelevant as long as both parties are committed to playing an equal part in determining its focus and direction in 'free flow' (i.e. in co-constructing the 'curriculum'). In a sense, 'initiation' is taken in turns as different material and symbolic resources are drawn upon, and each playful learning episode is extended as a more or less unique improvisation. As children develop the capability and are motivated to play with peers, the EYFS guidance encourages practitioners to continue to provide children with a rich range of experiences and resources to draw upon in collaborative play and to support them in developing a greater awareness of their development and learning. Ultimately, children will take pleasure in learning for its own sake and restrict their 'play' to scheduled playtimes, they will engage in more disciplined creative activities, and in a variety of games with rules (Siraj-Blatchford, 2009).

The particularly strong impact of pre-school on young children's language development and their peer sociability (Chapter 6) is an important finding and in pre-school settings that have higher quality and more highly qualified (teacher trained) staff the benefits for children's outcomes are stronger. Our use of a mixed method design (Siraj-Blatchford *et al.*, 2006) with rich qualitative and other case study data has illuminated such relationships through evidence on the way SST fosters children's learning and development.

A good deal of valuable illustrative material has been included in the EYFS practical guidance to show how this sort of progression works in practice. But ultimately the success of the initiative will inevitably depend on the quality of the initial and continuing training of early years educators. They need to develop a deep understanding of the pedagogic principles if they are to develop expertise in applying them in a wider range of collaborative teaching and learning contexts.

References

Alexander, R.J. (2008) *Towards Dialogic Teaching: Rethinking Classroom Talk*, York: Dialogos.

Bennett, J. (2004) Curriculum issues in national policy making. Keynote address to the ECCERA Conference, Malta, September 2, 2004, Paris: Organization for Economic Cooperation and Development.

Bennett, J. (2006) 'Schoolifying' early childhood education and care: accompanying pre-school intoeducation. Public lecture given at the Institute of Education, University of London, 10 May.

Bennett, J. and Tayler, C. (2006) *Starting Strong II: Early Childhood Education and Care*, OECD. Accessed 17.05.09: http://oberon.sourceoecd.org/vl=2049431/cl=33/nw=1/rpsv/~6682/ v2006n9/s1/p1l

Brostrom, S. (2006) Care and education: towards a new paradigm in early childhood education, *Child Youth Care Forum*, 35, 391–409.

Fröbel, F. (1826) *On the Education of Man (Die Menschenerziehung)*, Leipzig: Wienbrach.

Gage, N. (1985) Hard *Gains in the Soft Science: The Case of Pedagogy*, Phi Delta Kappa CEDR Monograph, Bloomington, IN, Indiana.

Mercer, N. and Littleton, K. (2007) *Dialogue and the Development of Children's Thinking: A Sociocultural Approach*, London: Routledge.

Montessori, M. (1909) *The Method of Scientific Pedagogy as Applied to Infant Education in The Children's Houses*, New York: Schocken Books.

Myrdal, A. (1945) *Nation and Family: A Swedish Experiment in Democratic Family and Population Policy*, London: Kegan Paul, Trench and Truber.

New Zealand Ministry of Education (1996) *Te Whāriki : Te Whāriki Matauranga monga Mokopuna o Aotearoa – Early Childhood Curriculum*, Wellington: Learning Media.

Oberhuemer, P. (2004) Controversies, chances and challenges: reflections on the quality debate in Germany, *Early Years*, 24(1), 9–21.

Owen, R. (1824) *An Outline of the System of Education at New Lanark*, Glasgow: Wardlaw & Cunninghame.

QCA/DfEE (2000) *Curriculum Guidance for the Foundation Stage*, London: QCA/DfEE.

Rogoff, B., Mistry, J., Göncü, A., Mosier, C., Chavajay, S. and Heath, B. (1993) Guided participation in cultural activity by toddlers and caregivers, *Monographs of the Society for Research in Child Development*, 58(8).

Sammons, P., Sylva, K., Melhuish, E., Siraj-Blatchford, I., Taggart, B. and Elliot, K. (2002) *The Effective Provision of Pre-School Education (EPPE) Project: Technical Paper 8a – Measuring the Impact of Pre-school on Children's Cognitive Progress*, Institute of Education, London: Institute of Education, University of London.

Sammons, P., Sylva, K., Melhuish, E., Siraj-Blatchford, I., Taggart, B., and Elliot, K. (2003) *The Effective Provision of Pre-School Education (EPPE) Project: Technical Paper 8b – Measuring the Impact of Pre-school on Children's Social/behavioural Development*, London: Institute of Education, University of London.

Sammons, P., Elliot, K., Sylva, K., Melhuish, E., Siraj-Blatchford , I., Taggart, B. and Smees, R. (2004) The impact of pre-school on young children's cognitive attainments at entry to reception, *British Educational Research Journal*, 30(5), 691–712.

Siraj-Blatchford, I. (2009) Conceptualising progression in the pedagogy of play and sustained shared thinking in early childhood education: a Vygotskian perspective, *Educational and Child Psychology*, 26(2), 77–89.

Siraj-Blatchford, I. and Siraj-Blatchford, J. (2001) Content analysis of pedagogy in the QCA/DfEE guidance, *Early Education Journal*, September issue.

Siraj-Blatchford, I. and Sylva, K. (2004) Researching pedagogy in English pre-schools, *British Educational Research Journal*, 30(5), 713–730.

Siraj-Blatchford, I. and Manni, L. (2008) *Effective Leadership in the Early Years Sector*, London: Institute of Education (Bookshop), University of London (Issues in practice series).

Siraj-Blatchford, I., Clarke, K, and Needham, M. (eds) (2007) *The Team Around the Child: Multi-agency Working in the Early Years*, Stoke-on Trent: Trentham Books.

Siraj-Blatchford, I., Sylva, K., Muttock. S., Gilden, R. and Bell, D. (2002) *Researching Effective Pedagogy in the Early Years*, DfES Research Report 365, London: HMSO, Queen's Printer.

Siraj-Blatchford, I., Sammons, P., Sylva, K., Melhuish, E. and Taggart, B. (2006) Educational research and evidence based policy: the mixed nethod approach of the EPPE project, *Evaluation and Research in Education*, 19(2), 63–82.

Siraj-Blatchford, I., Taggart, B., Sylva, K., Sammons, P. and Melhuish, E.C. (2008) Towards the transformation of practice in early childhood education: the effective provision of pre-school education (EPPE) project, *Cambridge Journal of Education*, 38(1), 23–36.

Siraj-Blatchford, I., Sylva, K., Taggart, B., Sammons, P., Melhuish, E.C. and Elliot, K. (2003), *The Effective Provision of Pre-School Education (EPPE) Project: Technical Paper 10 – Intensive Case Studies of Practice across the Foundation Stage*, London: DfES/Institute of Education, University of London.

Socialministeriet (2004) *Lov om ændring af lov om social service. Pædagogiske læreplaner for børn i dagtilbud til børn* (Act on Educational Curricula), København: Socialministeriet.

Strauss, A. (1987) *Qualitative Analysis for Social Scientists*, Cambridge, Cambridge University Press.

Sylva, K. (1997) The target child observation, in K. Sylva and J. Stevenson, *Assessing Children's Social Competence*, Slough: NFER Nelson.

Sylva, K., Melhuish, E., Sammons, P., Siraj-Blatchford, I. and Taggart, B. (1999) *The Effective Provision of Pre-School Education (EPPE) Project: Technical Paper 1 – An Introduction to the EPPE Project*, London: Institute of Education, University of London.

Sylva, K., Siraj-Blatchford, I., Taggart, B., Sammons, P., Melhuish, E., Elliot, K. and Totsika, V. (2006) Capturing quality in early childhood through environmental rating scales, *Early Childhood Research Quarterly, 21(1), 76–92.*

Taggart, B., Sylva, K., Siraj-Blatchford, I., Melhuish, E., Sammons, P. and Walker-Hall, J. (2000) *The Effective Provision of Pre-School Education (EPPE) Project: Technical Paper 5 – Characteristics of the Centres in the EPPE Study: Interviews*, London: Institute of Education, University of London.

Vygotsky, L. (1978) *Mind and Society: The Development of Higher Mental Process*, Cambridge, MA, Harvard University Press.

Wells, G. (1999) *Dialogic Inquiry: Towards a Sociocultural Practice and Theory of Education*, Cambridge: Cambridge University Press.

Wood, D., Bruner, J. and Ross, G. (1976) The role of tutoring in problem solving, *Journal of Child Psychology and Psychiatry*, 17(2), 89–100.

Chapter 9

Vulnerable children

Identifying children 'at risk'

Brenda Taggart

This chapter identifies and describes the characteristics of EPPE children who fall into 'at risk' or 'vulnerable' categories and investigates how pre-school can help ameliorate the adverse impact of disadvantage for such children, and support their development.

This chapter focuses on children who may be seen as 'at risk' because of poor educational or social/behavioural development. We discuss the ways in which we defined 'at risk' and 'vulnerability' for children in study. We describe the characteristics of children who we identified as falling into our definition of 'at risk' and discuss how this informs the notion of 'vulnerability'. We also examine the extent to which we can predict later identification of children with special educational needs (SEN) during Key Stage 1 (KS1) based on our findings. This is important because it may facilitate early identification of need and assist those working in the early years in supporting those most vulnerable groups of children and those at greater risk of poor outcomes.

In addition to presenting findings about the characteristics and consequences of 'vulnerability' and 'at risk' status for children, we also focus on the important question of how far educational provision such as pre-school can help ameliorate disadvantage. We have already discussed the positive impact of pre-school experiences in providing young children with a better start to primary school (Chapter 6) and have shown that such benefits last across Key Stage 2 (Chapter 7). Here we seek to show how pre-school makes a particular difference for vulnerable and at risk groups.

Issues of social inclusion and equity have been key themes throughout the EPPE research. Previous chapters have described the range of children and families included in the study and their differing experiences of early home learning, pre-school quality and academically effective primary schooling. Findings have pointed to the benefits for children of a combination of positive and stimulating early experiences in 'shaping' their later attainment and progress. Chapters 6 and 7 have described in detail the medium and long term benefits of these combinations and how they are important for all children, but particularly so for those coming from more disadvantaged backgrounds. This has important messages for those seeking to narrow the equity 'gap' and promote social inclusion. This focus on social inclusion prompted the research team to consider who are, and what happens to, children who are identified as likely to be at an educational disadvantage.

Educational disadvantage: two perspectives

This chapter reports on educational disadvantage from two different analytical perspectives:

a The research considered educational 'disadvantage' by focusing on children who at a very young age appear to be performing well below that of the majority of children of their age on their general cognitive and social/ behavioural profile. These children were defined as being 'at risk' of developing special educational needs (SEN). The project then explored factors which make children more 'vulnerable' to low attainment or poor social/behavioural development, and investigated what kinds of provision might act as a 'protective' factor and foster better developmental gains for young children while they are at pre-school and so increase the chances that they will move out of their initial 'at risk' status.

A second and alternative method of exploring the factors that either promote or inhibit educational disadvantage was:

b to consider which children, at different time points (age 5 and 10) score below or above their level of 'expected' performance given their background characteristics. This approach enables the factors that enhance the likelihood of over achievement to be contrasted with those that predict poorer outcomes (which we can regard as an indicator of greater 'vulnerability').

This chapter discusses some of the main findings of both of these different investigations (two sub-studies of the main EPPE research programme) and points to factors which can explain and help ameliorate differences in children's achievements and development that are related to their backgrounds.

Children 'at risk' of Special Educational Needs (SEN): background

The Warnock Report (DES, 1978) was the first large-scale investigation into children who need additional support from the educational system in order to achieve their maximum potential. Many, although not all of the recommendations from this comprehensive and land mark enquiry became part of the 1981 Education Act. The main part of the legislation concerned issues of equality, rights, and access to provision for children with both mild and profound learning difficulties. One of the key findings and probably most quoted part of the Warnock report was the acknowledgement that many children, as many as 20 per cent, may experience difficulties with learning at some stage during their school career. It took a broad based view of SEN rather than focusing only on those with the greatest needs. It also set the principle that wherever possible a child's special needs should be met in mainstream school rather than alternative provision (a special school or unit) and enshrined the rights of parents to be part of the decision making process in assessing a child's needs.

This led to the development of the Special Educational Needs Code of Practice on the Identification and Assessment of Special Educational Needs (DfE, 1994), the first national policy document to make clear to Local Authorities (LAs), schools, and parents, a system for allowing children to have a right, and access to additional support. Putting this system into operation proved to be challenging. Integrating pupils with special educational needs (SEN) into mainstream schooling and the development of 'inclusive' practices placed additional demands on both schools and individual teachers.

In 2001 a review of the SEN framework for support led to the issuing of a new statutory guidance booklet, 'Inclusive Schooling – Children with Special Educational Needs' and a revised Code of Practice (DfES, 2001). Unlike the previous Code of Practice the new framework placed more emphasis on early identification and referred specifically to provision in early years (para 1.23 – 1.29). At the same time (four years into the EPPE study) the Department for Education and Skills, subsequently the Department for Children, Schools and Families (DCSF), commissioned the EPPE team to conduct a separate investigation into young children 'at risk' of SEN. The focus of the investigation was to use a range of information to see how far it was possible to identify children with special educational needs (SEN) during the pre-school period in terms of either their cognitive or social/behavioural development, and to investigate links with a variety of child, parent and family characteristics. The investigation also sought to identify variations in the policies and provision offered by different pre-school centres and schools designed to support children with SEN. Some of the main findings of this sub-study are discussed below.

The Early Years Transition and Special Educational Needs (EYTSEN) study

The detailed findings of this aspect of the EPPE programme can be found in three Technical Papers, a DfES Research Report and Research Brief (see Appendix 3).

It was with the historical backdrop referred to above that the EYTSEN study was conducted. The aims of the EYTSEN study were:

1 To examine the impact of pre-school settings on the progress and development of children who may be seen as vulnerable or 'at risk' of developing SEN over the pre-school period and in transition to school until the end of Year 1.
2 To identify the characteristics of those children who are identified as 'at risk' for different measures of cognitive or social/behavioural development.

3 To analyse the distribution of the 'at risk' groups of children across different types of pre-school provider.

4 To analyse patterns of progress and changes in cognitive and social/behavioural development of the various 'at risk' groups across the pre-school period and into KS1, including the extent to which 'at risk' groups are identified as having SEN at primary school.

5 To identify pre-school centres' policies and practice in relation to the early identification of SEN as reported by centre managers.

6 To examine the relationship between pre-school centre quality characteristics and the subsequent progress and development of different 'at risk' groups.

7 To investigate parents' perceptions of whether their child has special educational needs (SEN) and their views and experiences of provision to support their child's needs.

Children 'at risk' of developing SEN

One of the initial challenges of the EYTSEN sub-study was to identify the children from the EPPE sample who were of particular interest to the investigation. This proved to be more complex than might initially be expected because definitions of, and the criteria for, the identification of SEN in very young children is contested. The project recognised that such needs can be viewed as social constructs, and that some aspects of need may be seen at particular points along a developmental continuum. Children's special needs may be perceived differently by parents, pre-school workers, and teachers (Hay *et al.*, 1999; Heiser *et al.*, 2000). At some time points particular children may be identified as giving cause for concern or be seen to show particular 'needs' but not at other time points. Likewise, different adults' understandings or perceptions of SEN can vary and will be affected by experience and training.

Young children develop differently, so changes in status in terms of 'showing' some form of 'need' may be expected to take place between the ages of 3 and 6 years, the period covered in the EYTSEN research (for further discussion of the issues surrounding the identification of special educational needs of young children see Scott and Carran, 1989; Roffey, 1999). Change over time, in children's status, cannot be attributed directly to pre-school or other interventions unless an experimental randomised controlled trial (RCT) is conducted but such studies are not always practical nor ethically desirable. The children in the EYTSEN study were not involved in an experimental RCT but rather represent naturally occurring variation in a sample of children in different types of pre-school provision. In contrast to an experimental design, the EYTSEN analysis provides a more realistic picture of pre-school experience and variation in young children's cognition and social/behavioural development. It therefore provides valuable insights into both the risk and incidence of SEN amongst different groups of young children at different ages. It also provided evidence concerning the nature

Table 9.1 Mean and standard deviation for national and EPPE sample on BAS General Cognitive Abilities (GCA) at age 3+ years

	National mean and standard deviation	EPPE sample mean and standard deviation
General cognitive ability	100.0 (sd=15.0)	91.6 (sd=14.0)
Special non-verbal composite	100.0 (sd=15.0)	93.6 (sd=13.0)

of pre-school provision for SEN and the impact of different types of provision on children thought to be most 'at risk' of SEN.

It should be noted at this point that the children in the EPPE sample came from regular pre-schools, not those designed for young children with multiple and profound medical disabilities. The latter were much more likely to receive support through hospital or specialist clinic facilities.

Rather than choose a narrow definition of formal reported/recorded 'special educational needs'(SEN), which few children at age 3 have, the project chose to concentrate on those children who we deemed as 'at risk' of developing SEN, given their profile at age 3. The identification focused on those children who, from their British Ability Scales (BAS, Elliot *et al.*, 1996) baseline assessment of General Cognitive Ability (GCA) scored one standard deviation below the national average (a score of 85 or below). Using national age standardised scales enabled us to compare the attainments of the EPPE sample with children nationally. The mean GCA for the sample was substantially lower than the national average of 100 (sd=15.0), at 91.6 (sd=14.0). This profile reflects the EPPE study's sampling strategy, which sought to include statistically viable sample sizes for individual pupil groups such as ethnic minorities and those of low socio-economic status, and thus focused on a range of local authority areas (rural, urban, ethnically diverse, shire county, etc.). Overall, approximately one-third (33 per cent) of the EPPE children were one standard deviation below the national average on the GCA scale at age 3+ which is approximately double the proportion expected in national terms.

In addition to making national comparisons, using the mean and standard deviation from our own sample, approximately 16 per cent of the pupils were 1 standard deviation below the EPPE samples average on the GCA scale (a score of 78 or below). Children scoring one standard deviation below for the EPPE sample can thus be seen to provide a tighter (more rigorous) definition of very low cognitive development and possible risk of subsequent identification of special educational needs (SEN) at school. We refer to these children in particular as being at 'strong risk' of developing SEN.

Identifying children 'at risk', *after* age correcting was extremely important, as the effects of age at this stage of children's development are pronounced.[1]

---

1   It should be noted here that 45 pupils did not take the verbal sub-scales due to language difficulties, but were assessed using the two non-verbal scales. A 'Special Non-verbal Composite' (SNC) was created from the two non-verbal scales for these

Table 9.2 Child, parent and home characteristics investigated in relationship to cognitive 'at risk' status

Child variables	Parent variables	Home environment variables
Gender	Mother's highest	Parents' emphasis on home
Ethnic group	qualification level	learning environment
First language	Mother's employment	(total)
Age at entry to pre-school	status	Frequency parent reads
Number of siblings	Mother's age	to child
Prematurity	Social class of father's	Frequency child taken to
	occupation	library
	Father's employment	Frequency child plays with
	status	letters/numbers
	Family average SES	Parents' emphasis on
	Marital status	teaching alphabet/letters
		Parents' emphasis on
		teaching songs/poems/
		nursery rhymes
		Frequency child paints or
		draws
		Frequency child plays with
		friends elsewhere (outside
		home)

What affects a child's 'at risk' SEN status for cognitive development?

We have already discussed the importance of child and family characteristics as influences on both cognitive and social/behavioural development (see Chapter 4). In this chapter we show how such characteristics can help us in the identification of those most 'at risk' defined by poor cognitive attainment at a young age.

Having established which children fell into our 'at risk' category at age 3+ we set out to explore the characteristics of these children and the relationship between various background characteristics and their attainment on the BAS scales. A number of background characteristics at child, family and home level were tested in our statistical models both individually and in combination for their impact on the likelihood of an 'at risk' classification. These variables have since been analysed and found to have predictive validity. The proportions of young children in the 'at risk' group are compared to those of the EPPE sample for each characteristic in turn, as well as the impact of multiple disadvantage (which shall be reported on later). The factors listed below in Table 9.2 were important characteristics in an 'at risk' profile for cognitive development. All of the statistical correlations are reported in full in the EYTSEN Technical Papers (see Appendix 3). Because these factors can be shown to increase the risk of a young child having very low cognitive development, they help us to identify groups who are more

---

children. This particular aspect of the project is reported on extensively in EYTSEN Technical Paper 1 (Sammons *et al.*, 2002b).

vulnerable due to their particular child and family characteristics, and experiences. Table 9.2 lists the characteristics explored in the analyses and below we report on why these characteristics were important.

Child characteristics

Gender

Gender has been identified as a factor that relates to pupil achievement from school entry through to GCSE and A level performance in England, with boys tending to underperform in comparison to girls at most phases. More sophisticated multilevel studies of pupil attainment and progress which control for the impact of other factors have provided more detail about variations in the size of 'gender effects' (e.g. Mortimore *et al.*, 1988; Sammons, 1995; Sammons and Smees, 1998; Tymms, 1999; Strand, 1999). Overall, a significantly higher proportion of boys than girls were identified as 'at risk' in terms of their cognitive attainments at entry to pre-school, although it should be noted that the majority of boys were not 'at risk'.

Ethnic group

Just under three-quarters of the EPPE sample's parents classified their child as of white UK heritage. All the non-white UK ethnic groups had a higher incidence of children included in the cognitive 'at risk' categories than the white UK group. This is likely to reflect both the verbal component of two of the BAS sub-scales (for children for whom English was not their first language), and the higher incidence of socio-economic disadvantage affecting such families. Sammons *et al.* (1999) explored this issue in some detail and found that, when account is taken of the impact of other factors, especially socio-economic status (SES) and parents' educational level, ethnic differences in cognitive attainment at entry to pre-school are reduced. We found that, for our EPPE sample, ethnic differences were not statistically significant in the non-verbal assessments used that were less dependent on language. As noted below, language status rather than ethnic group was a more influential factor.

First language

Proportionately more children who did not have English as their first language were included in each of the 'at risk' groups for cognitive assessments at entry to pre-school. Children who did not have English as their first language were also more likely to be identified as 'at risk' on the non-verbal risk classification. It should be noted that, as a group, children who did not speak English as a first language began pre-school significantly later than children whose first language was English, a factor also found to be related to cognitive development. Such children were also more likely to experience socio-economic disadvantage.

Age at entry to target pre-school

Children at 'strong cognitive risk' were significantly older at entry to the target pre-school than the not 'at risk' group, using groupings based on the internally standardised scores. However, there were no significant differences in age at entry in terms of the national cognitive 'at risk' definition.[2] This suggests that a later start to pre-school may have had a negative impact on cognitive development, possibly because of fewer opportunities to mix with a wider group of children and adults which can be particularly helpful in fostering language development.

Family size

A high proportion of children in each of the cognitive 'at risk' categories came from large families (more than three siblings, i.e. four children including the EPPE sample child). The relationship here is a complex one, as large family size (four or more children) is also strongly related to other characteristics including social class.[3]

Prematurity and low birth weight

Babies born weighing less than 2,500 grams (5lbs 8oz) are defined as low birth weight (Scott and Carran, 1989). In total 73 per cent of babies in our sample who had a low birth weight were reported by parents to have been born premature. Children born prematurely were over-represented in each of the cognitive 'at risk' groups at entry to the pre-school study (age 3+). Children identified as 'at cognitive risk' had significantly lower birth weights than those not identified. There is growing research evidence to suggest that children of lower birth weight tend to have poorer academic outcomes in later life (Richards et al., 2001; Sorenson et al., 1997; Martyn et al., 1996; Breslau, 1995). Scott and Carran (1989) also note that children under the normal birth weight range were more likely to require special education services. Low birth weight has been shown to be associated with mother's age, and educational level and social class.

---

2   The relationship with time spent at the pre-school before recruitment to the EPPE study and children's cognitive scores were also investigated. Partial correlations of age at start of pre-school and the BAS scores, controlling for age at testing, were carried out. The results indicate that children who started at their pre-school centre at an older age had significantly lower cognitive scores ({minus}0.13, $p<0.001$).

3   Children from large families were much more likely to have mothers with no qualifications (33.4 per cent compared to 15.7 per cent for only children and 15.3 per cent for 2–3 children), more likely to have an unemployed father (24.4 per cent compared to 7.8 per cent for only children and 10.0 per cent for 2–3 children), and more likely to have a father in unskilled manual work (4.8 per cent compared to 1.2 per cent for only children and 1.2 per cent for 2–3 children).

Parental characteristics

Mother's highest qualification level

There is strong evidence to suggest a significant link between the mother's educational level and young children's cognitive attainments for the project sample (see Sammons et al., 1999; Melhuish et al., 2001). A significantly large proportion of children in each of the cognitive 'at risk' classifications had mothers who reported they had no educational qualifications (over one-third for those at 'strong cognitive risk').

Mother's employment status

A larger percentage of 'at risk' children, than the overall sample of children, had unemployed mothers, and a lower percentage had mothers working (either part time or full time).

Social class of father's occupation

Much previous research has indicated that measures of parents' social class or occupational status are related to pupils' educational attainments at school (see Mortimore and Blackstone, 1982; Essen and Wedge, 1982). For this sample of pre-school children it can be seen that the father's social class level is associated with low cognitive attainment, with a smaller percentage of the children in the cognitive 'at risk' categories having fathers in the higher occupational groups. A higher proportion of children 'at risk' had fathers doing semi-skilled or unskilled manual work. Also it is notable that proportionately more of the 'at risk' group were recorded as 'father absent'.

Father's employment status

Fewer children at 'cognitive risk' had fathers who were reported to be in full time employment (for example 37.4 per cent of those at 'strong cognitive risk' had fathers in full time work, compared with 52.1 per cent of all children in the EPPE sample), and a somewhat higher proportion, though still a minority, had fathers who were unemployed.

Mother's marital status

Pre-school children living in single parent families were somewhat over represented in the cognitive 'at risk' categories. It should be noted that the factor single parent status is associated with lower levels of mother's qualification and SES. Elsewhere we have shown that single parent status by itself does not have a significant additional impact on attainment, when the influence of other factors, including SES and mother's qualification levels, is taken into account (Sammons et al., 2002a).

Home learning environment (HLE)

Earlier chapters have dealt with the importance of the quality of the HLE. Our analyses of this showed a strong net impact for individual measures related to children's HLE (parents engaging with children in activities to promote learning, i.e. reading to children, visits to libraries, teaching songs and nursery rhymes, etc.) and children's cognitive attainments at entry to pre-school, even after controlling for the influence of parents' SES and mother's educational level (Sammons *et al.*, 1999). The HLE index shows a greater association between cognitive development than family SES or mother's highest qualification level in the pre-school period (Melhuish *et al.*, 2001).

Young children identified as at 'cognitive risk' had significantly lower HLE scores than the sample as a whole. Children with the lowest home learning scores (0–13) were much more likely to be categorised as 'at risk' in terms of their cognitive attainment at entry to pre-school than children with higher scores.

What affects a child's 'at risk' SEN status for social/behavioural development?

Information about EPPE children's social behaviour was obtained at entry to pre-school using the Adaptive Social Behaviour Inventory (see Chapter 3). This is specifically designed to measure social/behavioural skills of pre-school children (Hogan *et al.*, 1992), and consists of 30 items completed by a pre-school centre worker who is familiar with the child (see Melhuish *et al.*, 2001 for more details). Previous analyses of the 30 items identified five underlying dimensions (or factors related to social behaviour): i) Co-operation and Conformity, ii) Peer Sociability, iii) Independence and Concentration, iv) Anti-social, and v) Worried/upset.

Three of these dimensions were examined as likely to be relevant to possible 'at risk' status for later social/behavioural difficulties (and later reduced to two). The Peer Sociability, Anti-social and Worried/upset factor scales were used to classify children who might be viewed as 'at risk'. Peer Sociability was chosen as a factor for special analyses as it is an important element of social development especially in very young children. It is especially important because it may help move children from an egocentric view of the world, held at a particular stage of development, to one that encompasses wider aspects of social adjustment (sharing, empathy, etc.). The Anti-social and Worried/upset scales were found to be fairly closely related and were combined to create a mean score.

Relationships with age were generally very weak for the social/behavioural factors and thus it was not considered necessary to correct for child age in creating the social/behavioural 'at risk' definitions.

Using the criterion of one standard deviation below the mean for the sample as a cut off, 20 per cent (564 children) were identified as 'at risk' on the mean Anti-social/Worried/upset scale, and eighteen per cent on the Peer Sociability scale (502 children). There was limited overlap between these two categories with around one

Table 9.3 Cross-tabulation of social/behavioural development 'at risk' classifications

	Not at risk Anti-social/Worried/upset		At risk Anti social/Worried/upset	
	n	%	n	%
Not 'at risk' Peer sociability	1877	(66.1)	398	(14.0)
'At risk' Peer sociability	462	(16.3)	102	(3.4)

in five (20.4 per cent) of children 'at risk' on the Anti-social/Worried/upset factor also being identified as 'at risk' in terms of poorer Peer Sociability. These represented only a small proportion of the total sample (102 children or 3.4 per cent).

In total, two-thirds (1877 or 66.1 per cent) of children were not identified as exhibiting difficulties in either social/behavioural dimension that might be seen as placing them 'at risk'.

Various characteristics of child, parent and home learning environment (HLE) have been shown to relate to children's social/behavioural development at age 3+ (see Chapter 4). Nonetheless, it must be stressed that relationships were generally very much weaker than in the analyses of cognitive attainment. These aspects were therefore investigated for the EYTSEN study in relation to the classification of children 'at risk' for social/behavioural measures.

Child characteristics

Gender

More boys than girls were identified as showing some behavioural difficulties for both Peer Sociability but not for Anti-social/Worried/upset categories at entry to pre-school study (age 3+ years).

Ethnic group

There are some indications that pre-school workers' assessments of children's social/behavioural development are associated with both ethnic group and language. It must be remembered that pre-school workers' perceptions are subjective and that few pre-school workers at the centres were of ethnic minority origin (see Taggart *et al.*, 2000). Cultural aspects may intervene. For example, slightly more Pakistani and Bangladeshi children were rated in the low scoring group for Peer Sociability; but speaking English as a second language may inhibit very young children's peer interactions at entry to pre-school (such children showed particular gains from attending pre-school which may be linked with English language acquisition). Slightly more children of mixed heritage or of Black Caribbean heritage were given higher scores in terms of the Anti-social/Worried/upset measure. Again it must be stressed that the proportions are low for all ethnic groups and may be confounded with socio-economic and other influences.

First language

Children whose first language was not English were not more likely to be identified as 'at risk' for Anti-social/Worried/upset behaviour but, proportionately, more were in the 'at risk' category for Peer Sociability. This may be related to communication problems where some children are only beginning to learn English.

Number of siblings

'Only children' were identified as more likely to exhibit Anti-social/Worried/upset behaviour, but less likely to show Peer Sociability problems. However, the number of siblings a child has is related to the age the child started at pre-school, with 'only' children starting much earlier than children from larger families ($p=0.12$, $p<0.001$). For example, the average start age for 'only' children is 32.6 months, compared with 38.3 months for children with four siblings.

Prematurity

Significantly higher proportions of premature children were identified 'at risk' for Peer Sociability problems. Children identified as 'at risk' for Peer Sociability were also found to have significantly lower birth weight than those not identified. By contrast, there was no evidence that prematurity or low birth weight was related to 'at risk' for Anti-social/Worried/upset.

Family characteristics

Mother's highest qualification level

There are indications that children whose mothers have no qualifications are over-represented in the group of children identified as 'at risk' in terms of Peer Sociability, while children whose mothers had degrees were somewhat under-represented. However, no significant differences were found for Anti-social/ Worried/upset.

Mother's employment status

As a group children whose mothers work full time start pre-school much earlier than those who do not work (mean age 29.9 months compared with 37.3 months), which may help explain why children with non-working mothers are more likely to be identified as 'at risk' on the Peer Sociability scale.

Social class of father's occupation

In contrast to the findings for cognitive attainment at entry to pre-school, father's occupation showed much weaker associations with social/behavioural development 'at risk' status. Children with absent fathers are slightly over-represented in the Anti-social/Worried/upset risk categories. There were some indications that children whose fathers were in higher SES groups had a slightly lower risk than those in lower social groups for Peer Sociability.

Father's employment status

Children whose fathers were in full time employment were under-represented in the group of children identified as showing poorer Peer Sociability and Anti-social/Worried/upset tendencies. Children whose fathers were not working showed an increased incidence of being 'at risk' for poor Peer Sociability.

Marital status

There were some indications that children whose mothers were never married and were single parents scored more highly in terms of Anti-social/Worried/upset, while those whose parents were married or living with a spouse (the largest group) were slightly under-represented. There were no differences in terms of 'at risk' for Peer Sociability by contrast.

Home learning environment (HLE)

The HLE scale has a positive relationship with Peer Sociability and is associated with less Anti-social/Worried/upset behaviour in analyses for the whole EPPE sample (see Melhuish *et al.*, 2001). Analyses of those classified as 'at risk', likewise indicate a statistically significant association for Peer Sociability.

There were significant differences between children in the highest or lowest categories of the HLE scale in terms of the proportions identified as 'at risk'. For example 15 per cent of those identified 'at risk' for Peer Sociability had the lowest HLE scores (0–13), compared with 9 per cent overall (and only 3.7 per cent of non-identified children). The effect was stronger for Peer Sociability than for Anti-social/Worried/upset. Children whose parents reported at interview that they never play with friends elsewhere were significantly more likely to be found in the 'at risk' classification for Peer Sociability. Children who played 1–2 times a week with friends showed fewer incidences of Peer Sociability problems. Thus a degree of exposure to playing with friends outside the home shows a more desirable impact on Peer Sociability than either higher or lower exposure.

'Multiple disadvantage' and cognitive 'at risk' status at entry to pre-school

There have been several studies that have looked at different classification of educational disadvantage (Sammons *et al.*, 1983; Alberman and Goldstein, 1970). Sammons *et al.* (1983) found that, amongst the Inner London Education

Table 9.4 Multiple disadvantage indicators

Child variables	Disadvantage indicator
First language	English not first language
Large family	Three or more siblings
Prematurity/low birth weight	Premature at birth or below 2,500 grams
Parent variables	
Mother's highest qualification level	No qualifications
Social class of father's occupation	Semi-skilled, unskilled, never worked,
Father's employment status	absent father
Young mother	Not employed
Lone parent	Age 13–17 at birth of EPPE child
Mother's employment status	Single parent
	Unemployed
Home environment variables	
Home Learning Environment (HLE) scale	Bottom quartile

Authority (ILEA) infant pupil (age 5–7) population, only 23 per cent experienced no factors that were classified as statistically significantly related to educational disadvantage, and approximately 25 per cent experienced three or more indicators of disadvantage.[4] In the ILEA study a strong relationship between multiple disadvantage and the number of pupils in the lowest verbal reasoning band was found at age 11 years, suggesting that the effect of disadvantage measures can be cumulative, though not necessarily additive. The analyses of children's outcomes at age 3+ show that 'at risk' children differed from the non 'at risk' group in terms of a number of child, parent and home environment characteristics reported above. Further analyses were conducted to investigate the impact of 'multiple disadvantage'. An index was created based on ten indicators in total: three child variables, six parent variables, and one related to the HLE. All the variables were chosen because they related to low baseline attainment when looked at in isolation (as described above). Where indicators were closely related, such as first language and ethnicity, only the most significant was included.

In all, just under a quarter of the EPPE sample (23.5 per cent) experienced none of the indicators of disadvantage we looked at, while 27 per cent experienced three or more indicators of disadvantage. Only a very small proportion (5.5 per cent) experienced five or more.

Multiple disadvantage shows a strong link with both the cognitive 'at risk' classifications for pre-school children used in the EYSTEN research. Within the groups of children identified as 'at risk' there was a much higher incidence of young children experiencing three or more indicators of disadvantage. For

---

4   The following indicators were used in the data collection in 1981: Eligibility for free school meals, Large families, One parent families, Parental occupation, Behaviour difficulties measured by class teacher, Pupil mobility, Fluency in English, Ethnic family background.

Table 9.5 Multiple disadvantage and percentage of children identified at cognitive risk

Number of factors	All children		Cognitive risk	Strong cognitive risk
	n	%		
0	637	23.5	11.3	7.0
1–2	1345	49.6	43.9	38.1
3–4	575	21.3	34.1	40.0
5+	151	5.5	10.7	15.0

example, using the strong 'cognitive risk' categorisation, within the group of children experiencing no indicators of disadvantage, only around one in twenty (5.2 per cent) were identified as 'at risk'. By contrast, within the group of children experiencing five indicators of disadvantage, nearly half (47.5 per cent) were identified as 'at risk'. This strong association provides pointers that may help our understanding of the factors which may influence the development of later SEN.

Combating disadvantage through pre-school

As EPPE was set up to investigate the impact of pre-school on young children's outcomes, the team were interested in whether or not pre-school could be viewed as a 'protective' factor to ameliorate some of the risk to children of developing SEN due to their background characteristics. Having established that some children were more 'vulnerable' than others, could pre-school help these children and if so what kinds of pre-schools were most likely to 'lift' children out of their SEN 'at risk' status?

In order to establish whether or not pre-school could be viewed as an ameliorating factor we conducted two analyses:

1   Comparing the 'at risk' status of EPPE children at age 3 when they entered pre-school, with their status at age 5 when they entered school. At age 3 a third of the sample showed low cognitive attainment. By entry to school this figure had dropped to a fifth.

2   Comparing the 'at risk' status of EPPE children at entry to school (in reception classes) with those of the 'home' group who had no pre-school experience. Far more of the 'home' group (51 per cent) showed some form of SEN compared to the EPPE sample (around 21 per cent) for cognitive attainment. This included 44 per cent of 'home' children who were 'at risk' for Reading and 37 per cent for Mathematics. In addition, 'home' children were significantly more likely to be identified from teacher assessments as having 'Emotional' and 'Peer' problems at this age. This analysis was after taking account of the higher levels of disadvantage in the 'home' group.

Both of these analyses suggest that pre-school has a very positive impact on young children's cognitive and social/behavioural development and so can be viewed as an effective intervention which can help improve children's development and thus provide more 'vulnerable' children with a better start to primary school (these analyses supplement those on the overall impact of pre-school in Chapters 6 and 7 that also pointed to positive benefits for all children). Here we show particular benefits in the reduction of the proportion classified as 'at risk' at a younger age.

What kinds of pre-school are most likely to move children out of 'at risk'

A detailed analyses of the patterns of movement 'in' and 'out' of risk up to the end of Year 1 (see Sammons et al., 2004) revealed that children who attended integrated centres and nursery school (most commonly referred to now as Children's Centres) were more likely to move children out of 'at risk' status. Children from the integrated centres were also much more likely to move out of 'at risk' status for Pre-reading by the time they started primary school. Children from nursery schools were also more likely to move out of 'at risk' status for Early Number Concepts. By contrast, proportionately more children who attended nursery classes moved into 'at risk' status for GCA, Pre-reading and Early Number Concepts. Children who attended local authority day nurseries showed a greater likelihood of moving into 'at risk' status for Early Number concepts.

Overall more children in all forms of provision tended to move out of than into 'at risk' status for Anti-social/Worried/upset. For Peer Sociability relatively more children in integrated centres, playgroups, and nursery classes moved out of than into 'at risk' status. Moreover, when examining parental views of children's SEN status, those parents whose children had attended pre-school were more likely to recognise when their children were experiencing difficulties (as compared to other children) than the parents of children who had not attended pre-school, see Taggart et al. (2004).

In addition, children who had attended any pre-school were significantly less likely to be reported as having special educational needs (SEN) by teachers (one in four) than the 'home' group (four in ten) during Key Stage 1 (KS1) of primary school (Sammons et al., 2004; Taggart et al., 2006).

These results suggest that certain forms of pre-school provision may be of particular benefit to children aged 3+ who are 'at risk' or more vulnerable in terms of low cognitive attainment and poor social behaviour. Integrated centres and nursery schools show the most positive outcomes for movement out of 'risk' for several measures, especially for cognitive outcomes. Integrated centres, nursery classes and playgroups show most positive movement for the social/behavioural outcome of Peer Sociability (for further details on the impact of pre-school see Sammons et al., 2002a, 2003).

Studying different child trajectories: exploring 'vulnerability' and 'resilience'

Another method of examining educational disadvantage is to consider which children, at different time points (ages 5 and 10) score below or above their level of 'expected' attainment given their background characteristics. Those who do better than expected, if they had experienced adverse background circumstances, have succeeded 'against the odds'. For some they may have done better than expected given many disadvantages and may be seen as especially resilient, but others may have done even better than expected given already favourable circumstances. This approach enables two concepts which we may view as forms of 'resilience' and 'vulnerability' to be investigated in relation to children's attainments in Literacy and Numeracy. These concepts are of interest to those concerned to promote greater equity in education.

The Equalities Review and Promoting Equality in Early Years study

In March 2006 the research team were asked to give a presentation on children's attainment at age 7 to the newly set up Equalities Review team, a group commissioned by the government's Cabinet Office to report on social equality across the life course. Following from this, EPPE was contracted to provide the evidence on early years for the final report, Fairness and Freedom (The Equalities Review, 2007), and also to undertake a separate study to provide an evidential base for practical recommendations that could enhance the life chances and academic success of children who fare poorly at school and are at risk of social exclusion.

The EPPE report Promoting Equality in the Early Years (EPPE Team, 2007) brought together important strands of social inequality relevant to the early years phase of education and focuses specifically on the impact of pre-school and the importance of child, family and home learning environment (HLE) characteristics on children's development during their early years.

Part of this sub-study was to identify differences in children's cognitive and social/behavioural development in order to shed light on why some children and families succeed 'beyond the odds' and how understanding such resilience can lead to improvements in policies and services for young children and their families. The work contained in this report (see Melhuish et. al., 2007) is particularly relevant to this chapter on 'vulnerable' and 'resilient' children.

Developing a definition of 'resilience'

Resilience is a concept which needs to be clearly defined. The definition often adopted is one based upon the absolute level of attainment or development. This is problematic in that children from very disadvantaged backgrounds may show some improvement over others in similar circumstances yet still not attain a high level. In the work conducted for the Equalities Review, the EPPE Team approached resilience by considering the child's attainment in Literacy and Numeracy in terms of whether the child attained above or below 'expectations' given a range of background characteristics (child, family, etc. referred to in previous chapters). In order to establish what is expected for a child, attainment in Literacy and Numeracy is considered as a function of the child's characteristics (birth weight, previous developmental problems, age, gender, FSM), parent and family characteristics (education, SES, income, number of siblings, home language), and pre-school experience. The statistical method used is to establish a multilevel model for each child outcome which we called the demographic model. Variables controlled in the demographic multilevel models were: age, birth weight, developmental problems, English as an additional language (EAL), number of siblings, mother's education, father's education, family SES, household income, eligibility for free school meals (FSM), and time in pre-school.

In these models results vary somewhat from outcome to outcome but the results typically indicate that overall, higher birth weights, educated parents, high incomes and professional households predict higher Literacy and Numeracy scores at ages 5 and 10. On the other hand, having EAL, being eligible for FSM, and experiencing early developmental problems predicts lower test scores. These findings are in line with the work on identifying those 'at risk' described earlier.

For each outcome the models provide a predicted or expected score for a child given the characteristics pertaining to that child. However, children's actual attainment can deviate from that predicted by the demographic model. We considered a child's observed attainment in terms of whether it is above or below the expected score (based on the demographic model).

Where a child's attainment is above the expected, then that child can be regarded as showing positive resilience. Where a child's attainment matches expectation then resilience is typical (in line with those predicted) and where a child's attainment is below that expected they were considered as having negative resilience or were vulnerable. Hence the difference between predicted and observed attainment constitutes children's level of under- and over-attainment in Pre-reading and Numeracy scores, and therefore can be treated as a score of resilience. In other words the resilience score is the degree of deviance from the expected attainment based on the child's demographic and background factors.

This enabled the project to look at particular background characteristics, not already included in the construction of the resilience measure, individually to explore their impact on a child's attainment and whether or not they had any significant effect on children's resilience. Given the findings from the EYTSEN analyses previously reported, there were some key background characteristics which were worthy of further exploration in this alternative analyses.

What might affect resilience?

A wide range of child, family and home learning environment (HLE) characteristics (as previously described) were compared in the models. These included a range of social/behavioural outcomes such as Co-operation and Conformity, Pro-social behaviour and Anti-social/worried and Self-regulation traits, etc. These are often referred to as a measure of children's personal resources (non-cognitive) or 'soft' skills. There were only four factors in these analyses that showed statistically significant relationships and were therefore likely to exert a stronger influence on a child's resilience. The items were gender, the HLE, Self-regulation and ethnicity. Figures 9.1 and 9.2 below show these additional influences on Literacy and Numeracy alongside of ethnicity for comparison (at different time points).

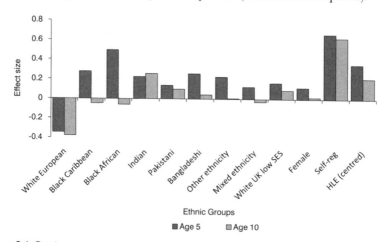

Figure 9.1 Predicting resilience in Literacy at 5 and 10 years

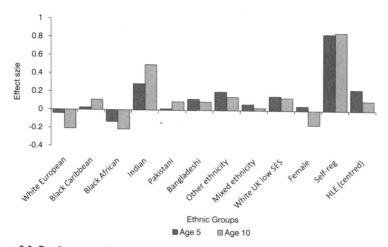

Figure 9.2 Predicting resilience in Numeracy at 5 and 10 years

Self-regulation

The strongest effect on children's resilience is their level of prior Self-regulation ('Independence and Concentration') measured at the start of school. This measure is based upon the ratings (1–5 scale) of the teacher most familiar with the child, on how the following items apply to the child:

- thinks things out before acting;
- not easily distracted;
- can move to new activity upon completion of task;
- can independently select and return equipment;
- does not fidget or squirm about;
- perseveres in face of difficulty;
- likes to work things out for self;
- not restless;
- sees task through to end.

The factors which predict the child's level of Self-regulation at the start of school are reported in full in Sammons *et al.* (2003). To summarise, being female, having parents with higher education levels and income, a more stimulating HLE, higher quality and longer duration of pre-school were all associated with increases in Self-regulation. Conversely, lower birth weights, eligibility for FSM, developmental and behavioural problems were all associated with decreases in Self-regulation.

Gender

Girls show more resilience in Literacy at ages 5 and 10, although the effect is stronger at age 5. For Numeracy there is barely a perceptible advantage for girls at age 5 and this has changed to an advantage for boys at age 10.

Home learning environment (HLE)

The HLE also has a strong, independent effect on resilience at ages 5 and 10, with higher early years HLE being associated with higher resilience; the effects being strongest at age 5 and also stronger for Literacy than Numeracy.

Ethnic group and other associations

Having established the contribution of ethnicity, gender, Self-regulation and the early years HLE to resilience, the research went on to investigate if the outcomes for gender, Self-regulation and the early years HLE differed by ethnicity. This possibility was examined by constructing multilevel models of resilience that included interaction terms for.

- ethnic group by Self-regulation;
- ethnic group by early years;
- ethnic group by gender.

The results of these analyses revealed that the effect of Self-regulation on resilience does not vary by ethnic group. Rather, across all ethnic groups, Self-regulation is strongly associated with resilient (better than expected) attainment in Literacy and Numeracy at ages 5 and 10. However, there are ethnic group differences in the effect of early years HLE and gender on resilience at ages 5 and 10.

Ethnic group and home learning environment (HLE)

At age 5 there are a few instances where the HLE is associated with a negative effect upon resilience. These are for White Europeans for Literacy, Black Caribbean and Pakistani children for Numeracy, and these negative effects are all small. Otherwise the effects of HLE upon resilience are positive and often large.

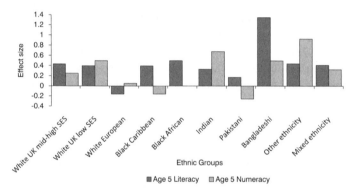

Figure 9.3 The effects of HLE on age 5 Literacy and Numeracy resilience by ethnic group

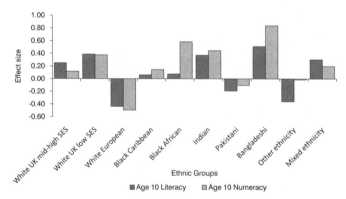

Figure 9.4 The effects of HLE on age 10 Literacy and Numeracy resilience by ethnic group

In the case of Bangladeshi children the effects are very large indeed. For most minority ethnic groups the effects of HLE is as large as or greater than the effect for the White UK group.

At age 10 the White European group is atypical in that HLE has a moderately large negative association with resilience for Literacy or Numeracy. There are negative effects for the Pakistani group but they are small and the 'Other ethnic minority' group also shows a negative effect for HLE on Literacy only. In all other cases the effects are positive and also for several groups the effects are larger than for the White UK group (Bangladeshi and Indian overall, and Black African for Numeracy).

The findings that the impact of early years HLE upon resilience is often greater for minority ethnic groups (despite sometimes lower overall level of HLE) than for the White UK group indicates that the HLE is a useful measure for understanding differences in the academic performance of children across most if not all ethnic groups.

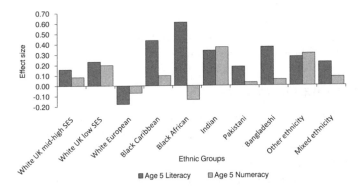

Figure 9.5 The effect of being female (over male) on resilience in Literacy and Numeracy at age 5

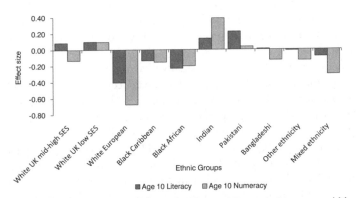

Figure 9.6 The effect of being female (over male) on resilience in Literacy and Numeracy at age 10

Ethnic group and gender

The analyses for gender by ethnic group interactions reveal that the consequences of being female (as opposed to male) also vary by ethnic group.

At age 5, girls have an advantage in Literacy over boys, a pattern that cuts across ethnic groups (to varying degrees). The exception is the White European group, for whom being a girl predicts worse attainment over boys (compared to White UK middle–high SES). Among Black Caribbean and African groups, being a girl quite strongly predicts 'over-attainment' in Literacy at age 5.

For all other ethnic groups, with the exception of White Europeans and Black Africans (in Numeracy), being female has a weak to moderate positive effect on resilience at age 5. By age 10, the pattern is reversed – being a girl no longer has positive effects except for Indian and Pakistani groups where the positive effect is weak. In fact, being a girl predicts worse attainment than expected, particularly for White European groups. These results suggest that something is occurring differentially for girls and boys by Year 5 of primary school that causes girls' early advantage over boys to disappear and even reverse, after accounting for all other factors such as demographics, HLE, and Self-regulation. Such changes result in boys catching up somewhat with girls in their Literacy related abilities and making more gains in Numeracy in most groups.

Concluding comments

This chapter throws some light on the characteristics of children who are likely to be most 'at risk' of developing SEN and illustrates that pre-school can help to reduce this risk. We also show how different background characteristics influence various child outcomes at differing time points. Our results enable us to examine concepts of 'risk', 'resilience' (those who do better than predicted, succeeding against the odds) and 'vulnerability'. It has highlighted the way child, family and home learning environment (HLE) characteristics may lead some children to have lower attainment or poorer social/behavioural development in the pre-school period and beyond, so helping us to understand the components of educational disadvantage that makes certain groups of children developmentally vulnerable.

No one definition of educational disadvantage or vulnerability can provide a complete picture but our data suggest that the concept of multiple disadvantage is an important one. Our results indicate that pre-school, especially high quality pre-school, can reduce the proportion of children identified as 'at risk' in terms of very low cognitive scores and so reduce the likelihood of later identification of SEN during Key Stage 1 (KS1). It also highlights the enduring impact of pre-school on children's later SEN status, with children who had attended pre-school being less likely to be reported as having SEN by teachers (one in four) than the 'home' group (four in ten) during KS1 of primary school (Sammons et al., 2004; Taggart et al., 2006).

There is considerable interest in policy developments that seek to 'narrow the gap' of academic achievement between the most advantaged and least advantaged children, and young people at all stages in education from pre-school to higher education. The range of analyses we have conducted enables researchers and policy makers to consider educational disadvantage from a number of perspectives. Having said this, there are some important consistent messages which cut across results.

There are particular child, family and HLE characteristics which are associated with and help predict more or less favourable outcomes, both individually and in combination, and these can make an important difference to a learner's trajectory. Targeted policies which seek to improve these in the short term (e.g. interventions to improve the home learning environment) and long term (e.g. increasing mothers' qualifications) will help to narrow the achievement gap. It is particularly important that children who experience 'multiple disadvantage' have access to early intervention services. Attendance at pre-school maximises the chances of early identification. Not only were children who attended pre-school more likely to have their early needs attended to by a professional but the EYTSEN finding that mothers whose children attend pre-school were more likely to recognise when their children were beginning to fall behind (Taggart *et al.*, 2004) is important. Providing support for families, especially in settings which provide health and parenting support can make very big differences to children's development.

Good quality pre-school can help to improve the long-term life changes of young vulnerable children and prevent the need for more costly interventions later in a child's life. We should not lower our expectations for such groups however, as we know that outcomes can change over time and by studying 'risk' and 'resilience' and the links with background and educational experiences we may be able to support children who are most vulnerable.

As children get older the factors which influence academic disadvantage exert different influences and these need to be borne in mind, especially when considering effects for different groups of children (ethnic group, gender, etc.). Nonetheless, one message is clear: good early experiences lay the foundation for children to thrive and help develop their potential by ameliorating the impact of social circumstances.

References

Alberman, E.D. and Goldstein, H. (1970) The 'at risk' register: a statistical evaluation, *British Journal of Preventative and Social Medicine*, 24, 123–125.

Breslau, N. (1995) Psychiatric sequelae of low birth weight, *Epidemiological Review*, 17, 96–106.

DES (1978) *Special Educational Needs: Report of the Committee of Enquiry into the Education of Handicapped Children and Young People* (Chair, M. Warnock), London: HMSO.

DfE (1994) *Code of Practice on the Identification and Assessment of Special Educational Needs*, London, Department for Education.

DfES (2001) *Special Educational Needs: Code of Practice*, London: DfES.

Elliot, C., Smith, P. and McCulloch, K. (1996) *British Ability Scales, Second Edition (BAS II)*. Windsor: NFER-Nelson Publishing Company Limited.

EPPE (Effective Pre-school and Primary Education 3–11) Team (2007) *Promoting Equality in the Early Years: Report to The Equalities Review*, London: DCSF, http://www.equalitiesreview. org.uk.

The Equalities Review (2007) *Fairness and Freedom: The Final Report of the Equalities Review*. London: HMSO. http://www.theequalitiesreview.org.uk/upload/assets/www.theequalitiesreview.org. uk/equalityreview.pdf

Essen, J. and Wedge, P. (1982) *Continuities in Childhood Disadvantage*, London: Heinemann.

Hay, D., Pawlby, S., Sharp, D., Schmucker, G., Mills, A., Allen, H. and Kumar, R. (1999) Parents' judgements about young children's problems: why mothers and fathers might disagree yet still predict later outcomes, *Journal of Child Psychology and Psychiatry*, 40(8), 1249–1258.

Heiser, A., Curcin, O., Luhr, C., Metze, B. and Obladen, M. (2000) Parental and professional agreement in developmental assessment of very-low-birthweight and term infants, *Developmental Medicine and Child Neurology*, 42, 21–24.

Hogan, A.E., Scott, K.G. and Bauer, C.R. (1992) The adaptive social behaviour inventory (ASBI): a new assessment of social competence in high risk three year olds, *Journal of Psychoeducational Assessments*, 10(3), 230–239.

Martyn, C.N., Gale, C.R., Sayer, A.A. and Fall, C. (1996) Growth in utero and cognitive function in adult life: follow up study of people born between 1920 and 1943, *British Medical Journal*, 312, 1393–1396.

Melhuish, E.C., Sylva, K., Sammons, P., Siraj-Blatchford, I. and Taggart, B. (2001) *The Effective Provision of Pre-School Education (EPPE) Project: Technical Paper 7 – Social/Behavioural and Cognitive Development at 3–4 Years in Relation to Family Background*. London: DfEE/ Institute of Education, University of London.

Melhuish, E., Sylva, K., Sammons, P., Siraj-Blatchford, I., Taggart, B. and Phan, M. (2007) *The HLE, Attainment and Resilience in The Equalities Review (2007) The Final Report of the Equalities Review*, London: HMSO. http://archive.cabinetoffice.gov.uk/equalitiesreview/ upload/assets/www.theequalitiesreview.org.uk/equality_review.pdf, pp. 63–8

Mortimore, J. and Blackstone, T. (1982) *Disadvantage and Education*, London: Heinemann.

Mortimore, P., Sammons, P., Stoll, L., Lewis, D. and Ecob, R. (1988) *School Matters: The Junior Years*, London: Open Books (republished by Paul Chapman, 1994).

Richards, M., Hardy, R., Kuh, D. and Wadsworth, J. (2001) Birth weight and cognitive function in British 1946 birth cohort: longitudinal population based study, *British Medical Journal*, 322, 199–203.

Roffey, S. (1999) *Special Needs in the Early Years: Collaboration, Communication and Co-ordination*, David Fulton: London.

Sammons, P. (1995) Gender, ethnic and socio-economic differences in attainment and progress: a longitudinal analysis of student achievement over nine years, *British Educational Research Journal*, 21(4), 465–85.

Sammons, P. and Smees, R. (1998) Measuring pupil progress at Key Stage 1, *School Leadership and Management*, 18(3), 389–407.

Sammons, P., Kysel, F. and Mortimore, P. (1983) Educational priority indices: a new perspective, *British Educational Research Journal*, 9(1), 27–40.

Sammons, P., Sylva, K., Melhuish, E.C., Siraj-Blatchford, I., Taggart, B. and Elliot, K. (2002a) *The Effective Provision of Pre-School Education (EPPE) Project: Technical Paper 8a – Measuring the Impact of Pre-School on Children's Cognitive Progress over the Pre-School Period*, London: DfES/Institute of Education, University of London.

Sammons, P., Smees, R., Taggart, B., Sylva, K., Melhuish, E.C., Siraj-Blatchford, I. and Elliot, K. (2002b) *The Early Years Transitions and Special Educational Needs (EYTSEN) Project: Technical Paper 1 – Special Educational Needs Across the Pre-School Period*, London: DfES/Institute of Education, University of London.

Sammons, P., Sylva, K., Melhuish, E.C., Siraj-Blatchford, I., Taggart, B. and Elliot, K. (2003) *The Effective Provision of Pre-School Education (EPPE) Project: Technical Paper 8b – Measuring the Impact of Pre-School on Children's Social/Behavioural Development over the Pre-School Period*, London: DfES/Institute of Education, University of London.

Sammons, P., Smees, R., Taggart, B., Sylva, K., Melhuish, E.C., Siraj-Blatchford, I. and Elliot, K. (2004) *The Early Years Transitions and Special Educational Needs (EYTSEN) Project: Technical Paper 2 – Special Educational Needs in the Early Primary Years: Primary School Entry Up to the End of Year 1*, London: DfES / Institute of Education, University of London.

Sammons, P., Sylva, K., Melhuish, E.C., Siraj-Blatchford, I., Taggart, B., Smees, R., Dobson, A., Jeavons, M., Lewis, K., Morahan, M. and Sadler, S. (1999) *The Effective Provision of Pre-School Education (EPPE) Project: Technical Paper 2 – Characteristics of the Effective Provision of Pre-School (EPPE) Project Sample at Entry to the Study*, London: DfEE/Institute of Education, University of London.

Scott, K. and Carran, D. (1989) Identification and referral of handicapped infants, in *Handbook of Special Education Research and Practice: Low Incidence Conditions (Vol.3)* (eds M. C. Wang, M.C. Reynolds and H.J. Walberg), Oxford, England: Pergamon Press, pp. 227–241.

Sorenson, H.T., Sabroe, S., Olsen, J., Rothman, K.J., Gilman, M.W. and Fisher, P. (1997) Birth weight and cognitive function in adult life: historical cohort study, *British Medical Journal*, 315, 401–403.

Strand, S. (1999) Ethnic group, sex and economic disadvantage: associations with pupils' educational progress from baseline to the end of Key Stage 1, *British Educational Research Journal*, 25(2), 179–202.

Taggart, B., Sylva, K., Siraj-Blatchford, I., Melhuish, E.C., Sammons, P. and Walker-Hall, J. (2000), *The Effective Provision of Pre-School Education (EPPE) Project: Technical Paper 5 – Characteristics of the Centres in the EPPE Sample: Interviews*, London: DfEE/Institute of Education, University of London.

Taggart, B., Sammons, P., Smees, R., Sylva, K., Melhuish, E. and Siraj-Blatchford, I. (2006) Early identification of special educational needs and the definition of 'at risk': The Early Years Transition and Special Educational Needs (EYTSEN) Project, *British Journal of Special Education*, 33(1), 40–45.

Taggart, B., Sammons, P., Smees, R., Sylva, K., Melhuish, E.C., Siraj-Blatchford, I. and Elliot, K. (2004) *The Early Years Transitions and Special Educational Needs (EYTSEN) Project: Technical Paper 3 – Special Educational Needs in the Early Years: The Parents' Perspective*, London: DfES/Institute of Education, University of London.

Tymms, P.B. (1999) *Baselines Assessment and Monitoring in Primary Schools: Achievements, Attitudes and Value-Added Indicators*, London: David Fulton.

Chapter 10

A linked study
Effective pre-school provision in Northern Ireland

Edward Melhuish

The EPPNI study used a comparable design to the original EPPE research and thus replicates aspects of EPPE in a different context in the UK: Northern Ireland. This chapter makes comparisons between the findings of research on the impact of pre-school in two different contexts and examines the implications for early years practices.

Background

Following discussions with the EPPE team the Department of Education in Northern Ireland (DENI) became interested in supporting a similar study in Northern Ireland. Hence they funded the Effective Pre-school Provision in Northern Ireland (EPPNI) project to start in 1998, a year after EPPE was set up. In Northern Ireland at that time there were six types of pre-school setting that 3 and 4 year old children might attend. Four of these, playgroups, private day nurseries, nursery schools and nursery classes, were structurally rather similar to pre-school centres of the same type in England. However, in Northern Ireland in remote rural areas where the population was not great enough to sustain the usual type of pre-school centre, 3 and 4 year old children might also be enrolled into the same settings as reception age children in primary schools. In some cases where there were few 3 and 4 year olds the children were mixed into the 'reception class', but where there were a greater number (usually 8 or more) of 3 and 4 year olds they might be grouped into a 'reception group' and separated from the rest of 5 year olds. In the EPPNI study, all types of pre-school centre in Northern Ireland were included in the study. However, in order to simplify sampling, the nursery schools and nursery classes were treated as one type. Thus there were 5 pre-school types in the EPPNI sample: nursery schools/classes, playgroups, private day nurseries, reception classes and reception groups.

As with the EPPE study in England, the EPPNI study took account of pre-existing differences between children and their families at the start of the pre-school period in order to understand the possible effects of pre-school experience upon children's development. Information on the characteristics of the parents, families, and children was collected by parental interview at the start of the study, including data on parents' labour market participation, socio-economic characteristics,

Table 10.1 Pre-school types

Type	Number of centres	Number of children recruited
Nursery schools/classes	16	189 (22.5%)
Playgroups	15	157 (18.8%)
Private day nurseries	19	118 (14.1%)
Reception classes	9	103 (12.3%)
Reception groups	21	118 (14.1%)
Home		152 (18.2%)

qualifications, marital status and age as well as the family's composition, ethnicity and language, the child's health, development and behaviour, the child's activities in the home, the use of pre-school provision and childcare history.

The EPPNI study and sample

As with the EPPE study in England, the EPPNI research in Northern Ireland was designed to enable the linking of three sets of data: (1) information about children's attainment and development (at different points in time); (2) information about parents and the home, and (3) information about pre-school experiences (type of centre and its characteristics). The EPPNI study included 685 children from 80 pre-school settings as well as 152 children without pre-school centre experience (the home group). Pre-school centres were randomly chosen from the five Education and Library Board areas in Northern Ireland. Children and their families were selected randomly in each centre to participate in the EPPNI Project. In order to examine the impact of no pre-school provision, an additional sample of 152 children with no pre-school experience were recruited from the Year 1 classes which EPPNI children entered. All parents gave written informed consent for their children to participate. Table 10.1 below shows the composition of the EPPNI sample.

Table 10.1 shows the recruitment from different types of pre-school provision.

How do the pre-school groups compare?

The different types of pre-school group varied extensively in relation to parental socio-economic and educational status. Socio-economic advantage of the different groups in the study can be illustrated by considering mothers' educational qualifications, which shows a similar pattern across groups as other socio-economic indicators. The classification of mother's educational qualifications by pre-school types within the EPPNI sample is shown in Table 10.2.

As results for EPPE in England (see Chapter 4) the private day nursery group has a much higher percentage of mothers with a degree or higher qualification, reflecting their relative advantage. Similarly the relative disadvantage of the

Table 10.2 Educational qualifications of mother by pre-school type (% within each type)

Educational qualifications	Nursery school/class	Playgroup	Private day nursery	Reception class	Reception group	'Home' group
Degree or higher	15.5	21.0	49.5	13.9	14.1	10.6
HND, 18+ Vocational	11.2	13.4	11.1	19.8	12.3	13.9
A level	10.2	9.0	13.7	5.9	9.6	7.3
GCSE	38.0	35.0	22.2	32.7	37.7	25.8
Less than GCSE	25.1	21.6	3.5	27.7	26.3	42.4

'home' group is also clear with more mothers in this group having less than a GCSE qualification. The differences between the other four groups are not so great. Similar patterns of differences in the characteristics of children in different pre-school types are reflected in other educational and socio-economic variables.

What background variables relate to child development at the start of the study?

The personal, social and family characteristics of a child can influence their progress and development. Thus it is essential to establish the extent to which the background characteristics of children attending different centres and types of pre-school provision vary, as this study has done. Hence EPPNI can identify any possible pre-school effects on children's later educational outcomes, separately from other factors. When the children entered the EPPNI study they were assessed on cognitive and social/behavioural development. These data, together with data from the parental interview, were used to investigate social/behavioural and cognitive development at 3–4 years in relation to a range of parental, family, child, home and childcare factors. The explanation for cognitive development in the analyses is strong (i.e. it explains a large amount of variance in children's scores) whereas the explanation of social/behavioural development leaves much of the variation between children unexplained. This may be explained in part by the fact that the social-behavioural measures were completed by more than 100 practitioners using a coarse rating scale; whereas the cognitive and linguistic measures were administered 1:1 by a small team of highly trained researchers conforming to standardised testing procedures. It seems likely that variation in the sophistication and reliability of measurement available for the two aspects of development led to the cognitive analyses being stronger. However, it is also likely that children's social behaviour may be less influenced by background factors than cognitive outcomes. The findings at the start of the study can be summarised as follows:

Child

- Gender had a significant effect on cooperation/conformity and cognitive development; girls scored higher than boys on both.
- Children with previous behaviour problems were more likely to have lower cognitive development scores. Behaviour problems were also significantly associated with cooperation/conformity, peer sociability and anti-social behaviour. This indicates that early behaviour problems observed at home continue into the pre-school setting.

Parents and socio-economic factors

- Mother's qualifications were significantly related to peer sociability and worried/upset behaviour. Children whose mothers had attained a high qualification were rated higher on these variables.
- For cognitive development higher parental socio-economic status and higher mother's qualifications were both associated with higher cognitive scores for children.

Family

- Children with three or more siblings scored lower on cognitive development. Larger families may result in less parent attention being available for any individual child. This decreased individual attention from parents may be the reason for the effects on cognitive development.

Home

- Those children who had more experience of playing with friends at home showed higher cooperation/conformity and confidence.
- The variables, whether the child had a regular bedtime and rules concerning TV and video, could be regarded as a marker for the degree of structure in the child's home life. These variables were associated with increased confidence. A regular bedtime was also slightly associated with worried/upset behaviour.
- A higher home learning environment was associated with higher cognitive scores and this effect on cognitive development was particularly pronounced. After age, it was one of the variables with the strongest effect on cognitive development. Its effect was stronger than either social class or parental education, which have often been found to be amongst the strongest predictors of children's cognitive development in previous studies.
- The importance of the home learning environment indicates that what parents do (i.e. with children at home) is more important than who parents

are (i.e. demographic status) in regard to fostering children's cognitive development.

Early childcare history

- Being in group childcare (e.g. nurseries) before entering the study was slightly associated with increased anti-social and worried/upset behaviour.
- Those children who had attended the pre-school centre for longer periods before the start of the study scored higher on cognitive development. These children were primarily in private day nurseries.

The quality of pre-school centres in Northern Ireland in EPPNI

As with the EPPE study, information about the pre-school centres was collected through two methods. Interviews were conducted with all centre managers, and systematic observations, supplemented by interviews were used to provide profiles of the experience and activities (ECERS-R, ECERS-E and CIS) provided by the pre-school centres to the children in their care.

Average scores across the 80 centres in the sample approached 'good' on the ECERS-R but the ECERS-E ratings showed that the learning opportunities in maths and science were often limited and even inadequate. However, overall scores on the ECERS-R suggest that the quality of much provision in Northern Ireland is similar to that in other industrialised countries.

These results reflect the quality of pre-school centres based upon observations that relate to 'expert opinion' of good practice with pre-school children. While pre-school centres in Northern Ireland are doing quite well overall on ECERS-R, there are big variations between individual centres, with some doing rather poorly. Most sub-scales of ECERS-R show fair to good scores when averaged across all types of provision. However closer inspection within types of provision reveals some differences. Many centres were exciting places where children were challenged and supported in their learning and with sensitive, responsive interactions between staff and children. Unfortunately, other centres were characterised by hasty planning and poor implementation of the curriculum. The sub-scale 'pre-school activities' tended to show the lowest scores. This indicates that differentiated pre-school curriculum activities such as fine motor activities, art, music, movement, sand/water, nature activities, etc., have scope for improvement in pre-school centres in Northern Ireland.

The scores for the sub-scales of ECERS-R and ECERS-E for the EPPNI pre-schools differ markedly as shown in Fig. 10.1. It is clear that while EPPNI pre-schools are doing quite well on ECERS-R, they are scoring poorly on ECERS-E, which may be related to ECERS-E being based on the English Desirable Learning outcomes, which are not applied in Northern Ireland. However, the scores on the ECERS-E were lower generally than the ECER-R in England as well.

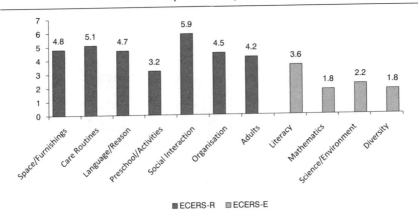

Figure 10.1 Sub-scale scores for ECERS-R and ECERS-E for pre-schools in EPPNI

There is less variation between types of centre in Northern Ireland than in England on ECERS-R. Overall nursery schools/classes score higher than other types of pre-school provision on ECERS-R with minor differences between the other types of provision. On ECERS-E the 'education sector' pre-school provision score higher reflecting their educational orientation, but all types of provision in Northern Ireland score poorly on ECERS-E. Pre-school centres in Northern Ireland score slightly higher overall than comparable centres in England on ECERS-R. This is due to the playgroups and the private day nurseries, but particularly the playgroups, scoring more highly on ECERS-R than in England. In contrast to the ratings on ECERS-R, the ECERS-E ratings reveal that the Northern Ireland centres do not score as highly as those in England on mathematics, science/environment and diversity. The differences by type of pre-school and the large differences between scores for ECERS-R and ECERS-E in Northern Ireland are illustrated in Figure 10.2.

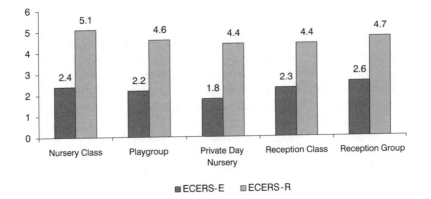

Figure 10.2 ECERS-R and ECERS-E scores by type of pre-school

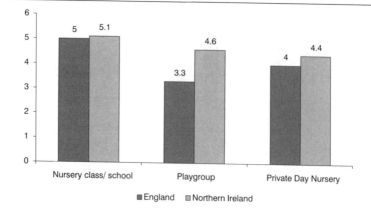

Figure 10.3 ECERS-R by type of centre in England and Northern Ireland

A comparison can be made for ECERS-R scores for Northern Ireland and England for types of centre in common in the EPPNI and EPPE studies. The differences between the countries can be examined by the type of pre-school as in Figure 10.3. In looking at the separate types of pre-school, the reasons for the differences in ECERS-R total scores can be seen clearly. The overall higher scores in Northern Ireland are due to the higher scores of playgroups and private day nurseries in Northern Ireland, whereas nursery classes/schools score almost exactly equivalently in the two countries. It is clear that on every ECERS-R sub-scale, playgroups in Northern Ireland score higher than playgroups in England. When private day nurseries in Northern Ireland are compared with those in England, they score higher on 'personal care routines', 'social interaction' and 'parents and staff', but lower on 'pre-school activities'. Nursery classes/schools in Northern Ireland score higher on 'personal care routines', but lower on 'pre-school activities' and 'parents and staff'.

Inspection of staff training differences between Northern Ireland and England revealed that the level of staff training in playgroups in Northern Ireland was substantially higher than that for staff in playgroups in the EPPE study in England. It seems likely that the higher observed quality ratings for ECERS-R in Northern Ireland as compared with England is related to the higher levels of staff training in Northern Ireland playgroups, while the lower scores on the ECERS-E may reflect differences in curriculum aims and provision between England and Northern Ireland or the lack of early education provision. The ECER-E was largely based on the emerging pre-school curriculum for England, which was more academically orientated than that of Northern Ireland. Hence the low scores on ECERS-E in Northern Ireland may reflect differences in curriculum emphasis.

The EPPNI findings on child development

Between 1998 and 2006 the EPPNI project had recruited its sample of 837 families and children, constructed developmental trajectories for children 3 and 8 years of age, and described the pre-school characteristics associated with children making a better start to primary school. This large-scale longitudinal study involved 80 pre-school centres and the research team collected and analysed very large amounts of data using diverse methodologies. The findings can be summarised as shown below.

Major findings at entry to school

Impact of attending any form of pre-school setting

Pre-school experience, compared to none, enhances children's development.

Having allowed for any differences in background factors that might affect development, 'home' children (those who had little or no pre-school experience) show poorer cognitive and social/behavioural outcomes at entry to school and at the end of Year 1 than those who attended pre-school. Also they are more likely to be identified as having some form of SEN.

Type of pre-school provision

The EPPNI project has compared children from each of the types of pre-school provision with children with very little or no pre-school centre experience (home group). In these comparisons a wide range of child, parent, socio-economic, home, family and early childcare variables have been included in analyses so that comparisons take place on a fair basis, i.e. 'a level playing field'. At the start of primary school, children from nursery school/classes showed the most benefit for cognitive development and children from reception groups showed no cognitive advantage over the home group. For social development children from playgroups showed the most advantage with all pre-school groups showing some advantage. A summary of overall benefits for the different pre-school groups compared with the home group is shown for cognitive and social development outcomes in Table 10.3.

Table 10.3 Overall developmental benefits associated with pre-school type at the start of primary school as compared with children with no pre-school experience

Developmental benefit	Nursery school/ class	Playgroup	Private day nursery	Reception class	Reception group
Cognitive development	3	1	2	2	0
Social development	1	3	1	1	2

Full-time versus part-time pre-school

At every stage of the study the possibility that there would be differences associated with full-time versus part-time attendance at pre-school was examined. At the start of primary school there were no differences between children who had full-time or part-time pre-school in terms of cognitive development. There were slight differences for progress in social development, which appeared to be the effects of one group catching up with the other as there were no differences in social/behavioural attainment.

Duration

The duration of attendance at pre-school was consistently found to be associated with better outcomes in the EPPE study in England, with every month of pre-school experience after age 2 years linked to better intellectual development and improved independence, concentration and sociability. However similar effects for duration were not found in the EPPNI study and this is likely to be because a lower level of variation in duration of pre-school was found in Northern Ireland than in England.

Quality of provision

The observed quality of pre-school centres is related to better intellectual/cognitive and social/behavioural development in children at the start of primary school. While good quality can be found across all types of early years settings, the evidence revealed that quality was higher overall in nursery schools and nursery classes. The quality of provision is likely to be affected by staff qualifications and training. The comparison of observed quality in playgroups between Northern Ireland and England strongly suggests that better staff training can improve quality of pre-school provision. Also the higher levels of observed quality and better child outcomes for nursery schools/classes is likely to be related to higher staff qualifications in these centres. It is of interest that ECERS-E, which measures the academically orientated aspects of pre-school activities, was equally predictive of cognitive and social/behavioural outcomes in Northern Ireland as in England. This was despite the fact that pre-schools in Northern Ireland scored lower on ECER-E overall and that the pre-school curriculum in Northern Ireland did not place as much emphasis on the activities measured by ECERS-E as was the case in England.

Peer group influences

The EPPNI study investigated the consequences of pre-school peer group influences upon children's development by testing for effects related to the composition of the peer group in terms of mother's qualifications (proxy for social class), cognitive ability and social characteristics. These aspects are correlated so that the peer group with the high average mother's qualifications will also likely be advantaged for children's cognitive and social development. At the start of primary school such peer group influences were present for cognitive and social development.

Vulnerable children

Where disadvantaged children attended centres that included children from mixed social backgrounds they showed further benefit than if they attended centres containing predominantly disadvantaged children. Children 'at risk' of learning or behavioural difficulties are helped by pre-school.

Major findings at end of Key Stage 1 (age 8 years)

Enduring effects: home versus pre-school groups

Advantageous effects of pre-school remained evident throughout Key Stage 1, although some outcomes were not as strong as they had been at school entry. The most likely explanation for the diminishing 'pre-school effect' is the powerful influence of the primary school on children's development. By the end of Key Stage 1 (age 8 years) the attainment gap is still evident for reading and mathematics, and was still evident at 7 years of age (last age social development measured) for some aspects of social development (e.g. the pre-school group were consistently less anxious).

Type of pre-school

The effects at the end of Key Stage 1 are present most strongly for children from nursery schools and classes, slightly less so for children from playgroups, less again for children from reception classes, but have largely disappeared for children from private day nurseries and reception groups.

The EPPNI project has compared children from each of the types of pre-school provision with children with very little or no pre-school centre experience (home group). In these comparisons a wide range of child, parent, socio-economic, home, family and early childcare variables have been included in analyses so that comparisons take place on a fair basis, i.e. 'a level playing field'. At every stage from the start of primary school up until the end of Key Stage 1, children who have been at nursery school or nursery class consistently show better cognitive social/behavioural outcomes. They are followed by children from playgroups, then the least benefits of pre-school appear for children from private day nurseries, reception classes and reception groups. The effects vary for different outcomes and for different periods in primary school. However it is possible to produce

Table 10.4 Overall developmental benefits associated with pre-school type for first four years of primary school as compared with children with no pre-school experience

Developmental benefit	Nursery school/class	Playgroup	Private day nursery	Reception class	Reception group
Cognitive development	15	10	5	4	0
Social development	9	9	2	1	2

an index of overall benefit for cognitive and for social behavioural outcomes by summing all the positive effects and subtracting any negative effects separately for cognitive and social outcomes over the first four years of primary school. Table 10.4 shows the result of this aggregation.

For cognitive outcomes the children from nursery school/class show the most benefit followed by the children from playgroups, then children from private day nurseries and reception classes, with children from reception groups showing no overall cognitive benefit compared to the home group.

For social/behavioural outcomes, children from nursery school/classes and playgroups show equivalent benefit, with children from the other types of pre-school showing a minimal advantage over the home group.

Full-time versus part-time pre-school

At every stage of the study the possibility that there would be differences associated with full-time versus part-time attendance at preschool was examined. For most comparisons there were no differences between children who had full-time or part-time pre-school. This result mirrors results in the EPPE study in England. There were a few differences for progress in aspects of social development, but these effects appeared to represent one group catching up with the other as there were no differences in attainment.

Duration

There were small benefits for social development found at the end of the first and second years of primary school.

Quality of pre-school

The observed quality of pre-school centres is related to better intellectual/cognitive and social/behavioural development in children throughout the first 4 years of primary school. The effects diminish with time in primary school but there are still some residual effects at the end of Key Stage 1 (age 8 years).

Good quality can be found across all types of early years settings in NI. However quality was higher overall in nursery schools and nursery classes. The quality of provision is related to staff qualifications and training. The comparison of observed quality in playgroups between Northern Ireland and England and also the relatively better child outcomes for playgroups in Northern Ireland strongly suggests that improved staff training can improve quality of pre-school provision, as these relatively better results for playgroups in Northern Ireland may reflect the higher levels of staff training in Northern Ireland playgroups. Also the higher levels of observed quality and better child outcomes for nursery schools/classes is likely to be related to the higher staff qualifications in these pre-school centres.

Peer group influences

The EPPNI study investigated the consequences of pre-school peer group influences upon children's development by testing for effects related to the composition of the peer group in terms of mother's qualifications (proxy for social class), cognitive ability and social characteristics. These aspects are correlated so that the peer group with the high average mother's qualifications will also likely be advantaged for children's cognitive and social development. Several findings showed that the children in more advantaged pre-school peer groups had a developmental benefit. Similar findings occurred in the EPPE project.

Vulnerable children

Many children continued to be 'at risk' of special educational needs at the end of Key Stage 1, with more of the 'home' children falling into this group even after taking into account background factors. There are a range of multiple disadvantages associated with children 'at risk' of learning or behavioural difficulties. These disadvantages include prematurity, low birth weight, more than three siblings, lower parent education and socio-economic status, and poorer home learning environment. Also such children are more likely to have shown developmental or behavioural difficulties in infancy. Children 'at risk' of learning or behavioural difficulties are helped by pre-school experience and the effects are greater the better the quality of the pre-school. This suggests that disadvantaged children will make better progress in pre-school centres with children from a mix of social backgrounds rather than in a uniformly disadvantaged centre. This has consequences for the siting of pre-school centres and their catchment areas.

The importance of the early home learning environment (HLE)

The quality of the early learning environment at home (where parents are actively engaged in activities with children) promoted intellectual and social development in all children. Although parents' social class and levels of education were related to child outcomes, the quality of the HLE was more important and only moderately associated with social class or mothers' qualification levels. What parents do is more important than who they are. Hence pre-school settings that do not include parent support/education are missing an important element in enhancing social and behavioural development.

Summary

The resonance between the results of the EPPE and EPPNI studies (see Chapters 5–7) is striking. In almost every case findings from EPPE and EPPNI are very similar. Such replication with different populations in different political contexts greatly adds to the credibility of the findings.

The EPPNI study has demonstrated the positive effects of high quality pre-school provision on children's intellectual and social behavioural development up to the end of Key Stage 1 in primary school (age 8 in Northern Ireland). The EPPNI research also indicates that pre-school can play an important part in combating social exclusion and promoting inclusion by offering disadvantaged children, in particular, a better start to primary school. The findings indicate pre-school has a positive impact on children's progress over and above important family influences.

The results show that type of pre-school centre is important, and indicate that better outcomes are associated with certain forms of provision. Quality of pre-school is also associated with more positive child outcomes. Likewise, the research points to the separate and significant influence of the HLE. These aspects (type and quality of pre-school, and HLE) are likely to be more susceptible to change through policy and practitioner initiatives than other characteristics, such as socio-economic status.

The project provides clear evidence of the benefits of pre-school education for children in Northern Ireland, and that children benefit more from nursery school, nursery class or playgroup than from other types of pre-school provision. The results indicated that these types of provision should be expanded in their coverage of the population rather than other types of provision. The public provision of reception classes and reception groups was associated with a low level of benefit, and governmental expenditure would achieve more for the children of Northern Ireland were resources redirected to the provision of nursery school, nursery class or playgroup provision for children currently receiving pre-school provision via reception classes or groups. Subsequent policy in Northern Ireland has taken such findings into account and reception classes and reception groups no longer receive children under the usual reception class age. It was also noticeable that private day nurseries in Northern Ireland also do not provide as much measurable benefit for children's development as do nursery school, nursery class or playgroups.

In addition to the benefits for cognitive and social development, the EPPNI study (in line with the EPPE findings) drew attention to the reduction of 'at risk' status of developing Special Educational Needs that is associated with good quality pre-school provision. This strengthens the economic case for good quality pre-school provision for all children as SEN is expensive in terms of individuals' development and public finances. Specific proposals related to vulnerable children include:

- Increasing the take-up of pre-school places by parents who would not usually send their children to pre-school (usually found in geographical clusters) would provide vulnerable groups of children with a better start to school and reduce their risk of developing SEN.
- Pre-school and school staff should be aware that boys may be at increased 'risk' of developing SEN for cognitive development and aspects of social development. Increased focus on the specific needs of boys, as learners, linked with appropriate staff development may have long-term benefits and help reduce the gender gap in SEN.
- Fostering active parental engagement with children and involvement in play activities that promote children's language, spatial skills and creativity, in particular, are likely to benefit children's subsequent cognitive and social development and attainment at school.
- The strong links between children's 'at risk' status and the experience of multiple disadvantage indicate that ways of effectively targeting additional resources to pre-schools and schools that serve high proportions of multiply disadvantaged families should be explored.

The linked projects (EPPE and EPPNI) have a unique contribution to make to 'evidence based policy' in early years education and care. Their findings are robust because they are based on sound and innovative research methods and the implications for policy are substantial at national, regional and local level. EPPNI set out to contribute to the debate about the education and care of young children, and the EPPNI research has targeted issues that could 'make a difference' to the lives of young children and their families. In these goals the EPPNI research has been successful.

Reference

Melhuish, E., Quinn, L., Hanna, K., Sylva, K., Siraj-Blatchford, I., Sammons, P. and Taggart, B. (2006) *The Effective Pre-school Provision in Northern Ireland Project, Summary Report*, Belfast: Stranmillis University Press. Available at http://www.deni.gov.uk/researchreport41.pdf

Chapter 11

Making a difference

How research can inform policy

Brenda Taggart

This chapter describes how EPPE has informed early years policy development in England through references to key policy documents.

Introduction

This chapter begins with a description of the policy context in the early 1990s and shows how EPPE evidence was used to inform (or not) a decade of policy innovation in early years education and care. Whilst much has been written about the impact of research on educational practice (Hargreaves, 1996; Siraj-Blatchford *et al.*, 2008) there are fewer examples of accounts that discuss the ways research can shape policy. Saunders (2007) identifies tensions and explores different roles and responsibilities for those with a 'policy remit for education' (p. 106) which serves to remind us of the difficulties encountered by researchers working with policy makers. This chapter describes the EPPE research as an example of a study that had policy change as an outcome, as advocated by Whitty (2007) and Davies *et al.* (2001).

Evidence-based policy making

The first chapter of this book sets out the historical background and policy context of early childhood education and care during the late 1980s and early 1990s leading up to the commissioning of EPPE. It discussed a number of large scale research projects (High/Scope, etc.) which have pointed to the consistent benefits of good quality early childhood experiences in promoting better development of the whole child. Despite this evidence there was little development in policies concerning early years before the late 1990s in the UK. For research to have an impact on policy development it helps if some of the following factors are evident:

- Timing – this is very important in policy terms as research has to be 'current' and fit in with a wider raft of political initiatives. This may involve an element of luck or serendipity in being 'in the right place, at the right time'.

- Sound methodology and reliable findings – policy makers and politicians must have confidence in the methods used and be able to rely on interpretations of the evidence.
- Clear messages – research findings need to be accessible and easily understood for a range of stakeholders.
- Be responsive to changing policy demands – researchers who recognise the shifting needs of policy makers and the time constraints in which they operate.

EPPE was fortunate in combining all of these elements. It could be argued that there would have been reform of policy in early years education and care without EPPE as it fitted a political agenda associated with social inclusion, but important for the Labour government in 1997 was evidence to support change. This was provided by EPPE and, as this chapter will explore, enabled reform to move forward with greater confidence of 'what works' in terms of some areas of policy and practice and the likely benefits of greater investment of resources in the early years.

The commitment to evidence-based policy was not without controversy at the time of the EPPE project, given the reputation of educational research in England in general. EPPE was commissioned during a period when educational research was under increasing criticism (Hargreaves, 1996; Tooley and Darby, 1998; and Hillage *et al.*, 1998) for its lack of rigour, inaccessibility, poor dissemination and poor cost-effectiveness. In addition, educational research was often accused of being out of touch with the needs of policy makers and failing to produce reliable findings in an acceptable time scale in order to inform key policy decisions. What helped to make EPPE more successful was that it encompassed three important policy agendas: the socio-economic, standards and research (described below) and this is important when considering its later impact on change. In 1997 a new Labour government came into power and made clear that it intended that its social reforms would be informed by research evidence (Humes and Bryce, 2001). The policy challenge was to transform services available for England's youngest children (aged 0–5), through a plethora of policy initiatives and legislation that sought to move the 'early years' sector from a 'patchwork quilt' to a 'seamless cover' of joined-up services. These services were to combine education and care and provide a smooth transfer from non-statutory to statutory schooling.

Families' need for childcare: the socio-economic agenda

Prior to the centre left 'New' Labour Party's electoral victory in 1997 policy in early years had a discernable split between 'care' and 'education'. Unlike some European countries (most notably in Scandinavia), pre-school provision in the UK at the turn of the last century was far from universally uniform. As non-statutory, the sector had grown according to the laws of the free market, and supply and demand. The system embraced both a growing voluntary and private sector alongside the maintained (state) sector. There were considerable geographical and socio-economic differences in the extent to which parents had access to a pre-school place for their child, and the nature of the provision itself varied widely (Sylva and Pugh, 2005).

The government was committed to 'concentrate resources on the essential tasks of combating unemployment and poverty' (Labour Party Manifesto, 1997). The two keys to delivering this promise were to lower the number of workless households and improve public services. The UK's workforce (like many other industrial countries) since the Second World War has become increasingly 'feminised' because more women are choosing to leave a purely domestic role to have a career commensurate with their academic qualifications, and households often rely on a woman's income to maintain levels above those of relative poverty. To maintain a female workforce requires adequate, 'organised' provision for young children. This was to be brought about by a raft of social policies including the introduction of Working Families Tax Credits and expanding child care (DfES, 2002) in order to encourage parents to return and stay in the active work force and to combat child poverty. Thus, the expansion and improvement of services to working families was key to this important piece of social reform. This bold commitment was summed up as follows:

> While the nineteenth century was distinguished by the introduction of primary education for all and the twentieth century by the introduction of secondary education for all, so the early part of the twenty first century should be marked by the introduction of pre-school provision for the under fives and childcare available to all.
>
> (Rt Hon. Gordon Brown, MP, Chancellor of the Exchequer (Her Majesty's Treasury, 2004a))

Raising educational achievement: the standards agenda

The end of the twentieth century saw an increased focus on educational 'standards' across all curriculum subjects and phases of education in the UK. The introduction of a National Curriculum (Great Britain, 1988) and national statutory assessments (DES and Welsh Office, 1988) for children at the ages of 7 and 11 years provided the backdrop to the debate about how well young children in England were performing compared to those in other countries. The development of international comparisons of standards in Literacy, Mathematics and Science[1] was a wake-up call to many governments (particularly Germany)

---

1   PISA (Programme for International Student Assessment), TIMSS (Trends in International Mathematics and Science Study and PIRLS (Progress in International Reading Literacy Study), see Mullis *et al.*, 2003,

concerned with a 'standards' agenda. The relative position of different countries on these international 'league tables' has added much to the debate about effective teaching, particularly in Reading and Mathematics (enabling students to access the curriculum), throughout each age phase.

This increased focus on standards during statutory schooling (age 5 onwards) led to an inevitable interest in, and questions being asked about, children's skills, attitudes and dispositions to learn at school entry. There was considerable concern about preparing children, especially those from disadvantaged backgrounds, for the challenges of the National Curriculum at the start of primary school. This turned the policy searchlight on early years education as one means of raising standards in primary schools.

The effects of early education: the research agenda

Internationally a number of key early years research studies had demonstrated the positive benefits of pre-schooling (see Chapter 1). Two influential randomised control trials; the Perry Pre-school study (Schweinhart *et al.*, 1993) and the Abercedarian study (Ramey and Ramey, 1998), both demonstrated positive effects of early education and care, especially for children from disadvantaged backgrounds. The Perry Pre-school study was especially important because, as a longitudinal study, it was able to provide evidence about the long term benefits that pre-school can bestow (in the US context). The study showed that early education (ages 3–5 years) improved high school grades, decreased delinquency and adult crime, and improved employment status and earnings. The often quoted economic argument that for each $1 invested in pre-school, $7.16 was saved in social, health and justice systems costs later on was persuasive in encouraging expansion in early years in the US (Barnett, 1996). But in the UK there was little research evidence to suggest that its system of pre-schooling was likely to replicate these outcomes.

The early 1990s saw some change in research interest in the early years. The Rumbold Report (DES, 1990) highlighted the potential for pre-school education to give children a better start at school. This was followed by the Start Right Report (Ball, 1994) that called for investment in universal pre-school education. In this influential report, Sylva (1994, Appendix C) reviewed the research evidence and made a convincing case for the positive effects of early education on young children's motivational as well as academic outcomes.

The EPPE findings

Given that these three agendas came together with the commitment of a new government, EPPE was well placed to supply evidence which informed the debate about the benefits to society as a whole, and children in particular, of good quality early years experiences. EPPE was able to explain clearly the significant positive effects of early childhood education on children's development. It showed that better quality, longer duration and the effectiveness of the pre-school setting attended made an important contribution to children's progress and attainment which could have lasting effects (Sammons *et al.*, 2004a, 2008a, 2008b). It also highlighted the relative strengths (expressed in Effect Sizes) of background characteristics on specific cognitive and social/behavioural outcomes. A key finding was the importance of the quality of the early years home learning environment (HLE) for ensuring children's long term success (Melhuish and Hall, 2007; Sylva *et al.*, 2004) and thus informed the development of policies intended to support parenting.

The impact of EPPE on policy

These findings contributed to the 'evidence base' for UK policy on the likely benefits of an offer of universal pre-school provision for young children and potential value of targeted services in disadvantaged communities. The remainder of this chapter will describe how important policy questions have been addressed by the EPPE research and show how this helped 'shape' developing policies and legislation through references to key policy documents.

In 2006 the Department for Education and Skills' Analytical Strategy (DfES, 2006a) stated:

> *Effective Provision of Pre-school Education (EPPE) at Key Stage 2*
> This project is helping to unpack the impact that pre-school education has on children's learning when they reach Key Stage 2. The results of the EPPE study have already had a significant impact on policy development in early years, especially through clearly demonstrating the vital influence of the quality of provision on successful outcomes. Continuation of the cohort will enable us to understand the lasting impact of early years experience and the factors which either enhance or negate this.
>
> (DfES, 2006a, p. 20)

EPPE's 'significant impact on policy development' is best considered through the published documents that refer to its influence and the importance of the research findings.

Prime Minister Tony Blair in 'Meeting the Childcare Challenge, The National Childcare Strategy' (DfEE, 1998) said, about children, that: 'good quality childcare . . . is vital to them growing up happy and secure in themselves, socially confident and able to benefit from education' adding that 'childcare has been neglected for too long' (DFEE, 1998, p. 3). This Green Paper paved the way for a major policy initiative outlined in 'Choice for Parents, The Best Start for Children: A Ten Year Strategy for Childcare' (Her Majesty's Treasury, 2004b). This landmark document sets out a long term vision on the delivery of newly reconfigured services which would fundamentally change the experiences of children under the age of 5. The ten year strategy paper is clear that 'the main source of analyses of the impact of pre-school provision on child development in the UK is the Effective Provision of Pre-School Education Project, (Her Majesty's Treasury, 2004b, p. 65).

This milestone strategy provides a policy rationale for the benefits of early education and repeatedly cites EPPE as providing wide ranging evidence on policy issues. The remainder of this chapter quotes the research evidence cited in the Ten Year Strategy illustrative of a range of policy questions EPPE responded to. It covers only a limited number of the policy implications of EPPE, namely those concerning centre-based provision. EPPE also reported on the importance of the contribution of the family to children's development through the quality of the HLE. This has influenced the development of policies to support families and communities such as the Sure Start Programme (see Melhuish and Hall, 2007).

Policy question 1: who benefits from pre-school education?

One of the key policy questions facing the government concerned the benefits of universal provision. The traditional view had been that early childcare, provided at the state's expense, was most profitably used strategically for disadvantaged families to enable poor children to 'catch-up' with their more advantaged peers (the rationale for early social services day care centres). The pilot voucher scheme introduced by the Conservatives in the early 1990s explored this. EPPE evidence showed that 'any pre-school experience can have clear positive effects on children's social, emotional and cognitive development' (Her Majesty's Treasury, 2004b, p. 8).

The finding that pre-school has benefits for ALL children (with attendance at pre-school being of a similar Effect Size to mother having an academic qualification at age 18 versus none) has led directly into policy development. This is not to say that the benefits for disadvantaged children are not of policy interest (see below), but it did provide the research evidence that suggests universal provision would be of benefit. The big policy shift announced in the strategy was twofold:

> 1. legislation for a new duty on local authorities in place by 2008 so that over time they will secure sufficient supply to meet the needs of families.

and

> 2. a goal of 20 hours a week of free high quality care for 38 weeks for all 3 and 4 year olds with this Pre-Budget Report announcing a first step of 15 hours a week for 38 weeks a year reaching all children by 2010.
>
> (Her Majesty's Treasury, 2004b, p. 1)

For the first time, pre-school provision in England was made universally available.

Policy question 2: at what age should children begin pre-school?

This has long been a contentious issue in the social discourse about young children and families. The twentieth century notion of the nuclear family with mum at home with the children has long been dismissed, but the debate about what age children gain benefits from group education and care has persisted. The strategy stated:

> Evidence from the Effective Provision of Pre-school Education (EPPE) project shows an early start to pre-school can have significant positive effects on children's cognitive and social development. For example, every additional month of quality pre-school from the age of two improves cognitive performance at the start of school, a gain that remains to at least age seven. Those who started in a good quality pre-school at two or younger were up to 10 months ahead of those without pre-school. The EPPE evidence also shows that an early start in pre-school improves children's social skills at entry to school.
>
> (Her Majesty's Treasury, 2004b, p. 8)

This notion of an 'early start' remains controversial as although EPPE reported largely positive and only one negative finding on institutional care, as the strategy states: 'However, the studies indicate that high levels of group care of poor quality below the age of three can have a small negative effect on behaviour for some children', p. 8. This finding resonates with other research (NICHD Early Child Care Research Network, 2004) that suggest that very early institutional (group) care, especially for long hours may not be in the best interest of some very young children. This finding added to the debate about what constitutes good care for children under the age of 2. There have been a number of policy initiatives to enable more parents to stay at home with babies:

> Statutory Maternity Pay, Statutory Adoption Pay and Maternity allowance will be extended from April 2007 to 39 weeks … to enable fathers to play a greater role in the crucial first year of a child's life the government intends to bring forward proposals … to give the mother the right to transfer a proportion of her maternity pay and leave to the father … giving parents more choice about how to arrange parental care for a new baby.
>
> (Her Majesty's Treasury, 2004b, p. 30)

Policy question 3: for how long should children attend pre-school?

On the question of duration, again the paper refers to EPPE findings:

Evidence from EPPE shows that the benefits are gained from regular part-time attendance through the week. Full-time attendance gives no better gains than part-time although EPPE suggests that pre-school experiences at all levels of quality and duration have positive effects on children's development compared with children who had no pre-school experience.

(Her Majesty's Treasury, 2004b, p. 8)

The findings on attendance have been used extensively across policy documents, most influentially in A Code of Practice on the Provision of Free Nursery Education Places for Three- and Four-Year-Olds (DfES, 2006b) and in the House of Commons' inquiry into Early Years (House of Commons. Education Sub-Committee, June 2000).

Policy question 4: can early childcare help children 'at risk' of developing special educational needs (SEN) and reduce the impact of social disadvantage?

Early identification for SEN is crucial, especially for children from disadvantaged backgrounds (see Chapter 9). This aspect of social disadvantage was an important research focus and a sub-study called the Early Transitions and Special Educational Needs (EYTSEN, see Sammons *et al.*, 2002b, 2004b; Taggart *et al.*, 2006) explores this in depth. An index of multiple disadvantage (Sammons *et al.*, 2002b) developed on the project showed that the higher up the index children appeared, the more likely they were to be 'at risk' of developing SEN. The strategy reports on EPPE evidence:

> EPPE data suggest that while one in three children were 'at risk' of having special educational needs at the start of pre-school, that proportion fell to one in five by the time they started primary school, suggesting that pre-school can be an effective intervention for the reduction of special needs' needs.
>
> (Her Majesty's Treasury, 2004b, p. 8)

Whilst not eliminating the impact of disadvantage, high quality pre-school education can provide children from lower income households with a better start to school. This has been important in policy development and has seen a pilot project to study the impact of free pre-schooling for under 2 year olds from disadvantaged backgrounds.

Policy question 5: what kinds of pre-school provide the best outcomes for children?

One of the key questions for EPPE was the impact of different types of provision on children. Multilevel statistical modelling enables individual 'centre' effects to be studied so that 'effective' centres could be identified and their characteristics described. EPPE findings associated with quality, type and the characteristics of the work force had a considerable impact on policy. The strategy sets out the EPPE evidence on quality:

> EPPE suggests that in comparison with children having no pre-school, all levels of quality and duration show a significant positive effect compared to none. The quality of pre-school experience is directly related to the intellectual, social and behavioural development of children. After taking into account the impact of child, family and home environment characteristics, evidence shows significant links between higher quality and better children outcomes, with children from high quality pre-schools possessing higher reading attainment and showing fewer conduct problems.

It goes on to say:

> evidence suggests that the effects can be substantial. EPPE analysis indicates that the difference in child development between having pre-school and not having pre-school is 4–6 months of development. For the highest quality integrated centres, the difference can be as much as nine months. This is a substantial difference given that it occurs over just two years. The combination of high quality provision and high duration shows a particularly strong effect.
>
> (Her Majesty's Treasury, 2004b, p. 66)

EPPE's finding on the importance of quality has been persuasive and accepted across the party political divide (Liberal Democrats, 2003).

The strategy also cites EPPE evidence on where quality can be found and factors that contribute to enhancing quality:

> EPPE conclude that good quality provision can be found across all types of pre-school settings but is higher overall in integrated learning and childcare centres, nursery school and nursery classes. Better quality pre-school centres are associated with better outcomes, with key explanatory factors being: staff with higher qualifications, staff with leadership skills and long-serving staff; trained teachers working alongside and supporting less qualified staff; staff with a good understanding of child development and learning and strong parental involvement.
>
> (Her Majesty's Treasury, 2004b, p. 66)

The EPPE qualitative case studies (Siraj-Blatchford *et al.*, 2003) gave detailed information for practitioners on aspects of effective practice and highlighted areas which might provide quality experiences for young children. These EPPE findings have been particularly influential and have been incorporated wholesale into Primary National Strategy (DfES, 2006c, p. 13)

Given the highest overall quality (and child outcomes) were in integrated centres, these settings, now known as Children's Centres have been pivotal to the new vision of early childcare services. Children's Centres, (part of Sure Start) in addition to providing and co-ordinating childcare, also support parents through a range of advice services (job seeking, parenting and study support). The policy expansion in this area has been profound: '525,000 additional childcare places have been created, benefiting 1.1 million children' (Her Majesty's Treasury, 2004b, p. 22), 1,279 Neighbourhood Nurseries have been opened (Her Majesty's Treasury, 2004b, p. 26), and 2,599 Children's Centres will be in place by 2008 (p. 1) with the promise of a 'Children's Centre in every community by 2010' (Her Majesty's Treasury, 2004b, p. 3.3). This is educational expansion in unprecedented terms and EPPE's recommendations have subsequently been subsumed into the 'Every Child Matters' agenda (HM Government, 2004).

Policy question 6: what kind of workforce?

In order to ensure quality, the strategy is clear that the government has '*a commitment to radical reform of the early years childcare workforce through a new qualification and career structure*' (Her Majesty's Treasury, 2004b, p. 43). This is to be achieved through a £125 million Transformation Fund to improve the workforce. The long term vision seeks out to 'ensure that all full daycare settings are led by a graduate qualified early years professional . . . and there will be single qualification framework and greater opportunities for existing workers to increase their skills' (Her Majesty's Treasury, 2004b, p. 45). In many local authorities this has meant a reconfiguring of the workforce to see how qualified teachers can be employed strategically across a number of settings. This is partly based on the EPPE finding that qualified teachers were associated with better quality learning environments and practices (Sylva *et al.*, 1999).

How did EPPE inform policy?

We have demonstrated in this chapter that EPPE was able to inform some aspects of policy because it provided robust answers to a range of research questions which had high policy importance. However, we believe this wasn't the only reason why EPPE was successful in policy terms. Other factors have contributed to this impact. During the period of the project the research team had a very clearly defined 'dissemination' strategy which ensured the research findings were accessible to a range of stakeholders. This included giving evidence at Parliamentary Select Committees, working with Local Authorities looking to reconfigure their early years services, giving 'key-note' address at conferences up and down the country and running many workshops for practitioners. The team was flexible in dealing with research queries across a range of government departments and conducted additional analyses for Her Majesty's Treasury and the Cabinet Office.

As well as informing policy development, the qualitative case studies provided detailed information on the day-to-day practices in more effective settings (see Chapter 8 and Siraj-Blatchford *et al.*, 2002, 2003). This aspect of the project proved especially valuable and has had a profound impact on practitioners (Siraj-Blatchford, *et al.*, 2008). The case study evidence, particularly on the use of 'sustained shared thinking', has been influential in the development of the curriculum and pedagogical practices, as outlined in Chapter 8 (see Department for Education and Skills (DfES), 2000, 2005, 2006).

Another important aspect related to policy influence has been the way in which EPPE worked alongside of the funders: the Department of Children, Schools and Families (formerly the Department for Education and Skills). EPPE, particularly during the early phases, developed a way of working which was based on 'knowledge exchange' whereby the researchers and funders worked collaboratively in overcoming difficulties. This fostered an environment that supported the use of research findings to inform and assist policy development (for more details see Sylva *et al.*, 2007).

Limitations of EPPE

EPPE has been able to answer a range of research questions but it cannot (and was never designed to) provide detailed evidence on all aspects of early years education and care. Clarke (2006) criticises EPPE for adopting what she terms as a mechanistic approach to early childhood education which sees pre-school education as

> essentially future-oriented (preparation for school), with little interest in the quality of the experience for its own sake and the benefits to children in the present. The focus is its effectiveness in generating certain outcomes as the first steps toward producing well-educated and qualified, responsible and well-behaved adults.

> (p. 710)

However, this criticism should be balanced with the emphasis EPPE places on the quality of young children's experiences, and through both observation and case studies tries to articulate the types of practices which enrich young children's lives and provide the challenges that facilitate intellectual and social development often unavailable to children elsewhere. This is especially important for children living in less stimulating and in some cases neglectful homes. We also argue that enhancing children's language and social/behavioural skills (such as peer sociability, independence and concentration) are important in their own right and enhance children's lives in the here and now as well as proving future benefits. Clarke also fails to acknowledge the vast array of literature on the benefits of high quality early learning experiences for their own sake. This literature has provided persuasive evidence of the importance of the early years as distinct from other phases of education (Anning and Edwards, 2006). EPPE was not commissioned to review the importance of pre-schooling but to investigate the *impact* of it. The research team took inspiration from the pioneers of early years education and care and were guided by previous research (see Chapter 12) in the field. Perhaps the unique contribution of EPPE has been to look at a range of evidence about the efficacy of pre-school and bring this together to describe the broad reach of influence pre-school has beyond its own age phase.

Inevitably the EPPE results show associations between likely predictive factors and child development; for example attending pre-schools. However, as the groups who use particular pre-schools are at least partly self-selecting, we cannot rule out absolutely other unmeasured factors that may co-vary with pre-school attendance and also affect outcomes. In order to counter this limitation EPPE has measured all the relevant child, parent, family and neighbourhood variables shown in previous research to influence child outcomes and have controlled for this. Hence while we cannot make causal attribution absolutely, it does seem by far the most likely explanation of the effects described.

EPPE was funded to explore pre-school experiences but chose not to ignore the contribution of the family and home, recognising that children do not wait until they go to school to begin learning. It was never designed to be a study of home learning. Clarke (2006) thinks that by measuring the HLE, EPPE reduces the

> child's home to its role in producing a particular outcome in the child's scores on a variety of scales. The things that parents or others do with children are described in terms of their contribution to producing a discrete set of attributes with a statistical correlation with other longer term goals, particularly educational outcomes.
>
> (p. 709)

EPPE has highlighted the importance of stimulating early learning experiences but cannot provide 'thick descriptions' of what makes for a rounded home learning environment. Nonetheless, by highlighting this we have added to the debate about early learning in the home and we hope that this stimulates further research in this field.

Similarly EPPE was not designed (or funded) to focus in depth on pedagogical practices and the role of the adult pre-school worker in children's learning. However EPPE took the opportunity to conduct interviews with staff members and observe their practice and this highlighted the importance of training and qualifications in settings of 'excellent' quality with good child outcomes. The English reform of the workforce recognises the importance of trained teachers but the government chose instead to develop the role of the Early Years Professional (CWDC, 2006). This qualification does not confer qualified teacher status but is a degree equivalent in status. Those holding the qualification are on less beneficial pay and conditions compared to qualified teachers. EPPE cannot answer questions about the long term impact of this major change to the early years workforce (see Chapter 2). In the future the impact will need to be evaluated through well designed research. This is an example of policy being 'informed' but not always 'influenced' by research evidence.

Another example of this would be the finding related to 'dose' of pre-school. The EPPE evidence suggests that duration is important (see Chapter 6) and children who attended part time, typically having half day sessions over a week (attending either every morning or every afternoon) were showing similar scores to those who attended full time. This 'drip feed' approach provides continuity both for children and staff. Children can maintain relationships and build on their immediate experiences. Staff can 'scaffold' learning better and make short, medium and long term plans. However, the universal free places allocation takes little account of this approach and provides for more parental 'flexibility' in accessing provision. The free allocation may be taken in whole day 'blocks', which may fit in better with patterns of work for parents but provides less continuity for children (Early Education, 2008).

Whilst EPPE can inform policy makers, it has no control over how the research is used in policy development and implementation. Many findings have been used extensively and well, whereas some others have attracted less attention. The work of the researcher is to contribute to the debate by providing evidence, disseminating their work, critically engage with other researchers and discuss the implication with all those who are interested in improving the lives of young children.

Discussion

The examples above show that the EPPE project has at times contributed to early years policy development during the first two terms of the Labour government in England, by providing sound and persuasive research evidence. It could be argued that the EPPE research was 'pushing on an open door' in policy development in that its findings coincided with growing recognition of the need to develop early years education and care in England. Whilst the time was ripe for reform to this non-statutory sector, the counter argument is that without this research evidence base the extent and speed of the reform (made possible by the Treasury) would have been more precarious. EPPE has provided information across government departments and has informed successive Treasury Spending Reviews.

The last decade has seen major changes to the three agendas identified at the beginning of this paper and EPPE has contributed to all three. The 'socio-economic agenda' has changed significantly with extra investment in disadvantaged communities (Sefton, 2004). The current challenge is to focus on strategies that will improve the lives of children still living in poverty and those from ethnic minority families who are overrepresented in disadvantaged groups. EPPE has sought to contribute to this by providing evidence to the Cabinet Office's investigation into equality across the life course (EPPE 3–11 Team, 2007). The 'standards agenda' has broadened with an interlocking curriculum from ages 0–6 years old and a new focus on 'education' for children under 5. EPPE has identified important day-to-day practices that can assist practitioners in improving curriculum and pedagogy. The development of the workforce is crucial in delivering the 'standards agenda' and it will be interesting to see if the implementation of the Early Years Professional (CWDC, 2006) qualification for staff will live up to its promise of improving quality. The 'research agenda' has also been transformed. The availability of more extensive background information and more sophisticated analysis techniques enable us not only to study the impact (and size) of a range of factors but how factors interact with one another. The research challenge is to see how emerging results from a number of longitudinal studies (LYPSE, ALSPAC, etc.) can be synthesised for meaningful patterns and trends that have policy relevance.

EPPE has influenced policy because its findings are large scale and broadly representative, longitudinal and based on 'value added' analyses that established the measurable contribution of a range of influences on children's development and highlighted the factors that foster better educational outcomes. This has proved important to policies which identify the relative costs and benefits that might be expected to accrue from significant investments of public money to enhance early years services.

References

Anning, A. and Edwards, A. (2006) *Promoting Children's Learning from Birth to Five*, 2nd edn, Buckingham: Open University Press.

Ball, C. (1994) *Start Right: The Importance of Early Learning*, London: RSA.

Barnett, W.S. (1996) *Lives in the Balance: Age 27 Benefit-cost Analyses of High Scope/Perry Pre-school Program*, Monographs of the High Scope Educational Research Foundation, 11, Ypsilanti, MI: High/Scope Press.

Children's Workforce Development Council (2006) Early Years Professional Prospectus. Part of the Sector Skills Council, Skills for Care and Development, Leeds.

Clarke, K. (2006) *Childhood, Parenting and Early Intervention: A Critical Examination of the Sure Start National Programme*, Critical Social Policy 2006, 26, 699, London: Sage Publications.

Davies, H.T.O., Nutley, S. and Smith. P.C. (eds) (2001) *What Works? Evidence Based Policy and Practice in Public Services*, Bristol: Policy Press.

Department for Education and Employment (DfEE) (1998) *Green Paper: Meeting the Childcare Challenge*, Norwich: HMSO.

Department for Education and Skills (DfES) (2000) *Curriculum Guidance for the Foundation Stage*, London, QCA/DfES.

Department for Education and Skills (DfES) (2002) *Delivering for Children and Families: Inter-Departmental Childcare Review*, London: DfES/DWP/HM Treasury/Women and Equality Unit, HMSO.

Department for Education and Skills (DfES) (2005a) *DfES Sure Start Children's Centres Practice Guidance*, London: DfES.

Department for Education and Skills (DfES) (2005b) *Primary National* Strategy *Key Elements of Effective Practice (KEEP)*, London: DfES/SureStart.

Department for Education and Skills (DfES) (2006a) *Analytical Strategy*, Nottingham: DfES Publications, http://www.dfes.gov.uk/research/data/general/AS2006.pdf (accessed 06/02/07).

Department for Education and Skills (DfES) (2006b) *A Code of Practice on the Provision of Free Nursery Education Places for Three- and Four-Year-Olds*, Nottingham: DfES Publications http://www.surestart.gov.uk/_doc/P0002205.pdf (accessed 06/02/07).

Department for Education and Skills (DfES) (2006) *Primary National Strategy. Guidance on Curriculum and Standards. Improving Outcomes for Children in the Foundation Stage in Maintained Schools. Process-based Targets in the Foundation Stage*, London: DfES Publications.

Department for Education and (DfES) (2006d) *Improving Outcomes for Children in the Foundation Stage in Maintained Schools: Process-based Targets in the Foundation Stage*, Primary National Strategy/SureStart, London: DfES.

Department of Education and Science (DES) (1988) *The National Curriculum*, London: HMSO.

Department of Education and Science (DES) (1990) *Starting with Quality: Report of the Committee of Inquiry into the Quality of Educational Experience Offered to Three and Four Year Olds (Rumbold Report)*, London: HMSO.

Department of Education and Science and Welsh Office (1988) *Task Group on Assessment and Testing*, London: DES.

Early Education (2008) *Flexible Offer and Extension to the Free Early Education Entitlement Offer.* Position Paper 2, London: Early Education.

Effective Pre-school and Primary Education 3–11 (EPPE 3–11) Team. (2007), *Promoting Equality in the Early Years: Report to The Equalities Review*, London: http://www.equalitiesreview.org.uk.

Great Britain (1988) *Education Reform Act 1988*, London: HMSO.

Great Britain (2006) *Childcare Act 2006, Explanatory Notes*, Chapter 21, London: HMSO.

Hargreaves, D. (1996) *Teaching as a Research-Based Profession*, London: Teacher Training Agency.

Hillage, J., Pearson, R., Anderson, A. and Tamkin, P. (1998) *Excellence in Research in Schools*, London: Department for Education and Employment.

HM Government (2004) *Every Child Matters: Next Steps*, Nottingham: DfES Publications.

HM Treasury. (2004a) *2004 Spending Review: Stability, Security and Opportunity for All: Investing for Britain's Long-Term Future*, London: HM Treasury.

HM Treasury. (2004b) *Choice for Parents, The Best Start for Children: A Ten Year Strategy for Childcare*, Norwich: HMSO. http://www.hm-treasury.gov.uk/media/8F5/35/pbr04childcare_480.pdf (accessed 06/02/07).

House of Commons Session Education and Employment Committee (Education Sub-Committee) Early Years (2000) *Minutes of Evidence. Wednesday 21st June 2000. Evidence given by Professors Sylva, Siraj-Blatchford and Sammons*, London: The Stationery Office.

Humes, W. and Bryce, T. (2001) *Scholarship, Research and the Evidential Basis of Policy Development in Education, British Journal of Educational Studies*, 4 (3), 329–352.

Labour Party Manifesto (1997) http://www.labourparty.org.uk/manifestos/1997/1997-labour-manifesto.shtml.

Liberal Democrats (2003) *Early Years*. Consultation Paper No. 65, London: www.libdems.org.uk.

Melhuish, E. and Hall, D. (2007) The policy background to Sure Start, in J. Belsky, J. Barnes and E. Melhuish (eds) *Evaluating Sure Start: Does Area-based Early Intervention Work?* Bristol: Policy Press.

Melhuish, E.C., Sylva, K., Sammons, P., Siraj-Blatchford, I., Taggart, B. and Phan, M. (2007) *Effects of the Home Learning Environment and Pre-school Center Experience upon Literacy and Numeracy Development in Early Primary School, Journal of Social Studies Issues*, 64, 157–188.

Mullis, I.V.S., Martin, M.O., Gonzalez, E.J. and Kennedy, A.M. (2003) *PIRLS 2001 International Report: IEA's Study of Reading Literacy Achievement in Primary Schools*, Chestnut Hill, MA: Boston College.

NICHD Early Child Care Research Network (2004) Type of child care and children's development at 54 months, *Early Childhood Research Quarterly*, 19(2), 203–230.

QCA/DfES/SureStart (2003) *Foundation Stage Profile*, Sudbury: QCA Publications.

Ramey, C.T. and Ramey, S.L. (1998) Early ntervention and early experience, *American Psychologist*, 53(2), 109–120.

Sammons, P., Sylva, K., Melhuish, E.C., Siraj-Blatchford, I., Taggart, B. and Elliot, K. (2002) *The Effective Provision of Pre-School Education (EPPE) Project: Technical Paper 8a – Measuring the Impact of Pre-School on Children's Cognitive Progress over the Pre-School Period*, London: DfES/ nstitute of Education, University of London.

Sammons, P., Sylva, K., Melhuish, E.C., Siraj-Blatchford, I., Taggart, B. and Elliot, K. (2003) *The Effective Provision of Pre-School Education (EPPE) Project: Technical Paper 8b – Measuring the Impact of Pre-School on Children's Social/Behavioural Development over the Pre-School Period*, London: DfES/Institute of Education, University of London.

Sammons, P., Smees, R., Taggart, B., Sylva, K., Melhuish, E.C., Siraj-Blatchford, I. and Elliot, K. (2002) *The Early Years Transition and Special Educational Needs (EYTSEN) Project: Technical Paper 1 – Special Needs Across the Pre-School Period*, London: DfES/Institute of Education, University of London.

Sammons, P., Sylva, K., Melhuish, E.C., Siraj-Blatchford, I., Taggart, B., Elliot, K. and Marsh, A. (2004a) *The Effective Provision of Pre-School Education (EPPE) Project: Technical Paper 11 – Report on the Continuing Effects of Pre-School Education at Age 7*, London: DfES/ Institute of Education, University of London.

Sammons, P., Smees, R., Taggart, B., Sylva, K., Melhuish, E.C., Siraj-Blatchford, I. and Elliot, K. (2004b)*The Early Years Transitions and Special Educational Needs (EYTSEN) Project: Technical Paper 2 – Special Educational Needs in the Early Primary Years: Primary School Entry up to the End of Year 1*, London: DfES/Institute of Education, University of London.

Sammons, P., Sylva, K., Melhuish, E., Siraj-Blatchford, I., Taggart, B. and Hunt, S. (2008a) *The Effective Pre-School and Primary Education 3–11 (EPPE 3–11) Project: Influences on Children's Attainment and Progress in Key Stage 2: Cognitive Outcomes in Year 6*, London: DCSF/Institute of Education, University of London.

Sammons, P., Sylva, K., Melhuish, E., Siraj-Blatchford, I., Taggart, B. and Jelicic, H. (2008b) *The Effective Pre-School and Primary Education 3-11 (EPPE 3-11) Project: Influences on Children's Development and Progress in Key Stage 2: Social/Behavioural Outcomes in Year 6*. London: DCSF/Institute of Education, University of London.

Saunders, L. (ed.) (2007) *Educational Research and Policy-making. Exploring the Border Country between Research and Policy*, New York and London: Routledge.

Schweinhart, L.J., Barnes, H.V. and Weikart, D.P. (1993) *Significant Benefits: The High Scope Perry Pre-school Study Through Age 27*. Monograph of the High Scope Educational Research Foundation, No. 19, Ypsilanti, MI: High Scope Press.

Sefton, T. (2004), *A Fair Share of Welfare: Public Spending on Children in England*, CASE Report 25, Centre for Analysis of Social Exclusion, London: London School of Economics and Save the Children.

Siraj-Blatchford, I., Sylva, K., Muttock, S., Gilden, R. and Bell, D. (2002) *Researching Effective Pedagogy in the Early Years (REPEY) – DfES* Research Report 356, London: DfES, HMSO.

Siraj-Blatchford, I., Taggart, B., Sylva, K., Sammons, P. and Melhuish, E.C. (2008) Towards the transformation of practice in early childhood education: the effective provision of pre-school education (EPPE) project, *Cambridge Journal of Education*, 38(1), 23–36.

Siraj-Blatchford, I., Sylva, K., Taggart, B., Sammons, P., Melhuish, E.C. and Elliot, K. (2003) *The Effective Provision of Pre-School Education (EPPE) Project: Technical Paper 10 – Intensive Case Studies of Practice across the Foundation Stage*, London: DfES/Institute of Education, University of London.

Sylva, K. (1994) The impact of early learning on children's later development, in C. Ball (ed.) *Start Right: The Importance of Early Learning*, London: RSA.

Sylva, K. and Pugh, G. (2005) Transforming the early years in England, *Oxford Review of Education*, 31, 11–27.

Sylva, K., Siraj-Blatchford, I. and Taggart, B. (2003) *Assessing Quality in the Early Years: Early Childhood Environment Rating Scale Extension (ECERS-E): Four Curricular Subscales*, Stoke on Trent, UK and Stirling, USA: Trentham Books.

Sylva, K., Melhuish, E., Sammons, P., Siraj-Blatchford, I. and Taggart, B. (2004) *The Effective Provision of Pre-School Education (EPPE) Project: Technical Paper 12 – The Final Report*, London: DfES/Institute of Education, University of London.

Sylva, K., Taggart, B., Melhuish, E., Sammons, P. and Siraj-Blatchford, I. (2007) Changing models of research to inform educational policy, *Research Papers in Education*, 22 (2).

Sylva, K., Melhuish, E., Sammons, P., Siraj-Blatchford, I. and Taggart, B. (2008) *Effective Pre-school and Primary Education 3–11 Project (EPPE 3–11) Final Report from the Primary Phase: Pre-school, School and Family Influences on Children's Development during Key Stage 2*, Research Report No. DCSF-RR061, Nottingham: DCSF Publications.

Sylva, K., Siraj-Blatchford, I., Melhuish, E.C., Sammons, P., Taggart, B., Evans, E., Dobson, A., Jeavons, M., Lewis, K., Morahan, M. and Sadler, S. (1999) *The Effective Provision of Pre-School Education (EPPE) Project: Technical Paper 6 – Characteristics of the Centres in the EPPE Sample: Observation Profiles*, London: DfEE/Institute of Education, University of London.

Taggart, B., Sylva, K., Siraj-Blatchford, I., Melhuish, E.C., Sammons, P. and Walker-Hall, J. (2000) *The Effective Provision of Pre-School Education (EPPE) Project: Technical Paper 5 – Characteristics of the Centres in the EPPE Sample: Interviews*, London: DfEE/Institute of Education, University of London.

Taggart, B., Sammons, P., Smees, R., Sylva, K., Melhuish, E., Siraj-Blatchford, I., Elliot, K. and Lunt, I. (2006) Early identification of special needs and the definition of 'at risk': the early years transition and special education needs (EYTSEN) project, *British Journal of Special Education*, 33(1), 40–45.

Tooley, J. and Darby, D. (1998) *Educational Research: A Critique*, London: Office for Standards in Education.

Whitty, G. (2007) *Making Sense of Educational Policy*, London: Paul Chapman Publishing.

Chapter 12

Re-thinking the evidence-base for early years policy and practice

Kathy Sylva

This chapter focuses on the importance and impact of combining qualitative and quantitative methods in order to give more strength to research findings. It will show why large scale research is better for answering some questions and how inter-disciplinary teams can 'go further' in theory and method.

EPPE was commissioned at a time when the early years of children's lives were of low priority in government thinking and services. Researchers began recruiting children and families in 1997 from a landscape of provision very different from today, a decade into the twenty-first century. Some children remained at home, many were in voluntary and private settings, and many families 'made do' with a mix of informal, '*ad hoc*' childcare from family and friends. Beginning with its election victory in 1997 the new Labour government was committed to enhancing the lives of all young children – but especially to 'narrow the gap' between the life chances of rich and poor. This dramatic change in policy direction was soon followed by a new emphasis on policies for *families* as well as *children*, a consequence of new research on the importance of parents in maintaining social hierarchies (Feinstein *et al.*, 1998) or in breaking them (Scott *et al.*, in press).

From its election victory in 1997 the government was keen to use research findings to shape radical new policy for children. In the decade between 1997 and 2007 services for children – and increasingly their families – were expanded and centralised, with the Department for Education and Skills (later to become the Department for Children, Schools and Families – DCSF) taking on more responsibility for supporting young children and their families. In rapid succession England had: the Sure Start programme in disadvantaged neighbourhoods (1999), the Childcare Review (Department for Education and Skills, Department for Work and Pensions, HM Treasury, 2002), the Childcare Strategy (2002), the Nursery Education Grant for 4 year olds (2002), the Extension to the Nursery Education Grant to 3 year olds (2004), see Eisenstadt, 2009.

The embryonic early years curriculum of 1996 (Desirable Outcomes, Department for Education and Employment, DFEE) was expanded into Curricular Guidance for the Foundation Stage (2000) and Birth to Three Matters (2003). Finally in 2008 the combined programme of the education and care of young children was established as the Early Years Foundation Stage, which became law in 2008 (Department for Education and Skills, DfES). Curriculum and assessment reform was matched with major changes to inspection arrangements and a new emphasis on the professional development of staff, including the development of the Early Years Professional (DfES, 2006; Children's Workforce Development Council, 2008).

EPPE had to keep abreast of all this change, and tailor its methods and priorities to take into account a changing policy landscape. It responded to such rapid change by working in partnership with the government, professional bodies, and practitioners to design research methods that would be sensitive to emerging policy. On advice from policy makers and practitioners, EPPE's original design was altered one year after inception to include integrated centres (the fore-runners of today's Children's Centres) because of their growing importance in national policy and nursery schools. Once begun, EPPE also expanded its research focus to include more information on parenting, particularly the Home Learning Environment (HLE), in order to respond to changing policy. Instead of working with funders in a linear or one-way manner, EPPE engaged in two-way partnership (Sylva *et al.*, 2007) with policy officials from the (then) Department for Education and Skills, but also the Treasury and the Cabinet Office (Taggart *et al.*, 2008).

EPPE was scheduled to come to an end in 2003 when its several cohorts of children would have completed Key Stage 1 at age 7 (the second phase of education in England, following on from the Foundation Stage that ends around age 5). The government funded an extension of the research to age 11 at the end of Key Stage 2, allowing medium-term answers to the question 'What are the continuing effects of pre-school education?' and to study how they interact with the effects of primary schooling.

When the EPPE children had completed Key Stage 2 the key findings were:

- Attendance at pre-school led to short-term (end of KS1) and medium-term (end of KS2) benefits for all children in both cognitive and social-behavioural development.
- Children made greater developmental progress in settings with more highly qualified staff, especially if these staff were qualified teachers (QTS).
- The quality of provision (structural and process) in children's pre-school settings made a contribution to developmental outcomes that was *net* of child and family background characteristics, including the HLE.
- Children made more progress in settings that viewed cognitive and social-behavioural development as of equal importance. One of the ways practitioners can challenge and extend children's thinking is through challenging their minds in 'sustained shared thinking' (Siraj-Blatchford *et al.*, 2003).
- Children from all social classes benefited from pre-school. However pre-school for disadvantaged children had particularly important benefits. When they had experienced pre-school their level of attainment at the end of Key Stage 1 was such that they started Key Stage 2 with a Level 2 in Reading and Mathematics, the level of key skills needed to tackle the more

demanding curriculum towards the end of primary. (Note that the gap had not narrowed much, but the absolute level of attainment needed for progression to KS2 was achieved by children who had attended pre-school but not by those who did not.)

- The quality of the early HLE made an important contribution to children's development. In fact, it was more important than parental demographic characteristics such as occupation or income. The combined effects of a positive HLE and a high quality pre-school put children on a very strong developmental pathway to success.
- By the end of KS2, the positive benefits of pre-school were found to be greater for disadvantaged children (as measured, for example, by maternal qualifications) than they were for those from more favoured circumstances. By age 11 (end of KS2) EPPE found a disproportional benefit of pre-school, favouring the disadvantaged children and suggesting the sustained importance of early educational experiences.

Thus EPPE study has shown that pre-school not only provides all children with a better start to primary schools but that these positive benefits last in the medium term. Moreover, by the end of KS2, the benefits are greater for children from disadvantaged backgrounds. The key ingredients of quality (measured through the ECERS scores) are related to highly qualified staff, 'shared and sustained' interactions between children and adults, pre-school staff working with parents on children's learning, and adult support for children in talking through peer conflicts.

The EPPE findings in the context of other research studies

EPPE is a large study with a (broadly) nationally representative sample of children and families drawn in equal numbers from the main types of provision. It took place, however, in one historical interval and in just one country of the United Kingdom. Its conclusions and recommendations are strengthened when they coincide with those of other studies, including those from other countries. Chapter 10 in this book, by Melhuish has showed the great similarity between EPPE findings in England and EPPNI findings in Northern Ireland. The 'replication' of English findings in another UK country increases confidence in the broad picture. There have been many studies with similar findings in other countries and many of these have used different research methods on differing samples. For this reason, a few of the most important recent studies will be outlined so that comparison of EPPE findings with other research studies can be made. What have others found?

- EPPE was replicated in Northern Ireland (Melhuish in this volume) to explore similarities and differences in two countries within the UK. The findings in Northern Ireland have been similar to those in England with respect to the impact of pre-school on all children, the importance of quality, the early years HLE, and the variability between settings in both quality and impact. The great similarity between the findings in the two contexts within the United Kingdom allows confidence in the robustness and generalisability of the results and their interpretations.

- Short and medium-term positive effects of pre-school education have been shown conclusively in the US, Sweden, Norway, Germany, Canada, Northern Ireland and New Zealand. There are too many for a complete list, but Melhuish (2004) provides a good summary. Finally the large US National Institute of Child Health and Development (NICHD) study of more than 1,100 children in 11 regions of the US have shown small but consistent positive effects of pre-school care and education (NICHD ECCRN, 2002a; Belsky et al., 2007). This study also followed a cohort of children and used value-added measures. It sampled very few children in each centre, however, and could not establish the effects of individual centres.

- The effects of greater staff training and qualifications have been shown in the US (Peisner-Feinberg and Burchinal, 1997) and in Northern Ireland (Melhuish et al. this volume). Other studies, especially in the US, find few effects on children's outcomes of greater staff qualifications or education (Early et al., 2006). This may be due to the fact that many studies are carried out in day care settings with a narrow range of qualification levels, possibly too narrow a range to establish the effects of qualifications on children's development.

- The contribution of quality to children's developmental progress has been shown in many studies, often using the ECERS observational scale (Melhuish, 2004) and other quality assessments (NICHD ECCRN, 2002b; Mashburn, 2008).

- The NICHD (2002a) found that family characteristics have a greater impact on outcomes for children than pre-school factors. However, the effect of attending pre-school (versus not) on developmental progress is greater than the effect of social disadvantage. In addition, for children attending pre-school, the effect of attending a specific centre is about half that of all social background factors (NICHD, 2002a).

- Longer duration in centre-based care was found in EPPE to relate to better cognitive outcomes, more Independence and improved Peer Sociability at 5 years, but also to slightly higher scores on anti-social behaviour in a small number of children. These findings are similar to those in the US and Northern Ireland (NICHD ECCRN, 2002a; Melhuish, et al., 2002; Melhuish et al., 2006). Note that the NICHD finds continuing adverse effects on selected aspects of social development at age 10 whereas EPPE found that the earlier, adverse effects on social development are no longer apparent at the age of 11. Note that the positive effects of early entry into child care remain at the end of primary school, as do the positive cognitive effects.

- The findings on disadvantage are mirrored elsewhere (see Melhuish, 2004a; Kysel *et al.*, 1983; Magnuson and Waldfogel, 2005) and are the basis of policy initiatives all over the world (Young, 1996). Experimental studies on disadvantaged children and families often show significant gains for children who attend high quality early education and care (Schweinhart *et al.*, 1993).
- EPPE found sector differences, with higher quality and better outcomes in the maintained (or state) sector. This effect of 'type' has been found in a large North American study (Sosinsky *et al.*, 2009) showing highest quality in state (called 'public') provision, followed by private provision that is not-for-profit, and with for-profit centres showing the lowest quality.

EPPE is one of few studies (the only one in the UK) to demonstrate the role of pre-school education as an effective means of early intervention in special educational needs (SEN) (Sammons *et al.*, 2002; Melhuish *et al.*, 2006). This will require replication elsewhere.

In some findings, EPPE is indeed unique and has gone beyond previous research in the field. It is the first large-scale, multi-level modelling study to show convincingly that individual pre-school centres have lasting effects on children's development. Previous research has shown that *certain types of centres/programmes* or *certain types of children* benefit from pre-school education. EPPE has identified the effects of individual centres, and this has not been done before because it requires a relatively high number of children in each of the centres in the sample.

Reflections on methodology

An educational effectiveness design

Instead of following an experimental, small scale design, EPPE adopted an 'educational effectiveness' approach (see Chapter 3) that studied several thousand children from 'typical' pre-schools all across England. This large and varied sample allowed generalisation to children and families of diverse backgrounds who attended typical kinds of settings. The advantage of an experiment, however, is its control for selection effects, i.e. children/families who are randomly assigned to either experimental or control groups are similar to one another and recruited from the same population. EPPE had to control for possible 'selection' effects through statistical use of co-variates such as parental education, child's birth weight or the language spoken at home. The rich data on child, family and the early years HLE had to be taken into account before estimating the effects of pre-school.

A further advantage of the EPPE design was that recruiting through settings and not from birth or health/benefit records allowed many children in each centre to be studied, not just a few. The well-known studies such as the NICHD and the Cost, Quality and Childcare Outcomes research (CQCO Study Team, 1995) have studied approximately 1–4 children in each setting, making it difficult (if not impossible) to find the effects of any one setting on the children who attend it. EPPE recruited approximately twenty children from each setting and these clusters of children within each setting allow reliable testing of its effects on children.

The government's funding of EPPE allowed intensive follow-up of children and parents, leading to low attrition and high response rates when compared to comparable studies. In addition, the researchers were able to assess young children in 1:1 individual testing, an expensive option but one that is necessary for the collection of robust and reliable assessments about development in very young children. Likewise, the initial parent interview that established family demographics and the HLE was carried out in 1:1 interviews with parents; EPPE did not rely on postal questionnaires or group discussions. Thus EPPE was able to collect a rich and detailed record of children and families to use in complex statistical analysis calling for larger samples and reliable measurements. In addition these data enabled us to explore interaction effects such as the way that the HLE and quality *combine* in shaping outcomes.

EPPE's use of mixed methods

Siraj-Blatchford *et al.*, 2006 and Sammons, *et al.*, 2005 have written of the advantages of a mixed methods approach to policy relevant research. Both argue that the qualitative element of EPPE did more than 'illustrate' the quantitative findings; it led to new findings and novel interpretations. For example, the informal observations and the semi-structured interviews in the REPEY study (Siraj-Blatchford *et al.*, 2002) found that 'sustained shared thinking' was at the heart of children's advances in understanding or skill. Through the case studies we learned about the diverse ways that adults can support children's learning through modelling, instruction, open questioning – and these insights came from the qualitative data analysis. This deepened considerably our understanding of good practice in settings whose children had positive developmental trajectories. After establishing the important role for adult 'guidance' and 'scaffolding', the researchers then refined the coding categories in the quantitative Target Child observations. Thus the quantitative analyses were able to inform and alter the qualitative ones. They also enabled rich description of practice that helped practitioners access our findings. The vignettes and direct quotations have been used to support continuous professional development.

EPPE's over-sampling of high quality settings and of disadvantaged children

From the outset EPPE wished to investigate the effects of different kinds of provision on children's development, while focusing in detail on those from disadvantaged backgrounds. Centres varied in terms of sector, staffing, structural and process quality. In order to make a robust test of the effects of high quality or of exposure to trained teachers, for example, EPPE had to sample sufficient numbers of settings with high quality scores or highly trained staff. For this reason EPPE did not select a sample that was nationally representative of settings across the country. To do this would have led to a final sample that was strongly weighted to the private and voluntary sectors as these are the most numerous. By sampling approximately *equal numbers of settings* in the maintained, voluntary, and private sectors, EPPE invited many settings of very high quality, led by trained teachers, to join the study. So, although EPPE selected its centres through random procedures, it did this after stratifying according to sector and type. By over-sampling pre-schools of higher quality, EPPE was able to study the effects of high quality on children's development, something that would not have been possible with proportionally representative sampling strategy. A stringent test of the effects of quality required a wide range of quality scores in the sample of settings, and many other studies have not sampled across such a range.

At the very beginning, EPPE over-sampled children from disadvantaged backgrounds. This was done for two reasons: they were particularly important to the research aims, and these children are the ones who often drop out of research. By the time the EPPE children reached the end of primary school, and after attrition, the EPPE sample was broadly representative of children and families across the country.

Informing policy through working in partnership with policy makers

We believe that EPPE has confirmed many findings on Early Childhood from elsewhere, especially the effects of poverty on children and of high quality pre-school. However, in some areas EPPE has broken new ground in design and findings related to:

- the interaction of the HLE with pre-school quality;
- the interaction of pre-school and primary school effects;
- the possibility of using qualitative and quantitative methods in an iterative way (see Chapters 3 and 8);
- demonstrating compositional effects, e.g. the effects on any child's development of the characteristics of other children/families in their particular centre.

By the end of the first phase of research in 2004, the 'patchy' early years provision found nationally in 1997 had been transformed into a large and complex system of services, both universal and targeted. EPPE had to change its design as it progressed to keep pace with evolving policies.

EPPE was not conceived as an exercise in 'pure science'. From its very beginning the researchers intended to produce robust answers to key policy questions concerning the care and education of young children. However, EPPE's answers to policy questions take into account the social contexts in which young children live, making the findings relevant to policy concerning pre-schools, primary schools and families. The policy recommendations of this very large and complex study that relate to Early Childhood fall into six clusters:

Universal entitlement to pre-school will benefit all children

Children who did not attend pre-school (the home group) did not make a strong start to school; they were especially lacking in the cognitive, linguistic and self-regulation skills that make a child 'ready to learn'. Overall, positive pre-school effects were still found in children's scores in English, Mathematics and Peer sociability at the age of 11.

Improving quality will improve outcomes for all

Sector is important and its effects last to age 7: quality was higher in the maintained sector (replicated in the Millennium Cohort Study (MCS) nationally representative study by Mathers et al., 2007). By the end of KS1, EPPE children who had attended the maintained or state sector (integrated centres that had been nursery schools) had made more progress than those who had attended pre-schools in the voluntary or private sectors. For equality of opportunity, there needs to be a 'level playing field' in the various sectors of provision. What is the reason for sector effect – is it trained teachers?

Targeted resources are needed: disadvantaged children benefit more from high quality than their advantaged peers. Lack of high quality pre-school is a loss of particular significance for children from multiply disadvantaged backgrounds.

The Early Years workforce needs up-skilling: qualifications of staff underpin high quality provision. Children make more progress when they attend settings with highly qualified staff. Staff with full qualified teacher status (QTS) were often found in the higher quality settings, especially those settings that scored high on aspects of pedagogy that lead to cognitive development and a strong start to school.

The combining of care and education should be at the heart of services for children and families

Our study shows that settings that combined care and education, along with nursery schools, had very high quality of provision for young children's learning and development. Importantly, their children made more progress than children in all other types of provision, except for nursery schools whose children, in general, did as well.

Supporting the Home Learning Environment in families

This will improve development in disadvantaged children. Parental characteristics such as education, and to a lesser extent employment, are related to children's progress, but even more important than demographic characteristics are the activities parents engage in routinely with their children. The Early HLE continues to exert a powerful influence on children's development throughout pre-school and primary education, and services that enhance these 'educative' features of parenting should contribute to better outcomes for children.

A 'balanced' pedagogy (between cognitive and social/ emotional goals, between guided and free play) needs to be maintained in pre-school settings

Case studies of excellent settings (defined as those where children made more progress than would have been expected from their backgrounds) showed that children made more progress in settings where cognitive and social goals were seen as complementary and equally important for all children.

Conversations focused on children's activities matter: staff and children in 'Excellent' settings engaged more in *sustained shared thinking* compared to settings with only moderate-to-good children's outcomes. Pre-schools can be particularly effective at enhancing children's language skills, especially at the start of school. Sustained shared thinking also encourages children to be curious and adept at problem-solving.

Freely chosen activities can be balanced with adult extension of children's play. Staff in 'excellent' settings extended children's self-chosen activities, often through light-touch 'instruction' such as open questions or modelling.

'Early intervention' through universal services

Pre-schools of high quality can serve as an 'intervention' for vulnerable children. Children who are 'at risk' of poor development are less likely to be identified as having Special Educational Needs if they attend pre-school settings of high quality. Thus pre-school can contribute to the development of children's resilience (Hall *et al.*, 2009)

Summing up

The EPPE study has demonstrated the importance of early learning, whether at a pre-school setting or at home. The impact of pre-school has been studied in different ways, not just whether a child attends pre-school or not but also the effect of specific characteristics of settings such as quality, staff qualifications or sector. EPPE has shown how the duration of pre-school as well as specific characteristics of children and families matter too. Its large sample revealed complex patterns of use and benefits, especially as they relate to children who are multiply disadvantaged. These are the ones with the most to gain.

EPPE is innovative also in showing how pre-school and primary school interact as they influence children, with high quality pre-school acting as a buffer against less effective primary schooling. For some vulnerable children, the quality of their pre-school contributed towards resilience. In the case of children 'at risk' of SEN, high quality pre-school can reduce the risk of future identification as having a SEN in primary school. Children who experience high quality pre-school show better overall long term outcomes and it has been suggested that these children have 'learnt how to learn'. Interestingly, in the case of English, those who attended a low quality pre-school do no better at age 11 in a medium or highly effective primary school than in a low effective school. Perhaps the children from low quality pre-school setting had not 'learnt how to learn' and so were unable to 'latch on' to the opportunities offered in a medium to highly effective primary school.

Whilst the EPPE research has many strengths, it also had limitations. Large scale studies such as this cannot reveal particular 'local' conditions that make each pre-setting unique. The twelve case studies went some way towards explaining uniqueness, but what about the remaining 129 settings? Each of them was a unique blend of people and environments. EPPE revealed the factors that in general, across our sample, had an impact on children's development. This 'broad picture' was the original intention, with the important exception of the very detailed case studies of effective centres. Still, there was much that EPPE did not account for; case studies are ideal for studying uniqueness in individuals or in settings.

Another limitation of the EPPE design is its focus on processes and outcomes (skills, attitudes and practices) that lend themselves to quantification. EPPE did not study, for example, curiosity or creativity in children, not because they are unimportant but because they are so difficult to measure. We did not shy away from studying curiosity or creativity because of disinterest but because there is little agreement about how it should be assessed. However, EPPE has identified persistent and regular patterns in practices and outcomes that could be measured, that we know are important for children's present and their future lives.

And finally, the large scale and 'objective' nature of the EPPE design (with the important exception of the qualitative case studies) means that the individual 'voices' of participants are rarely heard. We interviewed and observed thousands of children, parents and staff, but most of what they said has been turned into a number! Other research studies have great strength in capturing and analysing the voice of participants; studies such as EPPE are complemented by small scale or qualitative research that goes beneath the surface to bring alive the voices of children and their carers. Such qualitative studies both document and interpret educational or parenting practices. The EPPE researchers interacted with practitioners and other professionals and used their advice to inform our methods. We also listened to children. But in thousands of pages of reporting on EPPE, these important voices are easily lost in a forest of graphs and charts! We therefore conclude this book with a toast of gratitude to the thousands of children, parents, professionals and policy makers who advised us, criticised us, allowed us access and told us tales of 'what happened yesterday'. *Every* number in *every* table derives from human conversations and observations. For each of these we are grateful.

The EPPE research has proved innovative in design and its bold research aims. The mixed methods approach has allowed the quantitative findings to be (cautiously) generalised while the qualitative findings illuminate the details of good practice. The case studies have put a spotlight on effective pedagogy and dispelled some myths about practice. However, this book is just the beginning of the EPPE story. Several thousand EPPE children are now teenagers and we continue to study the factors that shape their development.

References

Belsky, J., Vandell, D., Burchinal, D., Clarke-Stewart, M., McCartney, K.A., Owen, K. and the NICHD ECCRN. (2007) Are there long-term effects of early child care? *Child Development*, 78, 2.

Children's Workforce Development Council (2008) *Introduction and Information Guide. Early Years Professionals Creating Brighter Futures*, Leeds: Children's Workforce Development Council.

Cost, Quality and Child Outcomes Study Team (CQO) (1995) *Cost, Quality and Child Outcomes in Child Care Centers Public Report*, Denver, CO: Economics Department, University of Colorado-Denver. ED 386 297.

Department for Children, Schools and Families (DCSF) (2009) *Next Steps for Early Learning and Childcare. Reference no.: DCSF-00173-2009*. Retrieved 10 May 2009 at http://publications.dcsf.gov.uk/default.aspx?PageFunction=productdetails&PageMode=publications&ProductId=DCSF-00173-2009

Department for Education and Employment (1996) *Nursery Education Desirable Outcomes for Children's Learning on Entering Compulsory Schooling*, London: Schools Curriculum and Assessment Authority/DfEE (currently under review).

Department for Education and Employment (2000) *Curriculum Guidance for the Foundation Stage*, London: QCA.

Department for Education and Skills, Department for Work and Pensions, HM Treasury (2002) *Inter-departmental Childcare Review – November 2002. Delivering for Children and Families*, London: The Strategy Unit, Cabinet Office.

Department for Education and Skills (DfES) (2003) *Every Child Matters*, Norwich: HMSO.

Department for Education and Skills (2006) *Children's Workforce Strategy: the Government's Response to the Consultation*, Nottingham: DfES.

Department for Education and Skills (2008) *Early Years Foundation Stage Profile Handbook*, London: Qualifications and Curriculum Authority.

Early, D.M., Bryant, D.M., Pianta, R.C., Clifford, R.M., Burchinal, M.R., Ritchie, S., Howes, C. and Barbarin, O. (2006) Are teachers' education, major, and credentials related to classroom quality and children's academic gains in pre-kindergarten? *Early Childhood Research Quarterly*, 21(2) 174–195.

Eisenstadt, N. (2009) 10 years: what we have learned about children, parents and disadvantage. Paper presented at Parents Matter conference, 2009, organised by Longview.

Feinstein, L., Robertson, D. and Symons, J. (1998) *Pre-school Education and Attainment in the NCDS and BCSI*, London: Centre for Economic Performance.

Hall, J., Sylva, K., Mehuish, E., Sammons, P., Siraj-Blatchford, I. and Taggart, B. (2009) The role of pre-school quality in promoting resilience in the cognitive development of young children, *The Oxford Review of Education*, 35(3), 331–52.

Kysel, F., Varlaam, A., Stoll, L., and Sammons, P. (1983) *The Child at School: A New Behaviour Schedule. Research and Statistics Report No. RS 907/83*, London: Inner London Education Authority, Research and Statistics Branch.

Magnuson, K.A. and Waldfogel, J. (2005) Early education care and education: effects of ethnic and racial gaps in school readiness, *Future of Children*, 15(1), 169–196.

Mashburn, A.J. (2008) Quality of social and physical environments in preschools and children's development of academic, language, and literacy skills, *Applied Developmental Science*, 12(3), 103–127.

Mathers, S., Sylva, K. and Joshi, H. (2007) *Quality of Childcare Settings in the Millennium Cohort Study. Research Report 025*, London: DCSF.

Melhuish, E.C. (2004) *A Literature Review of the Impact of Early Years Provision upon Young Children, with Emphasis Given to Children from Disadvantaged Backgrounds*. Report to the Comptroller and Auditor General, London: National Audit Office.

Melhuish, E., Quinn, L., Sylva, K., Sammons, P., Siraj-Blatchford, I., Taggart, B. and Shields, C. (2002) The Effective Pre-school Provision in Northern Ireland Project, Technical Paper 5: Pre-school Experience and Cognitive Development at the Start of Primary School, Belfast: Stranmillis University Press.

Melhuish, E., Romaniuk, H., Sammons, P., Sylva, K., Siraj-Blatchford, I. and Taggart, B. (2006) *The Effective Pre-School and Primary Education 3–11 Project (EPPE 3–11):* The Effectiveness of Primary Schools in England in Key Stage 2 for 2002, 2003 and 2004, London: DfES/Institute of Education, University of London.

Melhuish, E., Sylva, K., Sammons, P., Siraj-Blatchford, I.,Taggart. B. and Quinn, L. (2006) *Effective Pre-school Provision in Northern Ireland (EPPNI) Summary Report*, Northern Ireland: Department of Education. Available at www.deni.gov.uk

National Institute of Child Health and Human Development Early Child Care Research Network (2002a) Early child care and children's development prior to school entry: results from the NICHD Study of Early Child Care, *American Educational Research Journal*, 39(1), 133–164.

National Institute of Child Health and Human Development Early Child Care Research Network (2002b) Child care structure-process-outcome: direct and indirect effects of child care quality on young children's development, *Psychological Science*, 13, 199–206.

Peisner-Feinberg, E.S. and Burchinal, M.R. (1997) Relations between preschool children's childcare experiences and concurrent development: the cost, quality, and outcomes study, *Merrill-Palmer Quarterly*, 43, 451–477.

Sammons, P., Sylva, K., Melhuish, E.C., Siraj-Blatchford, I., Taggart, B. and Elliot, K. (2002) *The Effective Provision of Pre-School Education (EPPE) Project: Technical Paper 8a – Measuring the Impact of Pre-School on Children's Cognitive Progress over the Pre-School Period*, London: DfES/Institute of Education, University of London.

Sammons, P., Siraj-Blatchford, I., Sylva, K., Melhuish, E., Taggart, B. and Elliot, K. (2005) *Investigating the Effects of Pre-School Provision: Using Mixed Methods in the EPPE Research*, *International Journal of Social Research Methodology*, 8(3), 207–224.

Schweinhart, L.J., Barnes, H. and Weikhart, D. (1993) *Significant Benefits: The High/Scope Perry Pre-School Study through age 27*, Ypsilanti, MI: High/Scope Press.

Scott, S., Sylva, K., Doolan, M., Price, J., Jacobs, B., Crook, C. and Landau, S. (in press) Randomized controlled trial of parent groups for child antisocial behaviour targeting multiple risk factors: the SPOKES project, *Journal of Child Psychology and Psychiatry* (JCPP).

Siraj-Blatchford, I., Sylva, K., Muttock, S., Gilden, R. and Bell. D. (2002) *Researching Effective Pedagogy in the Early Years*. Research Report 356, Nottingham, England: Department for Education and Skills.

Siraj-Blatchford, I., Sammons, P., Sylva, K., Melhuish, E. and Taggart, B. (2006) Educational research and evidence-based policy: the mixed method approach of the EPPE project, *Evaluation and Research in Education*. 19(2) 63–82.

Siraj-Blatchford, I., Sylva, K., Taggart, B., Sammons, P., Melhuish, E., and Elliot, K. (2003), *Technical Paper 10 – The Effective Provision of Pre-School Education (EPPE) Project: Intensive Case Studies of Practice across the Foundation Stage*, London: DfEE/Institute of Education, University of London.

Sosinsky, L.S., Lord, H., and Zigler, E. (2007) For –profit/nonprofit differences in center based child care quality: results from the National Institute of Child Health and Human Development Study of Early Child Care and Youth Development, *Journal of Applied Developmental Psychology*, 28, 390–410.

Sylva, K., Taggart, B., Melhuish, E., Sammons, P. and Siraj-Blatchford, I. (2007) Changing models of research to inform educational policy, *Research Papers in Education*, 22(2) 155–168.

Sylva, K., Melhuish, E., Sammons, P., Siraj-Blatchford, I. and Taggart, B. (2008) *Final Report from the Primary Phase: Pre-school, School and Family Influences on Children's Development during Key Stage 2 (7–11) DCSF RR 061*, Nottingham: Department for Children, Schools and Families.

Taggart, B., Siraj-Blatchford, I., Sylva, K., Melhuish, E. and Sammons. P. (2008) Influencing policy and practice through research on Early Childhood Education, *International Journal of Early Childhood Education*, 14, 2.

Young, M. E. (1996) *Early Child Development: Investing in the Future*, Washington, DC: The World Bank.

Appendix I

How children were assessed at different time points throughout the study

Table A1.1 Entry to pre-school (age 3.0 to 4 years 3 months)

Name of assessment	Assessment content	Administered by
British Ability Scales, 2nd edn, (BASII) (Elliot et al., 1996):	Cognitive development battery	
Block Building	Spatial skills	EPPE researcher
Verbal Comprehension	Verbal skills	EPPE researcher
Picture Similarity	Pictorial reasoning skills	EPPE researcher
Naming Vocabulary	Verbal skills	EPPE researcher
Adaptive Social Behavioural Inventory (ASBI) (Hogan et al., 1992)	Social behaviour and emotional adjustment	Centre staff

Children not fluent in English: assessed only on the non-verbal BAS II scales (Block Building and Picture Similarity) and social and emotional behaviour.

Table A1.2 Entry to reception class (age rising 5 years)

Name of assessment	Assessment content	Administered by
British Ability Scales, 2nd edn, (BASII) (Elliot et al., 1996):	Cognitive development battery	
Verbal Comprehension	Verbal skills	EPPE researcher
Picture Similarity	Pictorial reasoning skills	EPPE researcher
Naming Vocabulary	Verbal skills	EPPE researcher
Pattern Construction	Spatial skills	EPPE researcher
BAS Early Number Concepts	Reasoning ability	EPPE researcher
Letter Recognition	Lower case letters	EPPE researcher
Phonological Awareness (Bryant and Bradley, 1985)	Rhyme and alliteration	EPPE researcher
Adaptive Social Behavioural Inventory (ASBI – R) (Hogan et al., 1992)	Social and emotional behaviour, hyperactivity and settling-into-school	Class teacher

Children not fluent in English: assessed only on two of the non-verbal BAS II scales (Picture Similarity and Pattern Construction) and social behaviour. In addition they were assessed on BAS II Copying, a measure of spatial ability (Elliot et al., 1996), which was also administered by the EPPE researcher.

Table A1.3 Exit from reception class (sub-scale sample of 1,000+ children including all 'Home' children)

Name of assessment	Assessment content	Administered by
British Ability Scales Second Edition (BASII) (Elliot *et al.*, 1996):		
Early Number Concepts	Reasoning	EPPE researcher
Word Reading	Reading single words	EPPE researcher
Letter Recognition	Lower case letters	EPPE researcher
Phonological Awareness (Bryant and Bradley, 1985)	Rhyme and alliteration	EPPE researcher
Dictation Test (Clay, 1985)	Phonological approximation to written words	EPPE researcher
Adaptive Social Behavioural Inventory – Revised (ASBI – R) (Hogan *et al.*, 1992)	Social emotional adjustment behaviour, hyperactivity and settling-into-school	Class teacher

Children not fluent in English: Assessed only on the non-verbal BAS II scale (Early Number Concepts and Copying) and social behaviour.

Table A1.4 At end of Year 1 (age 6+)

Name of assessment	Assessment content	Administered by
Primary Reading: Level 1 (NFER-Nelson)		Class teacher
Maths 6 (NFER-Nelson)		Class teacher
Strengths and difficulties questionnaire (Goodman, 1997) for extended study	Hyperactivity, conduct problems, peer problems, emotional problems and prosocial	Class teacher

Table A1.5 At end of Year 2 – end of Key Stage 1 (age 7+)

Name of assessment	Assessment content	Administered by
Strengths and difficulties questionnaire (Goodman, 1997) extended for study	Hyperactivity, conduct problems, peer problems, emotional problems and pro-social	Class teacher
Attitudes to school questionnaire	Children's views on academic and social activities	Completed by child
Record of conduct / emotional problems		School records
National assessments	Reading, Writing and Maths: national assessments Science: teacher assessed	School records

Table A1.6 At end of Year 5 (age 10+)

Name of assessment	Assessment content	Administered by
Primary Reading: Level 2 (NFER-Nelson)		Class teacher
Maths 10 (NFER-Nelson)		Class teacher
Strengths and difficulties questionnaire (Goodman, 1997) extended for study	Hyperactivity, conduct problems, peer problems, emotional problems and pro-social	Class teacher
Attitudes to school questionnaire	Children's views on academic and social activities All about me and all about me in school	Completed by child
Record of conduct/ emotional problems		From school records

Table A1.7 At end of Year 6 – end of Key Stage 2 (age 11+)

Name of assessment	Assessment content	Administered by
National assessments	English, Mathematics and Science	From National Pupil Database
Strengths and difficulties questionnaire (Goodman, 1997) extended for study	Hyperactivity, conduct problems, peer problems, emotional problems and pro-social	Class teacher

Appendix 2
The Home Learning Environment at different time points

Pre-school

Frequency (measured on 7 point scale):

Is X read to?
Taken to the library?
Paint and draw at home?
Child plays with friends elsewhere (outside home)?

Parents' emphasis/frequency on teaching/playing with ABC/The Alphabet/ letters

Parents' emphasis/frequency on teaching/playing with numbers, any songs/ poems, parents' emphasis/frequency on teaching/singing songs/poems, nursery rhymes?

Collect evidence on the above by prompts on what is used, e.g. favourite books read, range of songs, nursery rhymes, etc., contexts for playing with numbers/ letters.

Key Stage 1

How often do you:

Play with EPPE child with toys/games/puzzles?
Play computer games with X?
Visits library with X?
Listen to X read?
Read to X?
Use computer with X educationally?
Do sport/physical activities with X?
Go on educational visits with X?

How often does X
Play with computer?
Play make-believe/pretend?

Paint/draw/make models?
Enjoy dance/music/movement?

How many hours of TV/video does your EPPE child watch on a typical weekday?

How often do you help your EPPE child with homework?

What time does your EPPE child usually go to bed?

Key Stage 2

How often do you do the following with X:

Join in games or play?
Visit the library?
Listen to X read?
Read to X?
Teach a school subject, e.g. geography, science, English?
Sport, dance or physical activities?
Go on educational visits such as museums, nature parks, farm, etc.?
Go shopping?
Play computer games, i.e. play station, X-Box, etc.?
Use a computer in educational ways, e.g. spelling or KS1 SATs CD Roms?
Use the internet for learning?
Use the internet for play/recreation?

How often does X do this on their own?

Plays games on computer or play station, X- Box, etc.?
Uses the computer for activities related to learning?
Uses the internet?
Paints, draws or makes models?
Enjoys dance, music, movement?
Reads on their own?

How many hours of TV/video does X watch on a typical weekday (not weekends)?

How many hours does your child spend playing onscreen games (computer, playstation etc.) on a typical weekday?

Does your child have a TV/video in their bedroom?

What time does your EPPE child usually go to bed during term time?

Does your child have their own mobile phone?

Does your EPPE child receive any kind of education/teaching *outside* school hours? What?

Appendix 3
The EPPE Technical Papers/Reports/Research Briefs

Technical Paper 1 – An Introduction to the Effective Provision of Pre-school Education (EPPE) Project.
  Published: Autumn 1999. Price £8.50
Technical Paper 2 – Characteristics of the Effective Provision of Pre-School Education (EPPE) Project Sample at Entry to the study.
Published: Autumn 1999. Price £4.00
Technical Paper 3 – Contextualising EPPE: Interviews with Local Authority Co-ordinators and Centre Managers.
  Published: Autumn 1999. Price £3.50
Technical Paper 4 – Parent, Family and Child Characteristics in Relation to Type of Pre-school and Socio-economic Differences
  Published: Autumn 1999. Price £4.00
Technical Paper 5 – Characteristics of the Centre in the EPPE Study: (Interviews).
  Published: Autumn 2000. Price £5.00
Technical Paper 6 – Characteristics of the Centres in the EPPE Sample: Observational Profiles.
  Published: Autumn 1999. Price £8.50
Technical Paper 6A – Characteristics of Pre-School Environments.
  Published: Autumn 1999. Price £8.50
Technical Paper 7 – Social/Behavioural and Cognitive Development at 3–4 Years in Relation to Family Background.
  Published: Spring 2001. Price £5.00
Technical Paper 8a – Measuring the Impact of Pre-School on Children's Cognitive Progress over the Pre-School Period.
  Published: Autumn 2002. Price £8.50
Technical Paper 8b – Measuring the Impact of Pre-School on Children's Social/behavioural Development over the Pre-School Period.
  Published: March 2003. Price £8.50
Technical Paper 9 – Report on Age 6 Assessment.
  Published: November 2004. Price £5.50
Technical Paper 10 – Intensive Study of Selected Centres.
  Published: Autumn 2003. Price £11.00
Technical Paper 11 – Report on the Continuing Effects of Pre-school Education at Age 7.
  Published: November 2004. Price £5.50

Technical Paper 12 – The final report: Effective Pre-school Education.
Published: November 2004. Price £5.50

Effective Pre-school and Primary Education 3–11 Project (EPPE 3–11): The Effectiveness of Primary Schools in England in Key Stage 2 for 2002, 2003 and 2004. Full Report. London: Institute of Education, University of London.
http://eppe.ioe.ac.uk/eppe3-11/eppe3-11%20pdfs/eppepapers/Tier%20 1%20full%20report%20-%20Final.pdf. Published: 2006

Effective Pre-school and Primary Education 3–11 (EPPE 3–11): The Effectiveness of Primary Schools in England in Key Stage 2 for 2002, 2003 and 2004, Research Brief No. RBX06-06. Nottingham: DfES Publications.
http://eppe.ioe.ac.uk/eppe3-11/eppe3-11%20pdfs/eppepapers/Tier%20 1%20Research%20Brief.pdf. Published: 2006

Effective Pre-school and Primary Education 3–11 Project (EPPE 3–11): Influences on Children's Attainment and Progress in Key Stage 2: Cognitive Outcomes in Year 5. Full Report. London: Institute of Education, University of London.
http://eppe.ioe.ac.uk/eppe3-11/eppe3-11%20pdfs/eppepapers/Tier%20 2%20full%20report%20-%20Final.pdf. Published: 2007

Sammons, P., Sylva, K., Melhuish, E., Siraj-Blatchford, I., Taggart, B., Grabbe, Y. and Barreau, S. (2007), *Effective Pre-school and Primary Education 3–11 Project (EPPE 3–11) Summary Report: Influences on Children's Attainment and Progress in Key Stage 2: Cognitive Outcomes in Year 5.* Research Report No. RR828. Nottingham: DfES Publications.
http://eppe.ioe.ac.uk/eppe3-11/eppe3-11%20pdfs/eppepapers/Tier%20 2%20short%20report%20-%20Final.pdf.

Sammons, P., Sylva, K., Melhuish, E., Siraj-Blatchford, I., Taggart, B., Grabbe, Y. and Barreau, S. (2007), *Effective Pre-school and Primary Education 3–11 Project (EPPE 3–11): Influences on Children's Attainment and Progress in Key Stage 2: Cognitive Outcomes in Year 5.* Research Brief No. RB828. Nottingham: DfES Publications.
http://eppe.ioe.ac.uk/eppe3-11/eppe3-11%20pdfs/eppepapers/Tier%20 2%20Research%20Brief.pdf.

Sammons, P., Sylva, K., Melhuish, E., Siraj-Blatchford, I., Taggart, B., Barreau, S. and Grabbe, Y. (2007), *Effective Pre-school and Primary Education 3–11 Project (EPPE 3–11): Influences on Children's Development and Progress in Key Stage 2: Social/behavioural Outcomes in Year 5.* Research Report No. DCSF-RR007. Nottingham: DfES Publications.
http://eppe.ioe.ac.uk/eppe3-11/eppe3-11%20pdfs/Tier2%20Final%20 Report%20SOCS.pdf.

Sammons, P., Sylva, K., Melhuish, E., Siraj-Blatchford, I., Taggart, B., Barreau, S. and Grabbe, Y. (2007), *Effective Pre-school and Primary Education 3–11 Project (EPPE 3–11): Influences on Children's Development and Progress in Key Stage 2: Social/behavioural Outcomes in Year 5.* Research Brief No. DCSF-RB007. Nottingham: DfES Publications.
http://eppe.ioe.ac.uk/eppe3-11/eppe3-11%20pdfs/Tier2%20Research%20 Brief%20SOCS.pdf.

Effective Pre-school and Primary Education 3–11 Project (EPPE 3–11): Variations in Teacher and Pupil Behaviours in Year 5 Classrooms and Associations with School Characteristics. Full Report. London: Institute of Education, University of London.
http://eppe.ioe.ac.uk/eppe3-11/eppe3-11%20pdfs/eppepapers/Tier%20 3%20full%20report%20-%20Final.pdf. Published: 2006

Effective Pre-school and Primary Education 3–11 (EPPE 3–11) Summary Report: Variations in Teacher and Pupil Behaviours in Year 5 Classes. Research Report No. 817. Nottingham: DfES Publications.
http://eppe.ioe.ac.uk/eppe3-11/eppe3-11%20pdfs/eppepapers/EPPE%20 dfes%20Tier3%20Final%20summary%20research%20report.pdf. Published: 2006

Effective Pre-school and Primary Education 3–11 (EPPE 3–11): Variations in Teacher and Pupil Behaviours in Year 5 Classes: Research Brief No. RB817. Nottingham: DfES Publications.
http://eppe.ioe.ac.uk/eppe3-11/eppe3-11%20pdfs/eppepapers/Tier%20 3%20Research%20Brief.pdf. Published: 2006

The Influences of School and Teaching Quality on Children's Progress in Primary School. Research Report DCSF RR07. Nottingham: DCSF Publications.
http://eppe.ioe.ac.uk/eppe3-11/eppe3-11%20pdfs/eppepapers/DCSF-RR028.pdf. Published: 2007

The Influences of School and Teaching Quality on Children's Progress in Primary School. Research Report DCSF RB07. Nottingham: DCSF Publications.
http://eppe.ioe.ac.uk/eppe3-11/eppe3-11%20pdfs/eppepapers/DCSF-RB028.pdf. Published: 2007

Tracking and Mobility over the Pre-School and Primary School Period: Evidence from EPPE 3–11. London: Institute of Education, University of London.
http://eppe.ioe.ac.uk/eppe3-11/eppe3-11%20pdfs/eppepapers/ TrackingMobility16Sept08.pdf. Published: 2008

Relationships Between Pupils' Self-Perceptions, Views of Primary School and their Development in Year 5. London: Institute of Education, University of London.
http://eppe.ioe.ac.uk/eppe3-11/eppe3-11%20pdfs/eppepapers/ RelationshipSelfPercpViewSchool16Sept08.pdf. Published: 2008

Influences on Pupils' Self-Perceptions in Primary School: Enjoyment of school, Anxiety and Isolation, and Self-image in Year 5. London: Institute of Education, University of London.
http://eppe.ioe.ac.uk/eppe3-11/eppe3-11%20pdfs/eppepapers/ Influences16Sept08.pdf. Published: 2008

Exploring Pupils' Views of Primary School in Year 5. London: Institute of Education, University of London.
http://eppe.ioe.ac.uk/eppe3-11/eppe3-11%20pdfs/eppepapers/ PupilsViewsYr5.pdf. Published: 2008

Final Report from the Primary Phase: Pre-school, School and Family Influences on children's development during Key Stage 2 (7–11). DCSF RR 061. Nottingham: The Department for Children, Schools and Families.
http://eppe.ioe.ac.uk/eppe3-11/eppe3-11%20pdfs/eppepapers/Final%20 3-11%20report%20DCSF-RR061%2027nov08.pdf. Published: 2008

Final Report from the Primary Phase: Pre-school, School and Family Influences on Children's Development During Key Stage 2 (7–11). DCSF RB 061. Nottingham: The Department for Children, Schools and Families.
http://eppe.ioe.ac.uk/eppe3-11/eppe3-11%20pdfs/eppepapers/Final%20 3-11%20rb%20DCSF-RB061%2027nov08.pdf. Published: 2008

Other related publications

Harms, T., Clifford, R.E. and Cryer, D. (1998) *The Early Childhood Environment Rating Scale: Revised Edition* (1998). Available from Teachers College Press, Columbia University, 1234 Amsterdam Avenue, New York NY10027

Sylva, K., Siraj-Blatchford, I. and Taggart, B (2003) *Assessing Quality in the Early Years, Early Childhood Environment Rating Scale Extension (ECERS-E): Four Curricular Subscales* (2003) Nottingham: Trentham Books.

Early Years Transition and Special Educational Needs (EYTSEN) Technical Paper 1: Special Educational Needs across the Pre-school Period. Published Autumn 2002. Price £8.00

Early Years Transition and Special Educational Needs (EYTSEN) Technical Paper 2: Special Educational Needs in the Early Primary Years: Primary School Entry up to the End of Year One. Published Summer 2004. Price £8.00

Early Years Transition and Special Educational Needs (EYTSEN) Technical Paper 3: Special Educational Needs: The Parents' Perspective. Published Summer 2004. Price £8.00

Ordering information

For EPPE Publications: the bookshop at the Institute of Education, Hammicks Education Bookshop, The Institute of Education, 20 Bedford Way, London WC1H 0AL. Tel: +44 (0)20 7612 6050. Fax: +44 (0)20 7612 6407: Email: ioe@ hammicks.co.uk www.jscampus.co.uk/ioe or visit the Department for Children, Schools and Families website at http://www.dcsf.gov.uk/research/ or the EPPSE website at http://eppe.ioe.ac.uk

Appendix 4

Social/behavioural dimensions at different time points (items associated with dimensions)

Table A4.1 The specific items associated with each social/behavioural dimension at entry to pre-school

Co-operation and conformity	Peer sociability
1 Is helpful to other children 2 Is obedient and compliant 3 Follows rules in games 4 Waits his/her turn in games or other activities 5 Cooperates with your requests 6 Follows household or pre-school centre rules 7 Says 'please' and 'thank you' when reminded 8 Is calm and easy-going 9 Shares toys or possessions	1 Understands others' feelings, like when they are happy, sad or angry 2 Is sympathetic toward other children's distress, tries to comfort others when they are upset 3 Can easily get other children to pay attention to him/her 4 Says nice or friendly things to others, or is friendly toward others 5 Will join a group of children playing 6 In social activities, tends to just watch others 7 Asks or wants to go and play with other children 8 Plays games and talks to other children
Confidence	**Anti-social**
1 Is open and direct about what he/she wants 2 Is confident with other people 3 Tends to be proud of things she/he does 4 Is interested in many and different things 5 Enjoys talking to you	1 Teases other children, calls them names 2 Prevents other children from carrying out routines 3 Bullies other children 4 Is bossy, needs to have his/her way
Worried/upset	
1 When you give him/her an idea for playing, he/she frowns, shrugs shoulders, pouts or stamps foot 2 Gets upset when you don't pay enough attention 3 Accepts changes without fighting against them or becoming upset 4 Is worried about not getting enough (where enough might include attention, access to toys, food/drink, etc.)	

Table A4.2 The specific items associated with each social/behavioural dimension at entry to primary school

Independence and concentration	Co-operation and conformity
1 **Thinks things out before acting** 2 **Easily distracted, concentration wanders** 3 Can move to a new activity on completion of a task 4 Can independently select and return equipment as appropriate 5 **Constantly fidgeting or squirming** 6 Perseveres in the face of difficult or challenging tasks 7 Likes to work things out for self; seeks help from teacher/other children only as a last resort; can work independently 8 **Restless, overactive, cannot stay still for long** 9 **Sees tasks through to the end, good attention span**	1 Tries to be fair in games 2 Is obedient and compliant 3 Follows rules in games 4 Can behave appropriately during less structured sessions, with no more than one reminder 5 Waits his/her turn in games or other activities 6 Co-operates with your requests 7 Follows school rules 8 Says 'please' and 'thank you' when reminded 9 Is calm and easy going 10 Can work easily in a small peer group 11 Shares toys or possessions 12 Accepts changes without fighting against them or becoming upset
Peer sociability	Anti-social/worried
1 Can easily get other children to pay attention to him/her 2 Will join a group of children playing 3 In social activities, tends to just watch others 4 Asks or wants to go and play with other children 5 Plays games and talks with other children 6 Is confident with other people 7 Will invite others to join in a game	1 When you give him/her an idea for playing, he/she frowns, shrugs shoulders, pouts or stamps foot 2 Gets upset when you don't pay enough attention 3 Teases other children, calls them names 4 Prevents other children from carrying out routines 5 Bullies other children 6 Is worried about not getting enough (where enough might include attention, access to toys, food/drink etc.) 7 Is bossy, needs to have his/her way

Note:
Goodman items are in bold

Table A4.3 The specific items associated with each social/behavioural dimension in Year 1 and Year 2

Self-regulation	Anxious behaviour
1 **Easily distracted, concentration wanders** 2 Can behave appropriately during less structured sessions 3 Can move to a new activity on completion of a task 4 Can independently select and return equipment as appropriate 5 Can work easily in a small peer group 6 Perseveres in the face of difficult or challenging tasks 7 Likes to work things out for self; can work independently 8 Shows leadership in group work 9 Can take responsibility for a task	1 **Often complains of headaches, stomach aches or sickness** 2 **Many worries, often seems worried** 3 **Often unhappy, downhearted or tearful** 4 **Nervous or clingy in new situations, easily loses confidence** 5 **Many fears, easily scared**
Positive social behaviour	Anti-social behaviour
1 **Considerate of other people's feelings** 2 **Shares readily with other children (treats, toys, pencils, etc.)** 3 **Helpful if someone is hurt, upset or feeling ill** 4 **Kind to younger children** 5 **Often volunteers to help others (teachers, other children)** 6 Will invite others to join the game 7 Says 'please' and 'thank you' 8 Apologises spontaneously 9 Offers to help others having difficulties with a task 10 Is sympathetic toward other children when they are upset	1 **Restless, overactive, cannot stay still for long** 2 **Often has temper tantrums or hot tempers** 3 **Constantly fidgeting or squirming** 4 **Often fights with other children or bullies them** 5 **Often lies or cheats** 6 **Steals from home, school or elsewhere** 7 Is calm and easy going 8 Teases other children, calls them names 9 Prevents other children from carrying out routines

Note:
Goodman items are in bold

Table A4.4 The specific items associated with each social/behavioural dimension in Year 5 and Year 6

Hyperactivity	Self-regulation
1 **Restless, overactive, cannot stay still for long** 2 **Constantly fidgeting or squirming** 3 **Easily distracted, concentration wanders** 4 **Thinks things out before acting** 5 **Sees tasks through to the end, good attention span** 6 Quickly loses interest in what she/he is doing 7 Gets over excited 8 Is easily frustrated 9 Is impulsive, acts without thinking 10 Can behave appropriately during less structured lessons 11 Fails to pay attention 12 Makes careless mistakes	1 Likes to work things out for self; seeks help rarely 2 Does not need much help with tasks 3 Chooses activities on their own 4 Persists in the face of difficult tasks 5 Can move on to a new activity after finishing a task 6 Is open and direct about what she/he wants 7 Is confident with others 8 Shows leadership in group work 9 Can take responsibility for a task
Pro-social behaviour	Anti-social behaviour
1 **Considerate of other people's feelings** 2 **Shares readily with other children (treats, toys, pencils, etc.)** 3 **Helpful if someone is hurt, upset or feeling ill** 4 **Kind to younger children** 5 **Often volunteers to help others (teachers, other children)** 6 Apologises spontaneously 7 Offers to help others having difficulties with a task 8 Is sympathetic to others if they are upset	1 **Often fights with other children or bullies them** 2 **Often lies or cheats** 3 **Steals from home, school or elsewhere** 4 Vandalises property or destroys things 5 Shows inappropriate sexual behaviour toward others 6 Has been in trouble with the law

Note:
Goodman items are in bold

Appendix 5
The Multiple Disadvantage Index

The Multiple Disadvantage Index was developed as part of the Early Years Transition and Special Educational Needs (EYTSEN) Project which focuses on the identification of children 'at risk' of SEN (see Sammons *et al.*, 2004b). An index was created based on ten indicators in total: three child variables, six parent variables, and one related to the Early years Home Learning Environment (HLE). All the variables were chosen because they related to low baseline attainment when looked at in isolation. Where indicators were closely related, such as first language and ethnic groups, only the most significant was included.

Child variables

- First language: English as an additional language (EAL)
- Large family: three or more siblings
- Pre-maturity/low birth weight

Parent variables

- Mother's highest qualification level: no qualifications
- Social class of father's occupation: semi-skilled, unskilled, never worked, absent father
- Father not employed
- Young mother (age 13–17 at birth of EPPE child)
- Lone parent
- Mother not working / unemployed
- Low Early years Home Learning Environment (HLE)

Appendix 6

Results from analyses of pre-school effects compared with those of family income and parents' employment status

The EPPE study had information on average yearly parental salary (before tax) in the form of seven bands (plus an 'unknown' category, where no salary information was available). The use of parent salary categories also allows direct comparisons with the influence of different amounts of pre-school in multilevel analyses. Note these data were collected in 2001/2 and relate to salary levels at this time.

Table A6.1 shows that parental salary is more closely related to young children's pre-reading than their language development. Furthermore, it can be seen that there are only significant differences in attainment between the no salary group (this would include those only on benefit income) and those on higher joint incomes (the band £37,500–£66,000 and the band £67,500 plus). The effect size is moderate to large for the highest salary level for pre-reading. For Language the positive impact of longer duration is more noticeable.

Table A.6.1 Comparison of effect sizes for parental salary and pre-school attendance

Salary groups – compared to no reported salary including not working/unemployed/parent absent, etc.	Pre-reading	Language
£2,500–£15,000	0.066	0.057
£17,500–£27,500	0.177*	0.091
£30,000–£35,000	0.143	0.113
£37,500–£66,000	0.315*	0.140
£67,500 plus	0.502*	0.222*
Salary not known (NK)	0.014	0.103
FSM (compared to not eligible)	–0.127*	–0.103

Duration of pre-school (compared with no pre-school attended, i.e. 'home' children)		
Under 1 year	0.123	0.456*
1–2 years	0.255*	0.379*
2–3 years	0.361*	0.421*
3 years plus	0.403*	0.591*

*$p<0.05$

Our results show that the effect size associated with just under one year of pre-schooling is 0.123 for the Pre-reading outcome, this is a little smaller than the effect of earned family income band £17,500–£27,500 versus no salary income. Interestingly the effect size associated with one year of pre-school for the Language outcome is significantly larger than for Pre-reading, while the impact of higher family earned income for Language is smaller.

We also examined the effect sizes for parents' employment status. These are generally smaller than those for family income or pre-school duration. The results reveal that parents' employment status is significantly related to Pre-reading attainment, with moderate positive effects (controlling for other significant predictors) for both parents working. Nonetheless, duration of pre-school has a stronger net impact.

Additional analyses explored the influence of quality and duration of attendance effects on child attainment at the start of primary school compared with. Pre school centres were divided into three groups: low (bottom 20 per cent), average (middle 60 per cent) and high (top 20 per cent) based on total ECERS-E R quality measure. Within each quality band, children were further divided on the basis of duration of attendance. It should be noted that due to the relatively smaller numbers in the low quality band, the sub divisions by duration are broader. Therefore direct comparisons for the low quality, low duration, are not possible. Table 6.5 shows the net effects for each of the sub-groups.

It can be seen that in comparison with the 'home' group, *all* levels of quality and duration show a significant positive effect compared with none. Overall, longer duration shows a greater benefit than low duration, irrespective of quality. However, the combination of high quality and high duration shows a particularly

Table A.6.2 Comparison of effect sizes for quality and duration

Pre-school group (compared with no duration, no quality i.e. the 'home' group)	Pre-reading	Language
Low quality, low duration (< 24 months)	0.254	0.602*
Low quality, average duration (24–36 months)	0.293*	0.540*
Low quality, high duration (36 months plus)	0.368*	0.529*
Average quality, very low duration (< 12 months)	0.153	0.459*
Average quality, low duration (12–24 months)	0.331*	0.459*
Average quality, average duration (24–36 months)	0.479*	0.528*
Average quality, high duration (36 months plus)	0.545*	0.672*
High quality, very low duration (<12 months)	0.256*	0.338*
High quality, low duration (12–24 months)	0.381*	0.526*
High quality, average duration (24–36 months)	0.346*	0.535*
High quality, high duration (36 months plus)	0.622*	1.010*

*$p < 0.05$

strong effect size (1.01) for Language, and fairly large effect for Pre-reading (0.62). To try to distinguish the separate quality effect we can calculate the net difference between low quality, high duration, and high quality, high duration. For Language (1.01–0.53), this gives an estimate of 0.48. For Pre-reading the difference is somewhat smaller at 0.25 (0.62–0.37).

Earlier EPPE analyses modelled the quality measure as a continuous scale in the value added analyses of children's cognitive progress over the pre-school period (but the 'home' group was not included in these models). The results also confirmed a separate significant effect for quality (as measured by the ECERS-E instrument) over and above a larger effect for duration. The combined effects of high quality and high duration are stronger than the effects found for the highest category of family earned salary.

Another approach is to consider the effectiveness of individual pre-school centres in promoting cognitive progress after controlling for all measured child, family, home and contextual factors. These differences in effectiveness are in turn the result of a range of differences between pre-school centres. Residual centre effects can be regarded as a proxy for the cumulative effect of all quality differences, not just those observed using one instrument.

For pre-reading the range of centre residual effects is 10.43 points on the Pre-reading scale. This is a difference between the best and the worst centre in a distribution that is approximately normal. Taking the pre-school centre that is one standard deviation below the mean as an averagely bad centre in terms of quality, and the centre that is one standard deviation above the mean as an averagely good centre in terms of quality. The difference between these is 2 SD units, which is 4.2. This could be regarded as a measure of the effect size of quality (average bad compared with average good). It is a relatively conservative estimate as it is considerably smaller than comparing the very worst with the very best, and the levels of quality compared are ones that are frequently present in the population of pre-school centres. This effect size for quality of 4.2 Pre-reading units is equivalent to approximately 4.15 months of development.

Similar computations for Language give an effect size for quality of 2.48 months of development, and for early number concepts an effect size for quality of 3.36 months of development.

The calculation of effect sizes for specific sub groups of children allows comparison with the effects attributable to other child, family or home environment characteristics. Of particular policy relevance are the comparisons with the size of family income effects and those of different durations of pre-school. In addition the analyses reported here have extended the study of the impact of different levels of quality and duration of pre-school.

Glossary

Age standardised scores Assessment scores that have been adjusted to take account of the child's age at testing. This enables a comparison to be made between the performance of an individual pupil, relative to a representative sample of children in the same age group throughout the country or, in this case, the relative achievement of the EPPE sample.

Baseline measures Assessments taken by the EPPE child at entry to the study. These assessment scores are subsequently employed as prior attainment measures in a value added analysis of pupils' cognitive progress.

Birth weight We used three classifications for birth weight. Above 2,500 gms is regarded as normal birth weight. Between 1,501 and 2,500 gms is regarded as low birth weight and below 1,500 gms regarded as very low birth weight (Scott and Carran, 1989).

British Ability Scales (BAS) This is a battery of assessments specially developed by NFER-Nelson to assess very young children's abilities. The assessments used at entry to the EPPE study and entry to reception were:
- Block building – visual-perceptual matching, especially in spatial orientation (only entry to EPPE study)
- Naming vocabulary – expressive language and knowledge of names
- Pattern construction – non-verbal reasoning and spatial visualisation (only entry to reception)
- Picture similarities – non-verbal reasoning
- Early number concepts – knowledge of, and problem solving using pre-numerical and numerical concepts (only entry to reception)
- Copying – visual–perceptual matching and fine-motor co-ordination. Used specifically for children without English
- Verbal comprehension – receptive language, understanding of oral instructions involving basic language concepts.

Caregiver Interaction Scale (CIS) This scale (Arnett, 1989) of adult–child interaction was completed after a sustained period of observation with the 26 items forming four sub-scales: 'Positive relationships', 'Permissiveness', 'Punitiveness' and 'Detachment'. The 'Positive relationships' identifies favourable aspects of adult–child interaction whereas the other three sub-scales represent unfavourable aspects.

Centre/School level variance The proportion of variance in a particular child outcome measure (i.e. Pre-reading scores at start of primary school) attributable to differences between individual centres/schools rather than differences between individual children.

Child background factors Child background characteristics such as age, birth weight, gender, ethnicity.

Contextualised models Cross-sectional multilevel models exploring children's cognitive attainment at entry to primary school, controlling for child, parent and home learning environment characteristics (but not prior attainment).

Controlling for Several variables may influence an outcome and these variables may themselves be associated. Multilevel statistical analyses can calculate the influence of one variable upon an outcome, having allowed for the effects of other variables. When this is done the net effect of a variable upon an outcome controlling for other variables can be established.

Correlation A correlation is a measure of statistical association between two measures (e.g. age and attainment) that ranges from + 1 to – 1.

Duration of pre-school In terms of the value added models, the duration of pre-school covers the time period between date of BAS assessment at entry to the EPPE study until entry to primary school. Note that the number of months of pre-school attended before the child entered the EPPE study is not included in this duration measure. A separate 'duration' measure of amount of time in pre-school prior to entering the study was tested but was not found to be significant (note that this 'duration' measure is confounded with prior attainment). In the contextualised models, duration of pre-school refers to the time period between entry to the target pre-school until entry to primary school. These duration measures provide a crude indication of length of pre-school experience.

ECERS-R and ECERS-E The Early Childhood Environment Rating Scale (ECERS-R) (Harms *et al.*, 1998) is based on child centred pedagogy and also assesses resources for indoor and outdoor play. The rating scale developed in England (ECERS-E) (Sylva *et al.*, 2003, 2006) was intended as a supplement to the ECERS-R and was developed specially for the EPPE study to reflect the Desirable Learning Outcomes (replaced by the Early Learning Goals), and the Curriculum Guidance for the Foundation Stage.

Educational effectiveness Research design that seeks to explore the effectiveness of educational institutions in promoting a range of child/student outcomes (often academic measures) while controlling for the influence of intake differences in child/student characteristics (see Teddlie and Reynolds, 2000).

Effect sizes (ES) provide a measure of the strength of the relationships between different predictors and the child outcomes under study, usually measured in standard deviation units. For further discussion see Elliot and Sammons (2004).

Family factors Examples of family factors are mother's qualifications, father's employment and family SES.

Hierarchical nature of the data Data that clusters into pre-defined sub-groups or levels within a system (i.e. young children within pre-school centres/primary schools, within LAs).

Home learning environment (HLE) characteristics Measures derived from reports from parents (at interview or using parent questionnaires) about what children do at home, for example, playing with numbers and letters, singing songs and nursery rhymes.

Intervention study A study in which researchers 'intervene' in the sample to control variables, i.e. control by setting the adult:child ratios in order to compare different specific ratios in different settings. EPPE is not an intervention study in that it investigates naturally occurring variation in pre-school settings.

Intra-centre/school correlation Measures the extent to which the scores of children in the same centre/school resemble each other as compared with those from children at different centres/schools. The intra-centre/school correlation provides an indication of the extent to which unexplained variance in children's progress (i.e. that not accounted for by prior attainment) may be attributed to differences between centres/schools. This gives an indication of possible variation in pre-school centre/school effectiveness.

Multilevel modelling A methodology that allows data to be examined simultaneously at different levels within a system (i.e. young children within pre-school centres/primary schools, within LAs), essentially an extension of multiple regression.

Multiple disadvantage Based on three child variables, six parent variables, and one related to the home learning environment which were considered 'risk' indicators when looked at in isolation. A child's 'multiple disadvantage' was calculated by summing the number of indicators the child was at risk on.

Multiple regression A method of predicting outcome scores on the basis of the statistical relationship between observed outcome scores and one or more predictor variables.

Net effect The unique contribution of a particular variable upon an outcome while other variables are controlled.

Pre-reading attainment Composite formed by adding together the scores for phonological awareness (rhyme and alliteration) and letter recognition.

Prior attainment factors Measures which describe pupils' achievement at the beginning of the phase or period under investigation (i.e. taken on entry to primary or secondary school or on entry to the EPPE study).

Quality of pre-school Measures of pre-school/centre quality collected through observational assessments (ECERS-R, ECERS-E and CIS) made by trained researchers.

Quality of teaching Measures from Year 5 classroom observations using the IEO (Stipek) and COS-5 (Pianta) instruments.

Sampling profile/procedures The EPPE sample was constructed by:

- Five regions (six LAs) randomly selected around the country, but being representative of urban, rural, inner city areas.
- Pre-schools from each of the 6 types of target provision (nursery classes, nursery schools, local authority day nurseries, private day nurseries, play groups and integrated centres) randomly selected across the region.

Significance level Criteria for judging whether differences in scores between groups of children, schools or centres might have arisen by chance. The most common criteria is the 95 per cent level ($p<0.05$) which can be expected to include the 'true' value in 95 out of 100 samples (i.e. the probability being one in twenty that a difference might have arisen by chance).

Social/behavioural development A child's ability to 'socialise' with other adults and children and their general behaviour to others measured by teachers'/pre-school staff ratings.

Socio-economic status (SES) Parental occupation information was collected by means of a parental interview when children were recruited to the study. The Office of Population Census and Surveys OPCS (1995) Classification of Occupations was used to classify mothers' and fathers' current employment into one of eight groups: professional I, other professional non-manual II, skilled non-manual III, skilled manual III, semi-skilled manual IV, unskilled manual V, never worked and no response. Family SES was obtained by assigning the SES classification based on the parent with the highest occupational status.

Standard deviation (sd) A measure of the spread around the mean in a distribution of numerical scores. In a normal distribution, 68 per cent of cases fall within one standard deviation of the mean and 95 percent of cases fall within two standard deviations.

Total BAS score By combining four of the BAS sub-scales (two verbal and two non-verbal) a General Cognitive Ability score or Total BAS score at entry to the study can be computed. This is a measure of overall cognitive ability.

Value added models Longitudinal multilevel models exploring children's cognitive progress, controlling for prior attainment and significant child, parent and home learning environment characteristics.

Value added residuals (pre-school effectiveness) Differences between predicted and actual results for pre-school centres (where predicted results are calculated using value added models).

Value added residuals (primary school academic effectiveness) Differences between predicted and actual results for primary schools measuring pupil progress across KS1–KS2 (see Melhuish *et al.*, 2006a, 2006b).

Index